THE COMPLETE GUIDE TO
ETF PORTFOLIO MANAGEMENT

THE COMPLETE GUIDE TO
ETF PORTFOLIO MANAGEMENT

THE *ESSENTIAL* TOOLKIT FOR PRACTITIONERS

DR. SCOTT M. WEINER

NEW YORK   CHICAGO   SAN FRANCISCO   ATHENS   LONDON
MADRID   MEXICO CITY   MILAN   NEW DELHI
SINGAPORE   SYDNEY   TORONTO

1 2 3 4 5 6 7 8 9   LCR   26 25 24 23 22 21

ISBN   978-1-264-25746-1
MHID   1-264-25746-5

e-ISBN   978-1-264-25747-8
e-MHID   1-264-25747-3

This publication is designed to provide accurate and authoritative information in regard to the subject matter covered. It is sold with the understanding that neither the author nor the publisher is engaged in rendering legal, accounting, securities trading, or other professional services. If legal advice or other expert assistance is required, the services of a competent professional person should be sought.

—From a Declaration of Principles Jointly Adopted by a Committee of the American Bar Association and a Committee of Publishers and Associations

Library of Congress Cataloging-in-Publication Data

Names: Weiner, Scott M., author.
Title: The complete guide to ETF portfolio management : the essential toolkit for practitioners / by Dr. Scott M. Weiner.
Other titles: Complete guide to exchange traded fund portfolio management
Description: New York : McGraw-Hill Education, [2021] | Includes bibliographical references and index.
Identifiers: LCCN 2020053386 (print) | LCCN 2020053387 (ebook) | ISBN 9781264257461 (hardback) | ISBN 9781264257478 (ebook)
Subjects: LCSH: Exchange traded funds. | Portfolio management.
Classification: LCC HG6043 .W45 2021 (print) | LCC HG6043 (ebook) | DDC 332.63/27—dc23
LC record available at https://lccn.loc.gov/2020053386
LC ebook record available at https://lccn.loc.gov/2020053387

Disclaimer
The views expressed in this book are the author's and do not necessarily represent the views of Janus Henderson Group.

McGraw Hill books are available at special quantity discounts to use as premiums and sales promotions or for use in corporate training programs. To contact a representative, please visit the Contact Us pages at www.mhprofessional.com.

For Lindsay, Brady, and Alex

Contents

PART III

The Primary Market and Launching an ETF

PART IV

The Three Ts and the Three Cs

Acknowledgments

I am incredibly grateful to so many people who have made this project possible and/or made this book better as a result of their support. I want to begin with my family. First and foremost, I want to thank my wife, Lindsay, and my children, Brady and Alex, who have been so supportive and encouraging from the beginning of this journey, even when writing took away more family time than expected. Though it may not be your preferred genre, this book is for you. Second, I am fortunate to have been raised by parents who were both lifelong educators, who demonstrated by example the importance of sharing knowledge and teaching. This book is a tribute to you and these values. Finally, my in-laws have also been an incredible source of guidance and support along this journey and so many others. Thank you.

I feel particularly blessed to have such a strong network of friends who have believed in this project from the start and have encouraged me to see it through to its end, including Scott Hershovitz, Scott Rao, Rebecca Katz, Damien Horth, and many others whose names I'll regret not including in this sentence. You have read and edited drafts, offered suggestions, connected me with others who have been so helpful, and supported me throughout—I can't thank you enough.

Professionally, I'm especially grateful to Enrique Chang, the Chief Investment Officer of Janus Henderson, for his support of this project, as well as many other colleagues who have provided information, guidance, and assistance along the way. Nick Cherney and I have worked together for almost a decade, and I am grateful for the many, many conversations we've had over the years about ETF portfolio management that have undoubtedly enhanced the value of this book's content. Benjamin Wang, my co-Portfolio Manager on a number of ETFs, and Zoey Zhu, a member of my Quantitative Strategy team, have both been instrumental in building our collective approach to ETF portfolio management, and I'm extremely grateful for their work and support every day. Special thanks to Cliff Weber, the Chairman of the Board of Trustees for the ETFs I manage, for sharing his experiences from the early days of ETFs and his extensive regulatory and broad industry knowledge; to Richard Hoge, Byron Hittle, James Kerr, and Allen Welch for their guidance over the years regarding the legal, regulatory, and accounting issues that arise in ETF portfolio management; and to Jay Kirkorsky and Paul Lyons, who have helped deepen my knowledge of the Capital Markets function. No ETF portfolio manager gets to do what he or she does without the support of a strong distribution team; many thanks to Steven Quinn, Dan Aronson, Shawna Macnamara, Lee Gross, and Taylor Ranney for their efforts.

Several people and organizations have been incredibly generous with their time and/or resources to provide support for this book. Steffen Scheuble, the CEO of Solactive AG, has been a longtime business partner of mine, and I appreciate his assistance with this project. Fellow ETF Portfolio Manager Antonio Picca and others made meaningful improvements to my discussion of active and fixed-income ETFs. Jean Zimmer provided valuable guidance and editing early on in the process. A special thank you as well to Bloomberg Finance L.P., Douglas Richardson at the Investment Company Institute (ICI), Ropes Gray LLP, and The MathWorks, Inc.

As the idea for this book was coming together, I sought the advice of a number of academics in the finance world whom I respect and admire, including Emanuel Derman of Columbia University, Stuart Gilson of Harvard University, and Tim Jenkinson of Oxford University. I'm so grateful for their feedback and encouragement.

Last, but certainly not least, I am deeply grateful to Stephen Isaacs of McGraw Hill and his entire team, especially Patricia Wallenburg and Amanda Muller, for bringing this project across the finish line. Stephen, your enthusiasm for the project from day one and your support every day since have made all the difference. Thank you.

Introduction

In the twentieth century, the dominant investment vehicle in the United States was the mutual fund, a pooled instrument from a number of investors that is professionally managed by a mutual fund company. Toward the end of the century, in 1993, however, the Securities and Exchange Commission approved an application for listing a mutual fund–like product that differed from the traditional mutual fund in several ways. In particular and most significantly, while mutual funds did not trade on exchanges like stocks, these new products would, with funds changing hands at a market-determined price as opposed to the net asset value (NAV) of the fund.*

With this innovation, the exchange-traded fund, or ETF, was born. Just over 25 years later, the ETF industry has grown substantially more than anyone in 1993 could have imagined, with over $5.5 trillion invested in more than 2,000 products in the United States alone.[1] The products cover virtually every sector of the financial landscape, from equities to fixed income, currencies to commodities, domestic to international. An investor seeking to find a product that provides exposure to some corner of the market is at least as likely to find that exposure in an ETF as he or she would in a mutual fund. In 2014 and almost every year since, flows into ETFs outpaced flows into mutual funds.[2] It is fair to say that not even a quarter of the way into the twenty-first century, the ETF has overtaken the mutual fund as the dominant financial instrument of the times.

---

* The NAV is the per-share value of the fund at the close of the business day.

For investment companies themselves, the advent of the ETF has had a profound impact on portfolio management. Portfolio management used to be about what you held in the portfolio at any given time; index-tracking products simply sought to hold the underlying positions of the index, and actively managed products sought to hold positions chosen by the portfolio manager (PM) without any mandate to necessarily track an index. In the ETF era, however, a mutual fund and an ETF that track the same index are managed by their respective portfolio managers in entirely different ways. Even actively managed portfolios in ETF structures are managed differently than actively managed mutual fund portfolios. It's no longer appropriate to simply teach—or learn—"portfolio management" full stop; we need to distinguish the practice dependent on the product.

This book is believed to be the first of its kind, dedicating its content entirely to the complete practice of managing ETF portfolios. It is intended for aspiring PMs and seasoned practitioners alike, and with the explosive growth in assets in the sector, ETF investors can also use this book to "look under the hood" of the products they own to see exactly how they run. Every ETF investor should know how the product operates.

All the basics of ETFs and the ETF portfolio management process are covered, and the book includes advanced topics in a wide array of areas as well.

In Part I, we concentrate on the ETF industry in the United States. This part reviews the regulatory framework that gave rise to the proliferation of ETFs, surveys the variety of ETF structures available in the marketplace, presents a snapshot of the marketplace as it looks today, and details the ETF ecosystem and the types of organizations that make the industry function day to day.

With this overview in place, we move on to Part II, where we delve into passive, or index-based, ETF portfolio management. We discuss the entire index process, covering how indices are defined and how PMs remain informed about all the intricacies captured within an index. We construct a hypothetical index to serve as the basis for an ETF to be managed throughout the book, and we lay the groundwork for what will happen when the index rebalances and how the rebalance will impact the ETF PM. The focus on index-based ETF portfolio management is intentional: as we will discuss later, we believe that a lot of the tools employed by index-based ETF portfolio managers can also be employed by active ETF portfolio managers.

Then, in Part III, we effectively launch a hypothetical ETF, as if we worked at an ETF sponsor. We discuss methods for seeding the fund at inception and describe the critical role the primary market plays in ETF portfolio management.

In Part IV, we present the Three Ts of ETF portfolio management—tracking error, transaction costs, and taxes—and the Three Cs of ETF portfolio management—cash, corporate actions, and custom in-kind baskets (CIBs). We discuss the trade-offs required as the PM seeks to minimize each of the Ts, and we consider how the three Cs impact the PM's ability to do so. We keep a focus on equity-based ETFs, as some of the key aspects of portfolio management that enable the efficiency of ETFs can be easily demonstrated by this asset class. The last chapter in this part addresses the process of portfolio rebalancing, which differs from the index rebalancing discussed in Part II.

In Part V, we expand the product set. We discuss how international ETFs present new challenges to the ETF PM, particularly around noncontemporaneous market timing.* Next, we turn to a growing segment of the ETF landscape: actively managed ETFs, i.e., those that are not formally tracking an underlying index. Despite the absence of an index to be tracked, some of the methods employed in passive ETF portfolio management are surprisingly relevant in the actively managed ETF space, as mentioned. We continue the focus on expanding the product set by exploring fixed-income ETFs—another growing segment of the ETF industry. We end Part IV by investigating leveraged and inverse products, those that seek daily returns equivalent to multiples of an index's return on a particular day. These products require different portfolio management strategies from those used for nonleveraged products.†

Finally, in Part VI, we consider situations where particular challenges make managing an ETF difficult. We begin with a chapter on market turbulence, as extreme volatility can wreak havoc on the ill-prepared ETF PM. Next, we discuss how representative sampling can be a preferred technique for indices that are hard to track in the passive space. If all else fails, it is possible for the fund sponsor to shut down an ETF, and we address the implications of this for the ETF PM in the final chapter.

---

* Our discussion pertains to ETFs domiciled in the United States.
† There are, of course, other asset classes or products that are not covered here, such as commodities, currencies, and derivatives-based strategies. We also primarily focus on open-end investment companies.

The overarching goals are to prepare aspiring PMs to handle the basics as well as some of the more nuanced situations that arise in ETF portfolio management and to give seasoned veterans insight into situations that either they haven't yet come across, or they have come across and were left puzzled about how to handle.

The days of PMs just having views on stocks, bonds, or asset allocation are over; the modern-day PM needs to manage not only the content of the portfolio but also the structure of the product. For the exploding ETF marketplace, this book will prepare you for that tall task.

Let's get started.

Notes

1. Bloomberg Finance L.P., Investment Company Institute.
2. Ibid.

THE COMPLETE GUIDE TO

ETF PORTFOLIO MANAGEMENT

PART I

The ETF Industry

Ask a professional athlete how to play his or her sport, and you're likely to get a description of the playing field and maybe even a bit of history before you get to the nuts and bolts of skill and strategy. In that vein, we begin our journey into exchange-traded fund (ETF) portfolio management by describing the environment in which the practice takes place before reviewing the act of portfolio management itself. The incredible rise of the ETF industry has its roots in the regulatory environment of the early 1990s. In Chapter 1, we provide an overview of that environment along with the growth narrative of the product in the ensuing decades. In Chapter 2, we provide an overview of the ETF ecosystem with a clear focus on how the ETF portfolio manager fits within the framework.

Birth of an ETF

Industries evolve through disruption and innovation. In some industries, it is hard to pinpoint when that disruption occurs; in others, there is a watershed moment that permanently changes the landscape. In some cases, that moment may not even be known at the time, but only through the lens of history does it become clear. Startups are laser-focused on disruption and innovation, desperate to be the company that upends the status quo. Business schools teach disruption and innovation, hoping to instill vision in future leaders to find those areas of an industry ripe for attack. Examples of disrupted industries where innovation changed the nature of the industry are virtually everywhere, from digital cameras displacing film-based products to liquid soap pushing out bar soap to take top spot in the personal hygiene market.

Putting aside the innovations that drove these new industries, what is striking about disruption and innovation is how disruption-proof the industries appear at the time they get disrupted. Take the mobile phone market (which, of course, disrupted the communications industry). In 2007, the cell phone hardware market was dominated by Nokia "brick" phones (a 53% market share), and mobile operating systems were also dominated by Nokia through its Symbian operating system (a 67% share). Nokia was the cell phone Goliath. The company had over a *billion* customers in 2007; *Forbes* magazine had dubbed Nokia, the "Cell Phone King";[1] the company, and its industry, appeared virtually untouchable.

But that year, Apple recognized the value in integrating a software platform (think "apps") with the hardware to access it (think "iPhone"), and a new paradigm in cell phones emerged, one that led to competition between the Android platform and iPhone's iOS platform. Cell phones were no longer "phones"; they were pocket computers with operating systems that moved the industry forward. Nokia failed to adapt, and now, instead of a Nokia brick phone in your pocket, you likely have an iPhone, or perhaps a Samsung, running on an iOS or Android operating system. In 12 years, the market share of Symbian went to zero, and the market shares for Android and iOS went, respectively, to 76% and 22%.[2]

A seminal moment for disruption in the investment management industry came in 1993. To set the stage, at that time, the investment landscape looked like the cell phone landscape. The dominant product was the mutual fund, a product in which multiple investors pooled funds that invested in securities to their mutual benefit (or demise). Regulations were firmly established that outlined how the products worked and the rules that investment companies were required to adhere to when running a mutual fund. About $6 trillion was invested in mutual funds in 1993.[3] The mutual fund industry appeared disruption-proof.

So how do you disrupt a multitrillion-dollar industry, one that is well regulated with a defined set of rules entrenched in the financial markets, transparent for every market participant to not only see but adhere to? Simple, actually: you change the rules. Working with State Street Global Advisors, the American Stock Exchange (AMEX), through its wholly owned subsidiary PDR Services, asked the Securities and Exchange Commission (SEC) to relax some of the requirements outlined in the regulations surrounding mutual funds. In doing so, AMEX took the first steps toward upending the mutual fund market, becoming the "Apple" in the asset management industry before Apple upended the cell phone industry. Specifically, the request was for the SEC to allow AMEX to list a fund—Standard and Poor's Depositary Receipts (SPDR) S&P 500® ETF Trust under the ticker "SPY"*—that would trade on the exchange just like a stock and relieve AMEX of several other restrictions imposed on mutual funds. With the SEC's approval, mutual fund disruption was under way, and while mutual funds still maintain a dominant position in the financial landscape, the ripple effect of that first product launch in 1993 is far-reaching.

---

* SPY is a unit investment trust; claims to securities are traded, not the securities themselves.

MUTUAL FUND REGULATORY ACTS AND EXEMPTIVE RELIEF

A deeper dive into the regulatory environment and how exactly SPY changed the industry is worthwhile, especially because the regulatory environment continues to evolve to this day, with the adoption of the SEC's new ETF Rule, which we cover below.

Four specific regulatory acts formed the foundation of the modern-day mutual fund industry: the Securities Act of 1933, the Securities and Exchange Act of 1934, the Investment Company Act of 1940, and the Investment Advisers Act of 1940. We won't spend much time on them; there are many places where the interested reader can find details about, or even read, these acts.* For our purposes, though, what is interesting is that within this labyrinth of rules, the folks behind the SPDR effort managed to find a few rules that they would ask the SEC to relax for them. In doing so, the ETF revolution was started. The focus was on the Investment Company Act of 1940, commonly referred to as the "'40 Act."

The '40 Act effectively governs mutual funds, establishing what it means to be an investment company, and was designed on the back of the acts of 1933 and 1934 to protect investors in the wake of the financial collapse that began in 1929. The SPDR application to the SEC asked for "exemptive relief," in other words, permission from the SEC to violate some of the rules set out in the '40 Act.

A standard exemptive relief application seeks relief from three key parts of the '40 Act, allowing the fund to (1) issue shares that are redeemable at the NAV (net asset value) in creation units only, (2) receive securities from and transfer securities to authorized participants (in-kind transactions), and (3) list those shares on an exchange to be traded according to market dynamics as opposed to NAV. That might sound technical, so let's break it down: Redemption in creation units puts a barrier between the investor and the fund sponsor. No longer could investors give a few shares back to the fund sponsor; rather they had to accumulate enough shares (a creation unit) to redeem those shares, which was often 50,000 shares or more. Disintermediating those transactions would be the authorized participants (APs), market makers that would stand between the end investor and the funds, facilitating these transfers of creation units. No longer would the end investor transfer shares to the issuer. APs could transfer securities in exchange for shares of the ETF

---

* See, for example, https://www.sec.gov/investment/laws-and-rules.

in a creation and submit shares of the ETF in exchange for a set of securities in the case of a redemption. These in-kind transactions would have significant implications, which we will discuss in depth. Finally, when mutual fund shareholders bought shares from or sold shares back to the issuer, they did so at NAV. The exemptive relief application asked the SEC to allow the shares to be traded on the market much like a stock would trade on an exchange.*, 4

Why has the granting of these relief requests been so instrumental in building a brand-new marketplace that has fundamentally changed the landscape of the investment universe? For one, investors seek liquidity—the ability to get in and out of securities at a transparent price at any specific time. The exchange-trading provision allowed funds that previously only traded at NAV at the end of the day—which, of course, would be unknown *during* the day—to be exchanged at any point in the day, just like an individual security. If an investor seeks to get out of a mutual fund position at 9:31 a.m., he or she must wait until the NAV is struck at the end of the day to know the price received for the shares.

Second, as we are going to see a lot in this book, ETFs created tax efficiencies relative to mutual funds that would have profound consequences for investors. In a nutshell, when shares of a mutual fund are redeemed and securities are sold by the mutual fund company to provide cash to the redeeming investor, if those shares are sold at a capital gain, that gain is distributed to *all* the mutual fund holders at year-end. Even if you have not sold any shares of the mutual fund, if someone else has, you could be (and often are) liable for the tax consequences of security transactions in the fund. Some of the structural features of ETFs—namely, the authorized participant feature and how transactions with APs were structured—in conjunction with the tax treatment for AP transactions, allowed for the isolation of one investor's activities from those of all the other investors. These provisions also allow for more efficient tax management of ETFs.

Finally, the open-ended structure of the ETFs and the creation and redemption mechanism with authorized participants created an arbitrage mechanism that aimed to keep secondary market prices in line with the NAVs of the products. This ensured that investors buying and selling in the

---

* There are often other relief requests that come with applications, such as lifting restrictions on position limits in investing in other funds and allowing for delays in processing redemption proceeds. Funds also request relief from certain provisions of the Securities Act of 1934 that chiefly deal with the distribution of ETF shares.

secondary markets would receive a "fair" price, i.e., a price closely reflecting the value of what was held in the portfolio. No one class of investors (e.g., institutions) would have any material advantage over any other class of investors (e.g., retail investors).

There are other reasons, of course, that have contributed to the growth of the ETF industry, including a lower fee model, a rise in indexing more broadly, and the growth of the registered investment advisory sector relying heavily on the products, as well as some novel investment concepts that have been packaged in ETF form. Taken with the tax efficiency and liquidity of the offering, it is no wonder the product has steadily taken market share since its debut.

THE ETF INDUSTRY TODAY

What started out back in 1993 as a relatively small ETF trust—the SPDR S&P 500 ETF Trust had about $6 million at inception—has grown into a substantial and important piece of the financial industry landscape. This growth, as we outline below, provides the core context for why this book is necessary. As of December 31, 2020, the SPDR S&P 500 ETF Trust had $332 billion in assets under management (AUM), an all-time high. In the last 25 years, since the advent of the ETF, the ETF market has grown to over $5.5 trillion in assets (see Figure 1.1).

In terms of assets, ETF assets have grown to over 20% of mutual fund assets. That doesn't sound like much, but looking at this headline number doesn't scratch the surface when exploring the ETF growth story. To understand why, consider the dominant position that mutual funds hold in the retirement industry. According to the *Wall Street Journal*, which cites the Investment Company Institute (ICI), "80% of the 56 million households who own mutual funds buy them through [employer-sponsored retirement plans]."[5] And the ICI estimates that 54% of mutual fund assets are held in retirement accounts, a sum of over $9.4 trillion in 2019 (and $9.9 trillion if money market funds are included).[6] Most of these retirement accounts don't even offer ETFs, primarily because (1) there would be considerable technological enhancements required on their platforms to accommodate intraday trading, (2) fees to plan administrators could be lower with ETFs, and (3) tax efficiency is not relevant in this sector of the investment industry. As a result, there is a large barrier to entry for exchange-traded funds.

FIGURE 1.1

ETF assets over time, United States

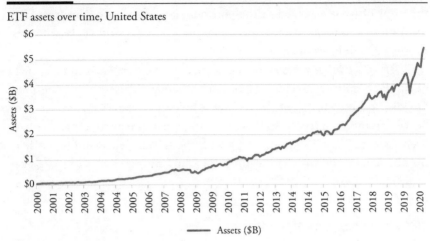

Source: Investment Company Institute, Bloomberg Finance L.P.
For the most up-to-date figures about the fund industry, please visit http://www.ici.org/research/stats.

Measured against the *nonretirement* assets, though, ETF assets have grown to roughly half the assets of the mutual fund industry when the playing field is leveled. When ETFs reach their inevitable tipping point in employer-sponsored plans, the rise of ETFs relative to mutual funds will be swift.

From a flows perspective, by at least one metric—trailing 12-month net new flows—ETF flows have exceeded net new flows into mutual funds from 2014 through 2019 (see Figure 1.2).* If this trend continues, and there is little reason to believe it will not, the ETF industry will ultimately surpass the mutual fund industry, especially if ETF-based defined contribution platforms gain a foothold in the retirement industry. According to some industry watchers, global ETF assets are expected to exceed $10 trillion by 2023,[7] and some estimates put ETF assets ahead of mutual fund assets by as early as 2024.[8]

---

* In the midst of the COVID-19 pandemic, a strong reversal took place, primarily due to over $1 trillion of flows into taxable money market mutual funds in March and April 2020 (*Bloomberg Finance L.P., Investment Company Institute*).

FIGURE 1.2

Rolling one-year ETF versus mutual fund flows

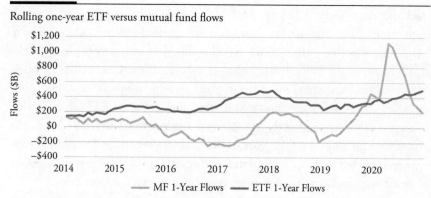

Source: Investment Company Institute, Bloomberg Finance L.P.

New product launches clearly favor ETFs as well. Since the year 2000, cumulative net new ETF launches have exceeded 2,000 products, while cumulative net new mutual fund launches have actually been negative (see Figure 1.3).

FIGURE 1.3

New product launches: ETFs versus mutual funds

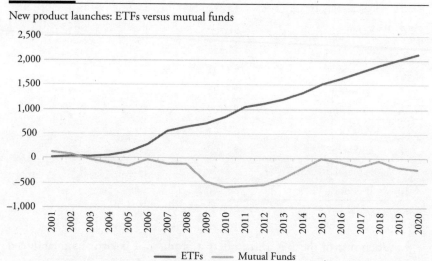

Source: Investment Company Institute, Bloomberg Finance L.P.

ETFs cover virtually every corner of the market. Pure beta products track the major indices, like the S&P 500. So-called smart beta products seek to provide beta to the market through newly created indices with alternative weighting schemes—often factor-based—aimed at outperforming a benchmark. Multiasset ETFs provide exposure to a set of markets such as equities, fixed income, currencies, and commodities, seeking to mimic the overall allocation of an investor's portfolio in one structure. There are ETFs that provide leveraged exposure to underlyings, inverse exposure to underlyings (when the underlying goes up, the ETF goes down, and vice versa), and nonlinear payouts constructed with options on underlyings of interest. There is no shortage of categories, and new categories seem to emerge on a frequent basis.

Many of the new product launches come from companies trying to compete with the dominant players in the market, the ETF Big Three: BlackRock, Vanguard, and State Street, whose assets dominate the ETF landscape (see Table 1.1).

TABLE 1.1

ETF Issuers by Assets (12/31/2020)

Rank	Issuer	AUM ($B)
1	iShares (BlackRock)	$2,014
2	Vanguard	$1,509
3	State Street	$ 848
4	Invesco	$ 295
5	Schwab	$ 198
6	First Trust	$ 109
7	VanEck	$ 53
8	ProShares	$ 47
9	WisdomTree	$ 41
10	JP Morgan	$ 40

Source: Bloomberg Finance L.P.

When one of the Big Three offers a product, it is virtually guaranteed to succeed, or at least maintain a profitable level of assets, due to its scale, infrastructure, and relationships to support and market the products. Many broker-dealers act as gatekeepers by requiring minimum asset levels and performance to be included on their platforms for use by financial advisors, and the larger firms have an easier time meeting those requirements. In contrast, one consequence of all this product proliferation is that lots of ETFs do not actually gather any significant assets, especially products issued by new companies hoping to make a splash in the ETF market. This is an industry where it is hard to survive as a small fish in a big pond.

The intense competition in the ETF industry has also led to a significant amount of fee compression, making ETFs even more attractive to investors, especially pit against their mutual fund counterparts. Many mutual funds charge 12b-1 fees, which are marketing fees that go to the broker that sold the fund, while ETFs do not charge 12b-1 fees. And some mutual funds charge "loads," fees that are paid when you enter your position ("front load") and fees that are paid when you exit your position ("back load") as well as redemption fees. Though less prevalent, these make the ETF more cost-efficient on a relative basis. Average dollar-weighted expense ratios in ETFs are currently approximately 18 basis points, more than 30 basis points lower than average dollar-weighted expense ratios for open-ended mutual funds.[9]

ETF RULE

In a sign of the times that recognizes just how far the ETF industry has evolved, the SEC, the primary body for securities regulation in the United States, proposed—and adopted—a new framework for the exchange-traded fund industry in 2019. Rule 6c-11, more casually known as the ETF Rule, drew widespread industry attention, with support from some of the largest ETF sponsors in the world.* The ETF Rule, which became effective on December 23, 2019, set a timetable for compliance with the substance of the regulation one year hence.

Some of the key provisions of the rule make it simpler for ETFs to come to market. In particular, many ETFs will no longer require exemptive relief applications, which are costly and time-consuming, and any ETFs that are eligible to rely on the rule will no longer be bound by their own exemptive relief orders. Further, *any* ETF relying on the rule will be able to use custom in-kind baskets (discussed in Chapter 12), including actively managed ETFs that had not had the benefit of this tool to manage taxes in their portfolios.

---

* See https://www.blackrock.com/corporate/literature/publication/sec-proposed-rule
  -exchange-traded-funds-092618.pdf.

There are also a number of disclosure-related requirements for ETFs that fall under the rule, including the requirement that funds post bid-ask spread information on their websites. Offsetting these disclosure requirements is the relaxation of the requirement for funds to post intraday indicative values.[10]

Much of what we present in this book is largely unaffected by the ETF Rule, but where a change is significant—particularly in our discussion of actively managed ETFs—we do our best to highlight it. In the next chapter, we review pieces of the ETF ecosystem and infrastructure that have supported the industry through the present and will continue to do so in the aftermath of the ETF Rule.

Notes

1. https://www.canalys.com/newsroom/smart-mobile-device-shipments-hit-118-million-2007-53-2006.
2. https://gs.statcounter.com/os-market-share/mobile/worldwide.
3. https://www.federalreserve.gov/pubs/bulletin/2000/1200lead.pdf.
4. https://www.barrons.com/articles/regulators-pass-streamlined-rules-for-etfs-1530316801.
5. Nick Ravo, *Wall Street Journal*, October 6, 2019, http://www.wsj.com/articles/etfs-get-all-the-buzz-but-mutual-funds-still-dominate-theres-a-reason-11570414020.
6. http://www.ici.org/pdf/2020_factbook.pdf, p. 184.
7. https://www.investors.com/etfs-and-funds/etfs/will-etfs-ever-replace-mutual-funds/.
8. http://www.investopedia.com/the-biggest-etf-trends-4776556.
9. Bloomberg Finance L.P., August 2020.
10. http://www.ropesgray.com/-/media/files/articles/2019/october/20191015_ETF_Article.pdf.

CHAPTER 2

The ETF Ecosystem

As we think about disruption in the investment arena, other instances of disruption become instructive. One case is particularly informative: Netflix's takeover of the video rental industry. It used to be the case that if you wanted to see a film that wasn't yet available on a cable station, you had to go to a physical store and hope that a copy of that film was available for rent. Blockbuster Video was the dominant player in the industry. A viewer would have to set up an account with Blockbuster, take the video home, and then return it a couple of days later or pay a late fee.

Netflix completely upended the Blockbuster model of video rental by offering a mail-in DVD service in 1997. The key to understanding why this happened was related to infrastructure: large retail stores with DVD-filled shelves were no longer necessary, but warehouses to process orders and returns were. Online membership portals operated in a fundamentally different manner than what had been a typical membership model of signing up for a membership card at the local Blockbuster store. Netflix needed *some* aspects of the old infrastructure—supply of product from Hollywood, for example—but newer technologies would be necessary for the company to get off the ground. Without the foundational infrastructure of the internet, Netflix could not have disrupted the video industry and succeeded to become the behemoth that it is today.

In a similar vein, the ETF industry also required a different infrastructure to function. And just as was the case in video rental, much of the needed infrastructure had existed already; you might say that the SPDR's biggest innovation was understanding how to use existing infrastructure as a foundation for a new business. Exchanges were in existence where stocks would trade; ETFs would use those to list funds instead of individual securities, and they would trade like stocks. Custodians existed for mutual funds; ETFs could leverage the custodial model already in place to handle a number of facets of ETF sponsorship. Clearing and settlement procedures around single stocks were already well established, and shareholder recordkeeping infrastructure was also firmly in place. In short, so much of what was necessary to make the ETF concept work was available in 1993, and this foundation, of course, has evolved and flourished since then.

In this chapter, we provide a brief overview of the ecosystem that supports the ETF industry.* At some point or another, a PM (or his or her firm) may interact with people who work at the custodian, or an index sponsor, or a regulatory agency. Who are these individuals, and what roles do they play? In what follows, we try to untangle the web of entities that work to make the ETF markets function.

Our exposition of the ETF ecosystem differs from other overviews in one crucial respect: we look at the ecosystem from the perspective of the ETF portfolio manager. This book is about portfolio management, and to that end, we seek a view of the ecosystem that lays out how the system supports the portfolio management function. As a result, we break the ecosystem down into two parts: first, we present the fund and some of its distinct parts, and then we follow that up with how the PM fits within the broader ETF ecosystem of external parties and partners.

THE ETF STRUCTURE AND THE PORTFOLIO MANAGER

The ETF structure consists of the formal trust that houses the ETF, the entity that sponsors the trust, and potential partners that are employed to manage parts of the ETF itself, including the investment advisor and the portfolio manager (see Figure 2.1).†

---

* The most complete discussion on the ETF ecosystem can be found in the Investment Company Institute's *Research Perspective*, a publicly available must-read for anyone particularly interested in the structural aspects of the ETF landscape; see https://www.ici.org/pdf/per20-05.pdf. We also recommend ETF Trends' analysis of the ETF ecosystem, which can be found at https://www.etftrends.com/etf-ecosystem.

† While we provide a general framework, there may be different structures that do not conform exactly to our exposition.

FIGURE 2.1

The ETF structure

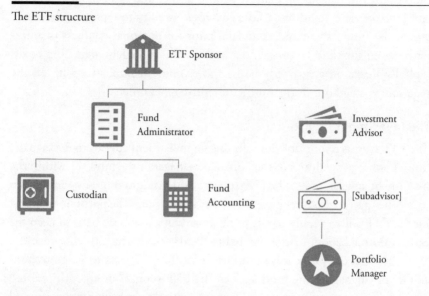

The ETF Sponsor and ETF Trust

The ETF sponsor is where it all begins: this is the company that seeks to launch a product. ETF sponsors range from giant asset managers like BlackRock and Vanguard to brand-new companies formed for the sole purpose of launching ETFs. Table 1.1 listed the largest ETF sponsors by assets. The sponsor decides the investment objective of the fund—whether it will be active or passive, what index to track in the case of a passive product, what the fees for the product will be, etc. The sponsor is also responsible for choosing parties to carry out certain tasks for administering the fund, including investment advisors, fund administrators, etc. Oftentimes these functions are carried out by entities related to the sponsor.

The ETF sponsor establishes the ETF through a trust that will formally house the fund and its board of trustees. The trust that houses the ETF is typically an investment company regulated by the Investment Company Act of 1940, and the trust is typically made up of employees of the ETF sponsor. The trust effectively separates assets in the fund from assets in the company that sponsors the fund.

The trust will produce the prospectus, which outlines all the details surrounding the fund, including the objective, fees, risks, policies, etc., and the board of trustees will assume oversight responsibility for a variety of functions of the fund, ensuring that the actions of the fund sponsor are fair to the end investor. The board has a fiduciary responsibility to represent the interests of the fund's shareholders and monitor for potential conflicts of interest between the fund's management and the fund's shareholders. The board typically meets on a quarterly basis, and monitors compliance with all the requirements laid out in the fund's exemptive relief order.*

The Investment Advisor

The ETF trust is responsible for selecting an investment advisor to manage the fund. Formally, the duties of the portfolio manager of the fund sits within the investment advisor, unless the investment advisor assigns those responsibilities to another party, who is then considered a "subadvisor." The portfolio manager for the ETF will generally report to the board on a quarterly basis to keep the board informed about matters related to the day-to-day investment process.

As just mentioned, it is not unusual for the ETF trust to assign responsibility for managing the fund back to the ETF sponsor or an entity related to the ETF sponsor. Often the ETF sponsor is an asset manager already, and the portfolio management function naturally fits within the firm's mandate. Still, the ETF trust is generally an investment company for the purposes of securities regulations, so the trust must assign the sponsor or a related entity to formally act as the investment advisor to the fund.

The ETF Fund Administrator

The ETF issuer will formally assign an entity to handle the administrative processes of running a fund, which includes (but is not limited to) fund accounting, custody, etc. Like the investment advisor, this entity is often affiliated with the ETF sponsor, and just as the investment advisor may subcontract out the advisory role, the fund administrator will generally subcontract out the fund accounting and custody responsibilities to an ETF agent.

THE BROADER ETF ECOSYSTEM

With an understanding of the internal structure in hand, we turn our attention to the many other types of firms or entities that play a role in making the ETF market function. While we provide a brief summary of many of these parties, the reality is that the portfolio manager will have limited interaction with many

---

* Or Rule 6c-11.

of them. For example, the portfolio manager, somewhat ironically, has little or no interaction with the investors whose capital he or she is investing.

Regulators

Several regulatory agencies play distinct roles within the ETF ecosystem.

The Securities and Exchange Commission

In addition to approving exemptive relief, the SEC is the primary regulatory agency in the United States that oversees securities markets. Various divisions of the SEC oversee different aspects of the ETF marketplace, including the Division of Investment Management, which regulates investment companies and investment advisors, and the Division of Trading and Markets, which primarily focuses on execution, including exchanges, broker-dealers, clearinghouses, etc.

The Financial Industry Regulatory Authority

Authorized by Congress, the Financial Industry Regulatory Authority (FINRA) is a nonprofit self-regulatory organization overseen by Trading and Markets, which seeks to "ensure the broker-dealer industry operates fairly and honestly." FINRA will audit member broker-dealers and bring enforcement actions and monitor compliance with rules that govern broker-dealer activities.

Commodity Futures Trading Commission

If the fund holds futures and/or options, it is subject to oversight by the Commodity Futures Trading Commission (CFTC), which is a US government agency that is responsible for overseeing these markets. An all-equity ETF, for example, would not be regulated by the CFTC, while an ETF that holds commodity futures would.

The Index Sponsor and Index Calculation Agent

Passive (or index-tracking) ETFs, by definition, require an index to be tracked. The index sponsor is a company that is responsible for computing and disseminating an index and publishing index values on a daily and intraday basis. Index values are typically published every 15 seconds during market hours for products which are linked to the index trades. The index sponsor is responsible for sending index files to subscribers (among them the investment advisor) so that they might manage a fund that tracks the index accordingly. Oftentimes these responsibilities are performed by an index calculation agent, a firm that is hired by the index sponsor to carry out this role. For PMs tracking an index, the index calculation agent is a critical partner. We delve into much detail regarding index calculation and the associated files in Chapter 3.

It is not uncommon for the index sponsor to be the same firm as the ETF sponsor or an entity related to the ETF sponsor. When an ETF sponsor is using its own index for the basis of a passive product, this is known as "self-indexing." We discuss self-indexing in Chapter 13.

The Exchange

The "E" in ETF stands for "exchange," of course, and each ETF is listed on one of the major exchanges. In the United States, that list includes the New York Stock Exchange, Nasdaq, and BZX (CBOE). Each exchange has a large set of requirements that the fund must meet to initially list and remain listed on the exchange. Once an ETF is listed (and maintains listing by adhering to the exchange's ruleset), shares of the fund can be traded in the same manner that shares of a company would be traded.

The Authorized Participants

As detailed in Chapter 1, exemptive relief applications include the request to route the creation and redemption of shares through authorized participants. These firms, some of the largest market makers and banks in the world, facilitate liquidity for ETFs and play a critical role in keeping secondary market prices in line with the NAV of each fund. APs are the only firms that can create or redeem shares of an ETF. The AP can (1) hold the shares of an ETF upon creation, (2) create or redeem shares on behalf of a client, or (3) trade those shares. As we will see in Chapter 5, transactions between the fund and the AP are primary market transactions in which the fund receives orders from the AP. Especially when the PM seeks customized primary market transactions (as we will discuss in Chapter 12), the relationship between the PM and the AP is critical in the mission to efficiently manage the portfolio. Often these interactions are facilitated by the investment advisor's capital markets desk.

Capital Markets

The capital markets desk is the investment advisor's link to all things market-related: APs and market makers, the exchanges, and ETF calculation agents.

The PM will rarely directly interact with these entities but will closely interact with capital markets to ensure smooth execution of primary market transactions with the fund's counterparties.

The ETF Agent

The ETF agent serves as a custodian for the securities and assets of an ETF. Large ETF agents dominate the market: State Street Bank and Trust, BNY Mellon, and Brown Brothers Harriman, to name a few. The agent will be a daily partner of the ETF sponsor, handling the movement of assets in and out of the fund and providing a number of services, such as fund accounting. The ETF agent will provide valuation services for the fund as well, posting the NAV of the fund on a daily basis after accounting for the fund's assets (and liabilities). The custodian may also handle securities lending operations, though they can be handled by a separate entity.

The Transfer Agent

The transfer agent processes shares of the ETF through the creation and redemption process, accounting for the primary market transactions that facilitate ETF share creation and redemption, typically via in-kind transfers.[1] This role is simplified by the fact that the shares are held book entry (that is, investors do not hold the actual certificates) at the Depository Trust & Clearing Corporation (DTCC).

The ETF Distributor

The ETF distributor is responsible for selling ETF shares and is a broker-dealer regulated by the Securities Exchange Act of 1934. In the case of the ETF distributor, shares are only sold to authorized participants. Effectively, since we can think about the sales of new shares in the context of a primary market, the distributor serves as the underwriter of the fund. The distributor may also engage in more traditional market and sales support.

The National Securities Clearing Corporation

The National Securities Clearing Corporation (NSCC), a subsidiary of DTCC, serves as a guarantor to the primary transaction in the event that the AP defaults. The NSCC is also the pivotal organization in the creation and redemption process, as the files that dictate in-kind transactions (portfolio composition files, or PCFs) are routed through the NSCC to authorized participants.

ETF Calculation Agent

The ETF calculation agent is responsible for publishing intraday indicative values (IIVs)* every 15 seconds typically during market trading hours, which are meant to reflect what the portfolio of securities held in the fund is worth and help to keep the value of the basket in line with the trading price. The 15-second intraday requirement is no longer enforced with the adoption of the ETF Rule. Still, this has been a staple of ETFs in order to promote price efficiency in the secondary market, and it is possible that firms may continue to print intraday IVs even if they are not required to do so.

Execution Desk

When a portfolio manager decides on what transactions he or she wishes to perform, instructions for those transactions are typically routed to execution traders, agents of the investment advisor who are responsible for placing the orders in the market and effecting the trades. The ETF PM may discuss certain transactions with the execution desk, for example assessing liquidity in the market for a particular security or deciding whether or not to trade on the close (a "market-on-close" order) or during the trading day. The PM will typically send the execution desk his or her trades through an order management system, which is generally a commercially available software system that will provide all the necessary instructions for the order to be completed.

Note

1. https://www.sec.gov/divisions/marketreg/mrtransfer.shtml.

---

* These are sometimes referred to as indicative optimized portfolio values (IOPVs) or intraday NAVs (iNAVs).

PART II

Passive ETFs

Our journey through ETF portfolio management will cover several kinds of ETFs. Since many of the concepts we develop will be applicable to most of them, and the majority of ETFs in the United States are "passive" ETFs—seeking to deliver performance similar to that of a published index—we begin the process by introducing the concept of an index. In this part we explore how indices work in some detail, and we construct a hypothetical index to use as a basis for several analyses later in the book. Our passive ETF product coverage will be a launching point for exploring active ETFs at a later stage.

CHAPTER 3

The Underlying Index

At the heart of the investment industry is what has been come to be known as "the market." To most investors, and even to laypeople across the world, the market typically refers to the stock market (though for some it could also refer to the bond market, commodity market, etc.). Every day, the primary way that millions of people check the market is by looking at the value of a market index. Major news networks, whether they are solely focused on business or not, often put the value of a market index on their screens and their websites, in their print media, etc. In fact, the concept of the market is so ubiquitous that we almost forget to ask what "the market" actually means. When we say or hear that the market is up 2% or down 3%, what we really mean is that some indicator of the performance of a set of securities is up 2% or down 3%.

Why do we care about market performance? In large part, we care because for those who invest, the goal is often to beat or to exceed market performance. "The market" becomes a benchmark for what you can expect to achieve in a portfolio that might reflect a broad array of securities. If you allow someone to manage your funds, and the return was 10% for the year, you might be happy, unless you learned that the market returned 20%. In that case, you would have wished that you simply invested in the "the market."

And it's that notion, "investing in the market," that brings us to one of the most fundamental aspects of the investment management industry: by pooling assets, investment managers can efficiently deliver portfolio performance to the everyday (or even institutional) investor that is designed to meet or exceed the market's performance. To be fair, mutual funds had been doing that long before the advent of the ETF, but the new structure (as we will show in subsequent chapters) was able to deliver that market performance far more efficiently.

Investment products broadly come in two forms. Some offer performance based on managers actively making decisions on what to hold in the portfolio on a day-to-day, or even minute-to-minute basis. These are called "active" products. The investor is banking on the active PM's ability to deliver strong investment performance, specifically the PM's skill at beating the market.* Conversely, "passive" or "index-based" investment products offer performance based on a published model, a strategy that is predetermined and is often very simply meant to match the market. The investor in this case is banking on the model to perform and the portfolio manager to be able to deliver performance in the fund similar (or as close as possible) to the performance of the model.

These terms, "active" and "passive," are often used in ways that may not be as intuitive as one might expect. For some, a passive product is simply a product that tracks a market capitalization–weighted index, like the S&P 500; any other product, even if it tracked an index, would be considered active because it deviated from the most basic market capitalization–based methodology. Conversely, there are some who would say that "active" relates to pure security selection—stock picking in the case of equities—and anything that relied on any type of model that took the decision-making out of the hands of the portfolio manager, no matter how complex or much it differed from market capitalization, would be considered "passive." For our purposes, we will use "passive" and "index-based" interchangeably, as a way to distinguish those products for which ETF PMs have an index to track, regardless of how that index is constructed.

We begin our journey through the portfolio management landscape with a focus on passive ETFs.† The underlying index that the ETF seeks to track holds the key to virtually all the investment decisions the ETF PM has to make. As such, in this chapter we introduce the concepts that serve as the basis for index construction and the mechanisms through which the ETF PM

---

* The market in this context could be a sector of the market or some other subset of the market.
† As we will demonstrate in Chapter 15 on active ETFs, much of what we learn here will be applicable to actively managed ETFs as well; and with the ETF Rule applying some of the important tax-efficiency features of passive ETFs to actively managed ETFs, there is even more overlap than there ever was in the past.

receives information pertaining to the underlying index, in the form of files from the index sponsor. We also introduce our own index, which will form the basis for much of our analyses in the coming chapters.

PASSIVE ETFS AND THE UNDERLYING INDEX

Passive ETFs are funds that track underlying indices. The underlying index is a predefined strategy. The underlying index holds certain amounts of financial instruments as prescribed in the index methodology document, a how-to guide for constructing the underlying index that is published by the index sponsor. Some indices are simple (e.g., hold a basket of stocks weighted by their free-float market capitalization). Others are quite complex (e.g., hold a combination of stocks and bonds and switch the ratio of stocks to bonds if certain signals are observed). Regardless of the relative complexity of the underlying index, it is the job of the portfolio manager of an ETF tracking a specific index to replicate that index as accurately as possible, therefore earning a return every day that mimics that of the index. Achieving precise index performance is the holy grail of index portfolio management, but as you will see, it is an impossible task.*

INDEX METHODOLOGY

Understanding how the underlying index is constructed is the most important thing for any passive ETF PM. It is the proverbial key to the castle, the Rosetta Stone. If a PM does not fully understand how the underlying index works, she will never track the returns closely. Fortunately, every index has an index methodology that specifically outlines how the index is constructed. A well-written index methodology document provides the PM with all the information she needs to manage the passive ETF tracking that index.

There are many choices that go into the design of an underlying index. The index sponsor might have any number of justifications for the choices made (or no justification at all). Below we outline some of the major choices that go into the design. We primarily focus on equities for illustrative purposes and address other asset classes later.

---

* As noted in Part IV, there are other objectives, including minimizing transaction costs and minimizing taxes.

Eligibility

What makes up the selection universe for the assets in the underlying index? For an all-equity index, for example, what types of equities can be held? For instance, is the index allowed to hold stocks from several countries, or are only US-based stocks acceptable? Typically, for many strategies, the "eligible universe" will consist of assets that have already been classified somewhere else, e.g., stocks that are in the S&P Index or stocks that are classified as financials according to an industry classification standard. Eligibility is generally also defined by a time period: it is not enough to say the eligible universe is the S&P 500 Index; rather, one must state that eligible stocks are those in the S&P 500 Index *as of a specific date.*

Selection Rules

Once the eligible universe is defined, the selection criteria must be established. The index sponsor is generally looking to build a unique index, so this is where indices differentiate themselves. Selection criteria could be fundamental in nature (e.g., selection based on earnings, P/E, etc.), market-based (e.g., selection based on volatility over the previous calendar year), or any combination of factors. Recent innovations in indexing have included such diverse factors as the gender of the board members of a company, a company's hiring practices for military veterans, and Wall Street analysts' price targets.

Weighting

Once the selection rules result in a selection set, the index sponsor must prescribe in what ratio the index holds the assets that meet the selection criteria. For example, a classic weighting scheme in many equity indices is to hold the selected assets (selection set) according to their free-float market capitalization (FFMC). If the total FFMC of all the stocks in an all-equity selection set is $100 billion, and a particular stock's FFMC is $3 billion, then that stock is given a weight of 3%. Oftentimes index sponsors will impose weight constraints within the underlying index. It is important for PMs to understand how and when an index component's weight is restricted. It is possible that an underlying index would reduce the weight of a security if that weight rose above some threshold; as we will see, this will likely require some action on the part of the ETF portfolio manager whose product tracks this index.

Calculation Day Versus Rebalance Day

Typically, the index sponsor will provide a lag between when calculations are performed to determine the composition of the underlying index and when that composition is implemented in the index. For example, a market capitalization–based index might use the market capitalizations for the eligible universe as of the last trading day in a quarter (e.g., December 31) to determine index weights; this day is known as the *calculation day*. Then, once the weights have been determined, they are converted into shares to be held per unit of the index on a particular day shortly thereafter. The day upon which the index composition is updated is known as the *rebalance day*. Indices generally rebalance at the close on the rebalance day.

Not all indices have a lag between calculation and rebalance days. Equal-weighted indices, where every constituent in the underlying index has the same weight, may have the calculation and rebalancing activity at the same time. The index sponsor will use the closing prices as of the rebalance day to determine the number of shares held in each constituent that would provide equal weighting across the index. All else equal, an index with a rebalance lag of zero is generally more challenging for a portfolio manager to track. We discuss this in more detail in Chapters 7 and 17.

Frequency of Rebalance

The index sponsor will establish a rebalancing schedule for each index. A common rebalancing frequency is quarterly, though there are indices that rebalance at different frequencies. The more rebalances in each year, the more work for the portfolio manager wishing to track the given index.

Income Treatment

Some securities provide investors with income; dividend-paying stocks are an obvious example. Once income is passed along to the investor, that value is no longer part of the security itself. This impacts the weight and value that a given security provides to the index, and the index sponsor must decide how to incorporate this value back into the index. Any value that is extracted from the index in the form of income to the investor must be "reinvested" into the index. This generally happens in one of two ways: either the income derived from a given instrument gets reinvested into that instrument, or the income gets reinvested across the rest of the portfolio. Understanding the income treatment for a given index impacts the way a portfolio manager of a tracking ETF will reinvest income in the tracking portfolio.

Corporate Actions

Securities, and their role in the corporate financial structure of companies, are not static. Stocks split, convertible bonds are converted, and often companies merge with and/or acquire other companies. These situations may have implications for indices. The index sponsor will generally describe what steps will be taken as it pertains to the index in the event a "corporate action" takes place. There are far too many possible corporate actions for every situation to be enumerated in an index methodology, but many of the more standard corporate actions are often covered. The rest are typically left to the index committee (see below). Since corporate actions are almost always announced ahead of time (we'll discuss what happens when they aren't in Chapter 11), the index committee generally has time not only to make a decision but to publicize that decision so that a portfolio manager tracking the index has an opportunity to adjust the portfolio accordingly. The index sponsor will also send out corporate action files to subscribers of the index so that they will understand how they will impact the index.

Index Committee

The index committee is part of the index sponsor and is the governing body of the index; the committee is empowered to make decisions regarding the index on an as-needed basis. Generally, all decisions made by the index committee are deemed to be final. Index committee decisions are also generally made public, in the interests of those who subscribe to the index and (more specifically for our purposes) those who manage a portfolio that tracks the index.

Maintaining awareness of the index committee's actions can be critical for an ETF portfolio manager. Consider what could happen if the index committee for a particular index decides to make a change in the way it rebalances the index and the PM doesn't process this information in a timely fashion. This could result in significant tracking error for the fund.

Force Majeure/Market Disruptions

"Force majeure" is a French term meaning "superior force." For the purposes of constructing an underlying index, force majeure refers to situations that are structural disruptions in the markets: when the New York Stock Exchange closes unexpectedly, when data fails to disseminate, etc. The index sponsor will generally provide guidelines for how the index will be calculated under such circumstances.

Prices and Sources

At the most basic level, an index is simply a set of weights and prices/returns. The index sponsor will state very clearly what prices are used to construct the index and what sources are used for those prices. Is the index value for a given day based on the closing price of a stock or the opening price? Are mid prices used, or are settlement prices used? Oftentimes securities will trade on more than one exchange; which exchange's price will be used in the index calculation? These details are always found in the index methodology.

There are occasions when an exchange may halt trading on a stock. This may be due to an impending corporate action or announcement, and the trading halt is designed to allow time for the market to incorporate the information release into price discovery in an orderly fashion. When the trading halt continues through the close of a trading day, however, there will not be a closing price to use for calculating index values. Typically, an index sponsor will have a pricing committee (which may be the index committee) determine a "fair value" for the position, so that the index may be calculated. In many cases, fair value might be the last traded price for the security, but that isn't always so: for corporate actions that involve a stock-for-stock acquisition, for example, the fair value may be a function of the stock price of the acquiror and the deal terms.

Intraday and End-of-Day Values

Indices that are tracked by ETFs generally "tick" during the day; that is, real-time intraday values are often published and disseminated. How often this takes place, during what hours, and how intraday values are calculated all provide important information when the portfolio manager is tracking the performance of the portfolio during the day relative to the index the ETF is tracking.

Holiday Schedule

The index sponsor will determine what days are holidays for the purposes of calculating the index and how holidays themselves impact the calculation. For example, in an index comprising international equities, will the index sponsor use a stale price for an equity whose market is closed for a holiday while the remaining markets are open? With accrued interest for total return indices, a clear specification of how interest accumulates over weekends and holidays ensures clarity for anyone wishing to replicate the index.

INDEX EXAMPLE: THE "STARTS WITH A" INDEX

Throughout this book we are going to use a standard index to illustrate many of the concepts that we explore. We will create the "Starts with A" Index, abbreviating the name by calling it the SWA Index.* SWA will be defined according to a formal set of index rules, i.e., the SWA Index methodology. Index methodology documents are often dozens of pages long; here we simply provide an abbreviated index methodology that highlights the key points:

SWA Index Methodology

1. The index base date and inception date are both 12/31/2020, the last business day of 2020, on which date the index level is set to 100. No rebalance takes place in January 2021, as the index is set to equal weights as of the close of 12/31/2020.
2. The eligible universe will be a set of randomly-generated hypothetical tickers that start with either the letter A or the letter B (see Table 3.1).†
3. The calculation day for the SWA Index will be the last business day of each calendar quarter (i.e., the last business days of March, June, September, and December).
4. The rebalance day will be the fifth business day of the calendar quarter (i.e., the fifth business day of January, April, July, and October), with the exception of January 2021.
5. As of the close on the calculation day, the largest 20 stocks from the eligible universe whose tickers begin with the letter A will be selected for inclusion into the index (the index constituents).

---

* Any reference to an actual index (past or present) is purely incidental. SWA, for the purposes of this book, is a hypothetical index.

† We assume that these tickers trade on a major exchange, and in the case where a ticker matches an actual stock that trades on an exchange, this is pure coincidence, and the ticker is not meant to relate to that security.

TABLE 3.1

Eligible Universe for the SWA Index

AABA	AEDV	AKOZ	BDIA	BHLT
AABD	AETR	AKRY	BDLZ	BIFV
AAQZ	AFDA	AKTA	BDVN	BILG
AAWL	AFOJ	AKVS	BELV	BITI
AAXX	AFYE	AKXI	BEMP	BIXR
ABEW	AGFZ	AKZO	BENJ	BJAP
ABTV	AGYB	ALCP	BFGE	BJXM
ABVW	AHBP	ALFN	BFLE	BJYD
ACBU	AHGG	ALTO	BFMZ	BKDV
ACGN	AHJQ	AMGP	BFNI	BLAJ
ACGT	AHOR	BAEF	BFRH	BLIW
ACOP	AHSK	BAGF	BFTR	BLKR
ACPL	AIAD	BAJW	BGAZ	BMCA
ACQM	AIGP	BAKQ	BGLU	BMIM
ADAX	AIYO	BAYR	BGQL	BMYK
ADPQ	AJBH	BBOF	BGUB	BNDJ
ADSV	AJGL	BCBX	BGVO	BNIT
ADXK	AKEK	BCSF	BGXT	BNLP
ADZI	AKIY	BCYD	BGZM	BNMT
AEAP	AKMW	BDAC	BHDA	BNNQ

6. The index constituents will be equally weighted as of the close on the calculation day.

7. Index constituent weights will be converted to share counts as of the close on the calculation day.

8. Notwithstanding corporate actions, the share counts will remain constant, and the weights will float into the close of the rebalance day. We discuss this in more detail in Chapter 4.

9. All dividends will be instantly reinvested pro rata across the index on the close prior to the ex-date.

10. Any takeover of a constituent in the index (for cash, cash and stock, stock, or otherwise) will result in the removal of that name from the index on the close of the day prior to the stock's delisting. The weight of that position is redistributed across the

remaining constituents. Other corporate actions are subject to interpretation by the index committee.

11. The (hypothetical) SWA Index Committee* has final say over the interpretation of the index methodology.

12. Prices, dividends, and all other relevant market data, including corporate actions, will be sourced from the (hypothetical) SWA Data Company. Closing prices will be those reported on the (hypothetical) SWA stock exchange for each index constituent.

13. Index business days on which the SWA stock exchange is closed are considered index holidays, and no index level will be published on these days.

INDEX FILES

A well-specified index methodology dictates exactly what positions constitute the index at any time, and it is critical for the ETF portfolio manager to understand all the intricate details contained in the documentation.† Fortunately, portfolio managers do not have to perform the calculations that dictate how the index will evolve (although we strongly advise replicating the methodology). Rather, the index sponsor will "publish" the index daily. Publishing the index consists primarily of two things: sending the index values at the close and in real time to an exchange and/or data dissemination service such as Bloomberg or Reuters and sending files that describe what is happening in the index to the index subscribers. For the PM of an ETF that tracks a particular index, subscribing to that index is obviously a necessary step.

Index files are the lifeline of any ETF PM whose product tracks an index. The first rule of index ETF portfolio management is to track the index. Without a detailed view of what is in the index at any one time and what might appear in the index on a going-forward basis as a result of corporate actions, dividends, and rebalances, the ETF PM will fail in his or her primary mandate.

---

* The author.

† Throughout this book, as is common practice, we will refer to "index holding" or "positions" as if the index is an actual portfolio. In practice, we know that the index is simply a construct and no positions are actually held, though portfolio managers will try to track indices.

By subscribing to an index, the ETF PM will receive several files to assist, including:

1. Index close and index open files
2. Pro forma close and pro forma open files
3. The corporate action file

We address index files and the corporate action file in this chapter, but defer to the next chapter the pro forma files as we introduce index rebalancing.

Index Close and Index Open Files

Index close and index open files reflect what is in the index at the close of business on a given business day and what will be in the index on the open of the following business day. The difference between these files will reflect two important things: dividends and corporate actions.

Index Close File

We begin with the index close file. In Table 3.2, we present the index close file for the SWA Index on 1/13/2021. A typical index close file contains index-level information, such as the name of the index, the reference date for the index information, and the index level.

In addition, the index close file will contain relevant information pertaining to each constituent, including identifiers such as tickers, CUSIPs and/ or ISINs (we display a hypothetical ID), names of the securities, country and currency information (for international constituents), and pricing.* Most importantly, the file will also contain index weights (the percentage of the index held in the security), index shares (the number of shares theoretically held in a portfolio with value equal to the index level), and index values (the value of the index shares held in the index).

Consider the index close file for SWA. On the close of 1/13/2021, the value of the SWA Index was 100.9317. The index consisted of 20 index constituents. Since the index weights were set on the index base date (12/31/2020), the index weights have not strayed too far from 5%. The largest weight in the index is AHJQ at 5.66%, and the smallest weight in the index is ADXK at 4.53%.

---

* For the ETF PM, identifiers may appear superfluous, but the systems used to process the files as part of the order management system often employ them.

TABLE 3.2

Index Close File for the SWA Index

Index	SWA Index
Date	1/13/2021
Index Level	100.9317

ID	Ticker	Country	Local Price	Currency	FX	Base Price	Weight	Index Shares	Index Value
US1001	AABA	US	$ 78.83	USD	1	$ 78.83	4.71%	0.0603	4.7508
US1003	AAQZ	US	$ 67.87	USD	1	$ 67.87	4.68%	0.0696	4.7212
US1004	AAWL	US	$ 64.10	USD	1	$ 64.10	5.19%	0.0817	5.2370
US1009	ACBU	US	$ 62.56	USD	1	$ 62.56	4.90%	0.0790	4.9422
US1010	ACGN	US	$ 39.59	USD	1	$ 39.59	5.14%	0.1311	5.1911
US1012	ACOP	US	$ 91.22	USD	1	$ 91.22	4.93%	0.0545	4.9710
US1018	ADXK	US	$ 26.28	USD	1	$ 26.28	4.53%	0.1739	4.5703
US1019	ADZI	US	$ 29.89	USD	1	$ 29.89	4.58%	0.1546	4.6195
US1024	AFOJ	US	$ 18.24	USD	1	$ 18.24	4.71%	0.2608	4.7577
US1026	AGFZ	US	$ 51.99	USD	1	$ 51.99	4.87%	0.0945	4.9127
US1028	AHBP	US	$ 71.13	USD	1	$ 71.13	5.35%	0.0759	5.3977
US1029	AHGG	US	$ 57.16	USD	1	$ 57.16	4.81%	0.0849	4.8518
US1030	AHJQ	US	$ 78.58	USD	1	$ 78.58	5.66%	0.0727	5.7121
US1033	AIAD	US	$ 32.14	USD	1	$ 32.14	5.32%	0.1669	5.3655
US1040	AKMW	US	$ 56.27	USD	1	$ 56.27	4.77%	0.0856	4.8177
US1042	AKRY	US	$ 98.28	USD	1	$ 98.28	5.11%	0.0524	5.1542
US1045	AKXI	US	$ 17.88	USD	1	$ 17.88	4.69%	0.2650	4.7385
US1046	AKZO	US	$ 76.50	USD	1	$ 76.50	5.53%	0.0729	5.5766
US1049	ALTO	US	$ 82.47	USD	1	$ 82.47	4.99%	0.0611	5.0369
US1050	AMGP	US	$ 14.78	USD	1	$ 14.78	5.56%	0.3794	5.6071

Closing prices for each of the index constituents are included in the index close file. Since it is possible to include foreign stocks in an index (or more to the point, to include stocks that price in a different currency than the base currency), currency information is also typically included in the index close file. In particular, the file will specify the local (closing) price of the security, the currency in which the local price is quoted, the FX rate that converts the local price to the base currency of the index, and the closing price of the security in the base currency. For domestic indices, local and base prices will be equivalent.

The Index Open File

While the index close file provides an exact representation of the index and its constituents at the close of an index business day, this representation only holds for that instant in time. Corporate actions, dividend processing, and rebalancing after the close lead to changes in the index that render the ICF obsolete at the open of the following index business day. As a result, the index calculation agent will send not only an index close file to subscribers, but also an index open file, which provides a representation of the index at the open on the following index business day.

Consider stock AKRY in the SWA Index, which goes ex-dividend on January 14. The declared dividend is \$1.5492 per share. This means that an owner of the stock is entitled to receive the dividend (on the payment date, usually a few days past the ex-dividend date) as long as he or she owns the stock on January 13. If an investor purchases the stock on the open of the ex-dividend date, that first owner is no longer entitled to the dividend. As a result, the stock is worth less on the open of the ex-dividend date than on the prior close. The stock is expected to open lower by the amount of the dividend per share. Since the shares closed at \$98.2845 on the 13th, they would be expected to open at \$96.7353 on the 14th.*

An index is a hypothetical portfolio, so it does not actually receive a dividend, but it must be the case that the value of the index does not drop simply because a security in the index portfolio goes ex-dividend. The index methodology, as mentioned, will typically discuss how dividends are handled within the index.

Table 3.3 shows how the dividend is treated in the SWA Index by presenting the index open file for 1/14/2021. First note that the index open file

---

* Often figures in the text are rounded for ease of exposition.

TABLE 3.3

Index Open File for the SWA Index

Index   SWA Index
Date   1/14/2021
Index Level 100.9317

ID	Ticker	Base Price	Weight	Index Shares	Index Value
US1001	AABA	$ 78.83	4.71%	0.0604	4.7583
US1003	AAQZ	$ 67.87	4.68%	0.0697	4.7286
US1004	AAWL	$ 64.10	5.20%	0.0818	5.2452
US1009	ACBU	$ 62.56	4.90%	0.0791	4.9499
US1010	ACGN	$ 39.59	5.15%	0.1313	5.1992
US1012	ACOP	$ 89.81	4.86%	0.0546	4.9022
US1018	ADXK	$ 26.28	4.54%	0.1742	4.5774
US1019	ADZI	$ 29.89	4.58%	0.1548	4.6268
US1024	AFOJ	$ 18.24	4.72%	0.2613	4.7651
US1026	AGFZ	$ 51.99	4.88%	0.0946	4.9204
US1028	AHBP	$ 71.13	5.36%	0.0760	5.4061
US1029	AHGG	$ 57.16	4.81%	0.0850	4.8594
US1030	AHJQ	$ 78.58	5.67%	0.0728	5.7211
US1033	AIAD	$ 32.14	5.32%	0.1672	5.3739
US1040	AKMW	$ 56.27	4.78%	0.0857	4.8252
US1042	AKRY	$ 96.74	5.03%	0.0525	5.0809
US1045	AKXI	$ 17.88	4.70%	0.2654	4.7459
US1046	AKZO	$ 76.50	5.53%	0.0730	5.5854
US1049	ALTO	$ 82.47	5.00%	0.0612	5.0448
US1050	AMGP	$ 14.78	5.56%	0.3800	5.6158

looks virtually identical to the index close file in terms of format. Almost all of the information contained in the file is exactly the same, and in fact on days where there are no corporate actions or dividends to be processed, the two files are indistinguishable. January 14, however, is not one of those days. Note how the base price information for AKRY has changed. These columns now reflect the expected open price of $96.74.

Since the index held 0.0524 share of AKRY (refer to Table 3.2), the total value of the dividend in index points is approximately 0.0812. As per the index methodology for the SWA Index, this dividend will be redistributed pro rata across all the index constituents (not just stock AKRY). As a result, we would expect slight increases in the index shares of *all* the remaining index constituents and a slight decrease in the weight of stock AKRY.

The index open file confirms this result. Take, for example, AABA. In the index close file, the index contained 0.0603 index share (recall shares are not rounded in the index files). In the index open file, the shares have been increased: now the index "holds" 0.0604 share. How is this share count computed? The total amount of dividends in index points divided by the index level is the percentage of the index that requires redistribution as per the methodology. Call this percentage "α." Each share count is bumped up by a factor of $1/(1 - \alpha)$, as shown in Table 3.4.

TABLE 3.4

Calculating Open Index Shares Ex-dividend

Index Shares of AKRY	0.0524
Dividends Per Share	$1.5492
Dividends in Index Points	0.0812
Index Level	100.9317
Alpha	0.0008
Multiplier	1.0008
Close Shares of AABA	0.0603
Open Shares of AABA (Close Shares × Multiplier)	0.0604

As a result, while index shares in the index open file may differ from those in the index close file, the index level will stay the same. Of course, those stocks that went ex-dividend will have a lower percentage of the index in the pro rata distribution method, since some of the position in the stock is redistributed to other stocks. If the index methodology prescribes that the dividend is reinvested in the dividend-paying stock, then the index value for that stock will remain unchanged.

Corporate Actions

Dividends are not the only significant events that contribute to differences in the index close and open files. Corporate actions are a major source of differentiation as well. The impact on the index open file, however, is largely the same: the index level needs to remain intact once the corporate action is processed, and the index open file will represent changes in the positions of the constituents as a result of processing the corporate action. Corporate actions include, but are not limited to:

- Stock splits
- Rights issues
- Tender offers
- Acquisition by another index constituent
- Acquisition by an acquiror outside the index
- Ticker changes (relevant for the SWA Index)

A corporate action file might look like what is presented in Table 3.5. In general, it contains the security in question, the ex-date of the particular corporate action, the type of corporate action, and any details related to the corporate action. As an example of a corporate acquisition, take a look at the fourth line in Table 3.5. It appears that AAQZ is acquiring AABA. The transaction is expected to be completed prior to the open on 5/6/2021, and the deal is a cash and stock transaction: each share of AABA will be replaced by $24.53 cash and 1.27 shares of the acquiring company, AAZQ.

TABLE 3.5

Corporate Action File

Ticker	Ex Date	Type	Acquiror	Acq Type	Ratio	Cash	Sub Price	Ann Date	Perc Cash
AABA	4/1/2021	Split	NA	NA	2	0	0	3/24/2021	NA
AAQZ	4/19/2021	Split	NA	NA	3	0	0	4/13/2021	NA
AFOJ	4/29/2021	Rights	NA	NA	0.4	0	$15	4/26/2021	NA
AABA	5/6/2021	Acquisition	AAQZ	Stock	1.27	$24.53	0	4/29/2021	50%

The corporate action file also tells us that AFOJ is offering its shareholders a rights issue, whereby holders of the stock prior to the open on 4/29/2021 may purchase additional shares in the company at a ratio of 0.40; for every five shares that a shareholder owns, he or she may purchase two additional shares at a subscription price of $15 per share.

The impact of these corporate actions will be addressed in more detail in Chapter 11.

CHAPTER 4

Index Rebalance

nherent in any index is the notion that what it is trying to capture and measure, by definition, evolves over time. Yesterday's index of largest companies does not necessarily comprise the same set of companies as tomorrow's: small companies grow, and big companies shrink. Some of the largest companies in the world today, like Amazon, for example, did not even exist when the first ETF was launched. If the S&P 500 Index had remained static in its composition, then Amazon would never have made it into the index. What is more, with it remaining static and with many of the original S&P 500 companies no longer in existence, calling it the S&P "500" would no longer be appropriate.

How the index changes its composition is at the core of what is known as the "index rebalance." The index methodology provides a ruleset that dictates how the index composition will be updated on a recurring basis. This typically involves both a calculation day, when the composition and weighting are determined, and the rebalance day, when the change is implemented. A portfolio manager tracking the index must have a way of being informed about these changes, since the index files described earlier simply characterize the index in its present form. A different set of files that characterize what the index will look like upon rebalance day is required for the portfolio manager to determine what transactions are necessary in the portfolio to track the index.*

---

* As we begin our discussion on the mechanics of index rebalance, it's important to read this material with your portfolio manager hat on. And as you read, ask yourself, how will the rebalance impact the way the portfolio is managed? In this chapter, we cover how the index evolves and what changes are occurring within it; in Chapter 13 we reframe the picture by focusing on the ETF portfolio and the necessary steps the portfolio manager must take to track the index if that is indeed his or her mandate.

PRO FORMA FILES

The pro forma files (also called "look-ahead files") serve this important function for the PM. The pro forma files generally have the exact look and feel of the associated index files, but the weights and composition reflected in the pro forma files differ from those of the index files. They tell the story of what the index will look like once all the rules regarding rebalance are considered. Pro forma files are produced from the calculation day up to and including the rebalance day and are adjusted for dividends and corporate actions just like index files are.

The Pro Forma Close File

Consider the index rebalance process for the end of the first quarter of 2021 for the SWA Index. On the close of March 31, the calculation day, the index closes at a level of 97.7002, and the index close file shows the composition of the index (see Table 4.1).

Recall that the index methodology for the SWA Index specifies that on the close of the calculation day, the top 20 stocks by market capitalization whose tickers begin with the letter A are included in the index. On March 31, that list comprised the stocks in Table 4.2.

A careful comparison of Tables 4.1 and 4.2 will show that AAWL and AKMW appear in the index close file but do not appear in the Top Market Cap list for stocks with tickers that begin with A. Two new stocks appear in the Top Market Cap list: AAXX and AKEK. This is natural: companies grow and shrink all the time, and just as we noted in the introduction of this chapter, indices evolve for this very reason. In this case, the fact that AAWL and AKMW seem to have shrunk in value relative to the other names in the eligible universe means that there is an opportunity for two new names to enter the index. Upon index rebalance, the index will no longer hold AAWL and AKMW and will replace those names with AAXX and AKEK.

It's not just enough to know that the names in the index will be replaced; we also need to know exactly *how* the stocks should be replaced: on quarter-end, the stocks that are to be in the portfolio on rebalance day are equally weighted. The positions are converted to shares, and barring corporate actions, the weights will float going into the rebalance day.

The index sponsor, in order to assist anyone tracking the index into the rebalance day, provides an index file that reflects the *anticipated* portfolio on

TABLE 4.1

Index Close File for the SWA Index

Index	SWA Index
Date	3/31/2021
Index Level	97.7002

ID	Ticker	Base Price	Weight	Index Shares	Index Value
US1001	AABA	$ 94.35	5.8794%	0.0609	5.7442
US1003	AAQZ	$ 62.27	4.4788%	0.0703	4.3758
US1004	AAWL	$ 52.55	4.4396%	0.0825	4.3375
US1009	ACBU	$ 80.89	6.6072%	0.0798	6.4552
US1010	ACGN	$ 39.48	5.3528%	0.1325	5.2297
US1012	ACOP	$ 91.98	5.1831%	0.0551	5.0639
US1018	ADXK	$ 23.82	4.2826%	0.1757	4.1841
US1019	ADZI	$ 31.72	5.0697%	0.1562	4.9531
US1024	AFOJ	$ 20.74	5.5939%	0.2635	5.4653
US1026	AGFZ	$ 44.17	4.3158%	0.0955	4.2165
US1028	AHBP	$ 73.54	5.7702%	0.0767	5.6375
US1029	AHGG	$ 54.30	4.7658%	0.0858	4.6562
US1030	AHJQ	$ 67.75	5.0921%	0.0734	4.9749
US1033	AIAD	$ 27.90	4.8169%	0.1687	4.7061
US1040	AKMW	$ 31.77	2.8126%	0.0865	2.7479
US1042	AKRY	$ 72.52	3.9324%	0.0530	3.8420
US1045	AKXI	$ 16.44	4.5045%	0.2677	4.4009
US1046	AKZO	$ 76.72	5.7832%	0.0736	5.6502
US1049	ALTO	$101.62	6.4180%	0.0617	6.2704
US1050	AMGP	$ 12.49	4.9013%	0.3833	4.7886

TABLE 4.2

Top Market Cap A Stocks (3/31/2021)

Rank	Ticker	Market Capitalization	Rank	Ticker	Market Capitalization
1	ACBU	$60,025,484,770	11	AAQZ	$40,323,822,566
2	AABA	$54,503,589,693	12	AHGG	$40,298,875,597
3	AHBP	$50,311,476,754	13	AGFZ	$39,672,315,391
4	ACOP	$48,571,897,597	14	ADXK	$39,627,488,113
5	ACGN	$48,321,577,044	15	AIAD	$39,014,253,031
6	ALTO	$46,056,620,488	16	AKZO	$38,506,773,892
7	AFOJ	$45,777,963,714	17	AKEK	$36,822,094,536
8	AHJQ	$45,442,987,850	18	AKXI	$36,112,831,524
9	AMGP	$44,240,541,992	19	AKRY	$34,714,371,527
10	ADZI	$42,177,957,869	20	AAXX	$33,226,243,093

rebalance day. This is the pro forma file. On the close of the calculation day, that file reflects the equally weighted portfolio, as shown in Table 4.3.

TABLE 4.3

Pro Forma Close File for the SWA Index

Index	SWA Index
Date	3/31/2021
Pro Forma Level	97.7002

ID	Ticker	Base Price	Weight	Index Shares	Index Value
US1001	AABA	$ 94.35	5.00%	0.0518	4.8850
US1003	AAQZ	$ 62.27	5.00%	0.0784	4.8850
US1005	AAXX	$ 31.80	5.00%	0.1536	4.8850
US1009	ACBU	$ 80.89	5.00%	0.0604	4.8850
US1010	ACGN	$ 39.48	5.00%	0.1237	4.8850
US1012	ACOP	$ 91.98	5.00%	0.0531	4.8850
US1018	ADXK	$ 23.82	5.00%	0.2051	4.8850
US1019	ADZI	$ 31.72	5.00%	0.1540	4.8850
US1024	AFOJ	$ 20.74	5.00%	0.2355	4.8850
US1026	AGFZ	$ 44.17	5.00%	0.1106	4.8850
US1028	AHBP	$ 73.54	5.00%	0.0664	4.8850
US1029	AHGG	$ 54.30	5.00%	0.0900	4.8850
US1030	AHJQ	$ 67.75	5.00%	0.0721	4.8850
US1033	AIAD	$ 27.90	5.00%	0.1751	4.8850
US1038	AKEK	$ 96.70	5.00%	0.0505	4.8850
US1042	AKRY	$ 72.52	5.00%	0.0674	4.8850
US1045	AKXI	$ 16.44	5.00%	0.2972	4.8850
US1046	AKZO	$ 76.72	5.00%	0.0637	4.8850
US1049	ALTO	$101.62	5.00%	0.0481	4.8850
US1050	AMGP	$ 12.49	5.00%	0.3910	4.8850

It bears mention that the index close file and the pro forma close file "coexist" on the calculation day (and as we shall see, on several subsequent days). The pro forma portfolio is a representation of a different but related index: the index that will replace the current index when the rebalance day arrives.

While the constituents in the index close file and the pro forma close file on the calculation day do not match, what does match on the calculation day is the level.* Virtually everything else looks and feels like the index close

---

* This isn't a requirement and may not always be the case.

close file, but this "shadow" index that we have constructed is based on the guidelines set out in the index methodology for rebalance.

The Pro Forma Open File

Now that we have established that the pro forma index is a shadow index that reflects what the index ought to look like upon rebalance, it should not be surprising that the pro forma open file functions exactly like the index open file: it is a corporate action–adjusted and dividend-adjusted version of the prior evening's pro forma close file. Table 4.4 shows the pro forma open file on the morning following the calculation day, 4/1/2021.

TABLE 4.4

Pro Forma Open File for the SWA Index

Index	SWA Index
Date	4/1/2021
Pro Forma Level	97.7002

ID	Ticker	Base Price	Weight	Index Shares	Index Value
US1001	AABA	$ 47.17	5.00%	0.1036	4.8850
US1003	AAQZ	$ 62.27	5.00%	0.0784	4.8850
US1005	AAXX	$ 31.80	5.00%	0.1536	4.8850
US1009	ACBU	$ 80.89	5.00%	0.0604	4.8850
US1010	ACGN	$ 39.48	5.00%	0.1237	4.8850
US1012	ACOP	$ 91.98	5.00%	0.0531	4.8850
US1018	ADXK	$ 23.82	5.00%	0.2051	4.8850
US1019	ADZI	$ 31.72	5.00%	0.1540	4.8850
US1024	AFOJ	$ 20.74	5.00%	0.2355	4.8850
US1026	AGFZ	$ 44.17	5.00%	0.1106	4.8850
US1028	AHBP	$ 73.54	5.00%	0.0664	4.8850
US1029	AHGG	$ 54.30	5.00%	0.0900	4.8850
US1030	AHJQ	$ 67.75	5.00%	0.0721	4.8850
US1033	AIAD	$ 27.90	5.00%	0.1751	4.8850
US1038	AKEK	$ 96.70	5.00%	0.0505	4.8850
US1042	AKRY	$ 72.52	5.00%	0.0674	4.8850
US1045	AKXI	$ 16.44	5.00%	0.2972	4.8850
US1046	AKZO	$ 76.72	5.00%	0.0637	4.8850
US1049	ALTO	$101.62	5.00%	0.0481	4.8850
US1050	AMGP	$ 12.49	5.00%	0.3910	4.8850

While we haven't formally addressed corporate actions, we note here that AABA announced a two-for-one stock split with an ex-date of 4/1/2021, meaning that every shareholder received two shares of AABA stock for every one the shareholder held just prior to April 1. The value of the position stays the same, meaning that the stock price adjusts to offset the additional number of shares; in this case the stock price is halved. Looking at the pro forma open file, we see that AABA still has a 5% weighting, only now the number of index shares has doubled, and the price ($47.17), which is the expected price on the open, is now half of what it was in the prior evening's pro forma close file ($94.35).

PRO FORMA FILES BETWEEN CALCULATION AND REBALANCE DAYS

The pro forma close file is the first look at what the new portfolio reflected in the index will look like, but it is the pro forma files published in the following days leading up to rebalance that deserve more attention. Recall that many indices, and in particular the hypothetical SWA Index, fix the weights only on the calculation day; as soon as the weights are converted to shares, it is the share count that rules the day going forward.* As a result, as market prices move in the days leading up to the rebalance, the share counts stay the same (assuming no corporate actions that would alter them), but the weights differ. Table 4.5 shows the pro forma close file on 4/1/2021.

The pro forma level and the index level differ as well, as shown in Table 4.6.

---

* Not all indices are constructed using fixed shares in the index. Some indices are constructed such that the weights in the index are fixed as of the rebalance day, not on the calculation day, and then converted to shares. As a result, the pro forma files will fundamentally differ, in that on each given day the index shares are chosen such that the portfolio weights equal the target weights as of the close of the rebalance day. This is atypical, but some ETFs that market themselves as equal-weighted products can follow indices that may have this structure.

TABLE 4.5

Pro Forma Close File for the SWA Index

Index	SWA Index
Date	4/1/2021
Pro Forma Level	97.0192

ID	Ticker	Base Price	Weight	Index Shares	Index Value
US1001	AABA	$ 45.03	4.81%	0.1036	4.6629
US1003	AAQZ	$ 60.17	4.87%	0.0784	4.7200
US1005	AAXX	$ 30.67	4.86%	0.1536	4.7116
US1009	ACBU	$ 82.28	5.12%	0.0604	4.9688
US1010	ACGN	$ 38.22	4.87%	0.1237	4.7288
US1012	ACOP	$ 92.29	5.05%	0.0531	4.9013
US1018	ADXK	$ 24.60	5.20%	0.2051	5.0455
US1019	ADZI	$ 31.36	4.98%	0.1540	4.8304
US1024	AFOJ	$ 21.83	5.30%	0.2355	5.1408
US1026	AGFZ	$ 43.14	4.92%	0.1106	4.7710
US1028	AHBP	$ 73.07	5.00%	0.0664	4.8537
US1029	AHGG	$ 54.13	5.02%	0.0900	4.8696
US1030	AHJQ	$ 70.47	5.24%	0.0721	5.0812
US1033	AIAD	$ 27.61	4.98%	0.1751	4.8341
US1038	AKEK	$ 95.16	4.96%	0.0505	4.8077
US1042	AKRY	$ 67.69	4.70%	0.0674	4.5597
US1045	AKXI	$ 16.09	4.93%	0.2972	4.7809
US1046	AKZO	$ 76.36	5.01%	0.0637	4.8618
US1049	ALTO	$108.49	5.38%	0.0481	5.2151
US1050	AMGP	$ 11.95	4.82%	0.3910	4.6743

TABLE 4.6

Index and Pro Forma Closing Levels Differ Post-Calculation

Index	SWA Index
Date	4/1/2021
Index level	97.4765
Pro forma level	97.0192

However, despite the differences in index levels and constituents, when the close of the rebalance day comes, the index must somehow reflect a basket that reflects the composition of the the pro forma file, not the current index file. This is the "magic" of the index rebalance.

INDEX REBALANCE: THE BASICS

The most important days of the calendar year for a passive ETF PM are the index rebalance days. These are the days when the composition of the underlying index will change at the end of the day. As we have outlined in this and the previous chapter, the ETF PM is not flying blind, but rather has been given all the information he or she needs to manage the index rebalance by way of the index and pro forma files.

The Basic Rebalance "Trade" in the Index

According to the index methodology, the SWA Index rebalances five days after each calculation day, which is the last business day of the calendar quarter. Since 3/31/2021 is a calculation day, 4/8/2021 is a rebalance day. Table 4.7 shows the progression of the index shares for each ticker on the rebalance day.

Going from left to right in the table, we see the index shares on the close prior to any rebalance, the index shares from the pro forma file on the close of the rebalance day, and the index shares from the index close file after the rebalance. The list of securities held in the index prior to rebalance is, of course, not the same as the list of securities in the pro forma file. The table shows that stocks AAWL and AKMW are held prior to the rebalance, but not in the pro forma index close file; at the close of the rebalance day, the weights of these securities will be zero. The table also shows that AAXX and AKEK, which are absent from the index prior to the rebalance, have nonzero weights in the pro forma index close file; at the close of the rebalance day, these securities will have been added to the index, replacing some of the weight taken out of the index by the removal of AAWL and AKMW.

In addition to the index shares differences, note how the pro forma level does not match the index level. This is generally the case after the calculation day: the two sets of index constituents are different, so we cannot expect the overall valuation of the baskets to remain the same since the calculation day. In the table, the pro forma level is 96.7529, while the index level closes at 97.4188 on the rebalance day. This means that the index shares from the pro

TABLE 4.7

The Index "Trade"

Index Date	SWA Index 4/8/2021	Index Date	SWA Index 4/8/2021	Index Date	SWA Index 4/8/2021
Index Level	97.4188	PF Level	96.7529	Index Level	97.4188

Ticker	Index Shares	Ticker	Index Shares	Ticker	Index Shares	Index "Trade"
AABA	0.1219	AABA	0.1036	AABA	0.1044	−0.0175
AAQZ	0.0703	AAQZ	0.0785	AAQZ	0.0790	0.0087
AAWL	0.0826	AAWL	0.0000	AAWL	0.0000	−0.0826
AAXX	0.0000	AAXX	0.1537	AAXX	0.1548	0.1548
ACBU	0.0799	ACBU	0.0604	ACBU	0.0609	−0.0190
ACGN	0.1325	ACGN	0.1238	ACGN	0.1247	−0.0079
ACOP	0.0551	ACOP	0.0532	ACOP	0.0535	−0.0016
ADXK	0.1758	ADXK	0.2053	ADXK	0.2067	0.0309
ADZI	0.1563	ADZI	0.1541	ADZI	0.1552	−0.0011
AFOJ	0.2637	AFOJ	0.2357	AFOJ	0.2373	−0.0264
AGFZ	0.0955	AGFZ	0.1107	AGFZ	0.1114	0.0159
AHBP	0.0767	AHBP	0.0665	AHBP	0.0669	−0.0098
AHGG	0.0858	AHGG	0.0900	AHGG	0.0907	0.0048
AHJQ	0.0735	AHJQ	0.0722	AHJQ	0.0727	−0.0008
AIAD	0.1688	AIAD	0.1752	AIAD	0.1764	0.0076
AKEK	0.0000	AKEK	0.0506	AKEK	0.0509	0.0509
AKMW	0.0865	AKMW	0.0000	AKMW	0.0000	−0.0865
AKRY	0.0530	AKRY	0.0674	AKRY	0.0679	0.0149
AKXI	0.2679	AKXI	0.2974	AKXI	0.2994	0.0315
AKZO	0.0737	AKZO	0.0637	AKZO	0.0642	−0.0095
ALTO	0.0617	ALTO	0.0481	ALTO	0.0484	−0.0133
AMGP	0.3836	AMGP	0.3913	AMGP	0.3940	0.0104

forma level need to be grossed up by a fraction to be equal in value to the basket of index shares in the index. For every 1 share in the pro forma level, we need 97.4188/96.7529 shares in the index, or 1.0069 shares. So instead of 0.0785 share of AAQZ, for example, we require 0.0790 share. Since we started the day with 0.0703 index share, the index rebalance requires a "trade" of 0.0087 share, as depicted in the rightmost column in the table, along with the final index shares on the close of the rebalance day. The index "trade" requires a complete liquidation of AAWL and AKMW; the trade amount is exactly equal to the holdings of the shares.

Aside from the securities that are added to replace those that are removed, there are many other securities that remain in the index but have a different index shares count in the index post-rebalance than they did pre-rebalance. This means that the index rebalance will include a "trade" in this security. We say "trade" in quotes because indices do not actually hold securities; rather, they reflect a hypothetical portfolio at points in time. Were this to be an actual portfolio, we could calculate the exact transaction in each of the securities required in the rebalance. We discuss the actual portfolio rebalance activity for the ETF PM in Chapter 13.

There is a subtle, but important, difference between a PM rebalancing a portfolio for the close and the index sponsor rebalancing the index *on* the close: the index sponsor updates the constituents with perfect information; that is, the sponsor knows the closing prices of all the constituents in the old (index) and the new (pro forma) portfolios when the rebalance take place. A PM rebalancing a real portfolio tracking this index, in contrast, would only have information prior to the close, so there would undoubtedly be error in the transaction. We discuss the impact of this imperfect information set in Chapter 7.

PART III

The Primary Market and Launching an ETF

The unique construct that emerged as a result of exemptive relief gives rise to two avenues of transactions in the ETF world: primary market transactions and secondary market transactions. Primary market transactions in the context of exchange-traded funds cover those transactions that occur between the AP and the fund, while secondary transactions cover market-based exchanges of securities held in the portfolio (as well as market-based exchanges of shares of the ETF).

In the next chapter, we describe in detail how the primary market transaction takes place, focusing our attention on the construction of the transaction and its impact on the portfolio. Then in Chapter 6 we begin our journey as theoretical portfolio managers by "launching" an ETF.

CHAPTER 5

ETFs and the Primary Market

The distinction between primary and secondary markets in finance plays a critical role in the ETF market. Primary markets refer to transactions that bring financial securities to the market or remove financial securities from the market; secondary markets refer to transactions that transfer those securities from one investor to another (for a price, of course). One of the most attractive features of ETFs, in contrast to mutual funds, is the ability to trade them on the exchange—in the secondary market—in real time. Mutual funds trade at their net asset value at day's end; ETFs have a bid and offer in the market at all times (a requirement for the lead market maker of each ETF).

Much of the magic behind ETFs, however, occurs in the primary market. When a classic mutual fund is sold by an investor, the mutual fund sponsor will receive the sell order and sell enough securities in the portfolio to return cash to the investor for the sale. The securities sold will match the portfolio composition more broadly, making the sale effectively a slice of the entire portfolio. Similarly, when an order is received to buy the mutual fund, the sponsor will purchase securities that match the composition of the portfolio and use the cash proceeds from the purchase for funding these transactions.

When an investor seeks to purchase or sell shares of an ETF, he or she will likely do so in the secondary market, where market makers facilitate transactions among buyers and sellers. For the majority of ETF transactions, there is no primary market activity. As a result, while the ETF is trading throughout the day, there is no need for the ETF PM to do anything as a result of this activity—the only thing changing is the end investor.

For large ETF orders, transactions often do take place in the primary market; however, the mechanism through which the transaction takes place differs considerably from the primary market mechanism in a mutual fund trade. In this chapter, we will describe how the primary market transaction, known as a "creation" or a "create" (a buy) or a "redemption" or a "redeem" (a sell), takes place.

CREATIONS AND REDEMPTIONS

Every share that is traded in the secondary market must first be created in the primary market. But how does this creation/redemption (C/R) process* occur? ETF sponsors will generally offer creation and redemption for a fixed number of shares, typically 50,000 or 100,000, known as a creation unit, or CU. Only designated parties can create shares—these parties are called "authorized participants," or APs. APs are market makers that are either creating the shares on behalf of a third party or creating the shares to hold some inventory of the ETF shares for future client purchases.

At a high level, the AP (through the distributor) informs the ETF sponsor of the create and the number of units desired. The ETF sponsor delivers shares of the ETF to the AP, and in return, the ETF sponsor delivers a basket of securities and/or cash that is equal in value to the shares of the ETF as of the NAV of the trade date. Transfers of securities are called "in kind." The transfers are depicted in Figure 5.1.

FIGURE 5.1

Primary market creation

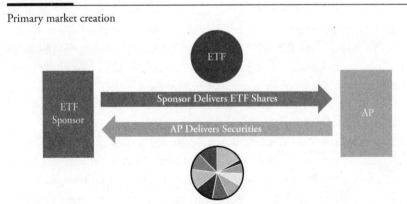

---

* For an excellent review of the C/R process, please see Rochelle Antoniewicz and Jane Heinrichs, "Understanding Exchange-Traded Funds: How ETFs Work," *ICI Research Perspective* 20, no. 5 (September 2014). Available at http://www.ici.org/pdf/per20-05.pdf.

The trade, by definition, is a "fair" trade: the values of the securities exchanged perfectly match by design. Similarly, when the AP wishes to redeem shares, instead of the ETF portfolio manager selling shares and using the proceeds to pay the investor (as in the mutual fund case described above), the ETF sponsor will transfer securities and/or cash to the AP equal to the value of the ETF shares being redeemed, and then the AP can sell those securities, resulting in a cash position in exchange for the redeemed ETF shares (see Figure 5.2).

FIGURE 5.2

Primary market redemption

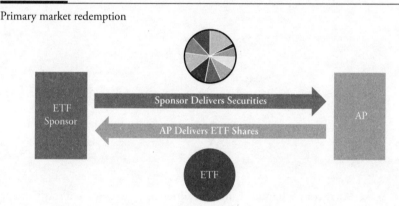

This process plays a critical role in the ETF ecosystem: it keeps secondary market prices in line with the NAV of the ETF. The basket of shares is designed to be equal in value to the NAV of the ETF shares, but is not necessarily going to be equal to the secondary market price of the shares. However, if the secondary market price is higher than the NAV of the shares, then the AP can create the shares at NAV and sell them in the market for a profit. Conversely, if the secondary market price is lower than the NAV, the AP can purchase shares in the secondary market and then redeem them at NAV with the ETF sponsor. As a result, subject to some friction related to transaction costs, secondary market prices are not meant to veer too far from the NAV of the funds.* Figure 5.3 shows the closing NAV and closing prices for SPY for May 2020. Note how the secondary market prices (the closing prices) hug the NAV (the primary market price) day in and day out. Because the absolute values are so close, it is hard to see the differentiation between the NAV and the closing prices, so on the right-hand axis, we show the premium/discount to NAV.

---

* There are, of course, exceptions, which we discuss in Chapter 18.

FIGURE 5.3

NAV versus closing price for SPY (May 2020)

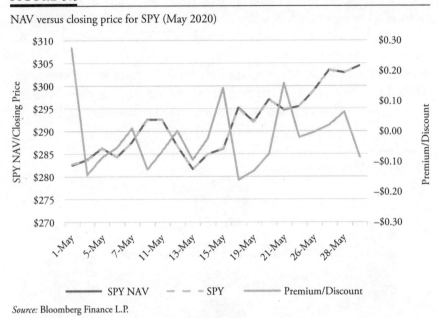

Source: Bloomberg Finance L.P.

As we learned in Chapter 2, intraday indicative values are also generally published throughout the day, so on a 15-second basis, market participants can check to see if secondary prices are in line with intraday NAV calculations.*

The importance of the AP and the ability to create and redeem shares cannot be overstated, and it all starts with what the AP delivers or receives in that transaction. The process sounds simple, but the devil is in the details.

THE PORTFOLIO COMPOSITION FILE

Just as the index and pro forma files we learned about in Chapters 3 and 4 gave index subscribers all the information they needed to know about the index, files will play a critical role in facilitating the primary market transactions that form the foundation for ETF trading. For APs looking to transact in an ETF, the portfolio composition file (PCF) is the primary resource: it can be thought of as the list of ingredients the ETF sponsor specifies pertaining

---

* We will discover in Chapter 18 that IIVs are not always a good source of indicative value for an ETF. Furthermore, intraday transactions may not post to the NAV until the following business day.

to one unit of the ETF. When an AP submits a create to the ETF sponsor, the ETF sponsor will expect to receive exactly what is specified in the PCF; when a redemption is submitted, the AP will receive exactly what is specified in the PCF. The PCF specifies the "basket" of securities in terms of shares and the amount of cash. In essence, this gives the AP the exact instructions for how the ETF sponsor wishes to transact in the primary market.

Constructing the PCF

Constructing the PCF is one of the most important exercises in the management of an ETF. Considering that any day an authorized participant can submit a creation or redemption order based on the PCF, it becomes quickly apparent that constructing the PCF is akin to constructing a trade that may, in fact, happen on any day. Getting the PCF right, therefore, is a critical exercise.

An ETF must submit a PCF that accurately reflects portfolio holdings.*In the case of an index-tracking ETF where the holdings file is meant to reflect the index as closely as possible, this is akin to submitting a file that reflects the index. We will walk through two methods of constructing the PCF: one from a portfolio holdings file and one from index files or pro forma files.

PCF from Holdings

At the close of trading on 1/29/2021, the portfolio holdings are as presented in Table 5.1. We show the amount of cash the portfolio has, the amount that has accrued that comes from dividends declared but not yet received, and the total number of shares in each of the securities in the portfolio along with their valuations. The current shares outstanding for the ETF are 400,000 shares, and a creation unit comprises 50,000 shares; in other words, there are 8 CUs outstanding. At the close on 1/29/2021, the NAV of the ETF is $25.38, so the NAV of 1 CU is simply 50,000 × $25.38, or approximately $1,269,168 (rounded). A representative "slice" of the portfolio for a 1-CU order would be 1/8 of the portfolio holdings, adjusted to round shares and whole lots.†

---

* Technically, a portfolio listing file (PLF) is submitted, which simply has the securities and position sizes. The PLF is then converted into a PCF, given prices, NAVs, etc.
† In this example, lot sizes are in unit increments, but for international portfolios, lot sizes are often multiples of 100 (see Chapter 14).

TABLE 5.1

SWA Portfolio Holdings

Index	SWA Portfolio
NAV	$25.38
Shares OS	400,000
AUM	$10,153,350

Ticker	Shares	Local Price	Market Value	Portfolio Weight
CASH	(2,249.52)	$ 1.00	$ (2,249.52)	−0.02%
Accrued	16,868.90	$ 1.00	$ 16,868.90	0.17%
AABA	6,049	$80.81	$488,844.28	4.81%
AAQZ	6,982	$73.91	$516,057.92	5.08%
AAWL	8,201	$60.21	$493,781.63	4.86%
ACBU	7,929	$64.58	$512,050.67	5.04%
ACGN	13,160	$43.97	$578,618.18	5.70%
ACOP	5,470	$90.92	$497,332.76	4.90%
ADXK	17,455	$28.77	$502,203.51	4.95%
ADZI	15,515	$30.24	$469,111.78	4.62%
AFOJ	26,182	$16.16	$423,014.50	4.17%
AGFZ	9,485	$53.52	$507,651.02	5.00%
AHBP	7,617	$75.26	$573,262.53	5.65%
AHGG	8,520	$58.40	$497,606.99	4.90%
AHJQ	7,296	$66.27	$483,538.19	4.76%
AIAD	16,757	$31.56	$528,780.71	5.21%
AKMW	8,593	$55.83	$479,779.78	4.73%
AKRY	5,264	$83.73	$440,729.18	4.34%
AKXI	26,598	$17.23	$458,225.89	4.51%
AKZO	7,317	$75.79	$554,530.48	5.46%
ALTO	6,130	$84.74	$519,446.99	5.12%
AMGP	38,083	$16.13	$614,160.56	6.05%

In Tables 5.2 and 5.3, we present two sections of the PCF for 2/1/2021 based on the holdings in the portfolio. The first section (Table 5.2) contains portfolio-level information, which includes information on the ETF as a whole and information on cash management, detailing how cash moves between the AP and the fund.*

---

* This section has been condensed for ease of exposition, but a PM might see a number of additional fields in a PCF. We explore some fixed-income–related fields in Chapter 16.

TABLE 5.2

SWA PCF Based on Holdings—Portfolio-Level Detail (2/1/2021)

SWA ETF			
Trade date	2/1/2021	Actual CIL	$ —
Settlement	T + 2	Actual cash	$ 2,182.46
Creation unit	50,000	Base market value	$1,266,234.84
NAV	$ 25.38	Basket shares	31,067
NAV per CU	$ 1,269,168.37	Estimated CIL	$ —
Shares O/S	400,000	Estimated cash	$ 2,933.53
Total net assets	$10,153,346.95	Estimated dividend	$ 707.10

TABLE 5.3

SWA PCF Based on Holdings—Security-Level Detail (2/1/2021)

ID	Ticker	Shares	Base Price	Base MV	Weight	CIL
US1001	AABA	756	$79.88	$60,388.33	4.77%	N
US1003	AAQZ	872	$73.91	$64,451.81	5.09%	N
US1004	AAWL	1,025	$60.21	$61,715.18	4.87%	N
US1009	ACBU	991	$64.58	$63,998.26	5.05%	N
US1010	ACGN	1,644	$43.97	$72,283.30	5.71%	N
US1012	ACOP	683	$90.92	$62,098.40	4.90%	N
US1018	ADXK	2,181	$28.77	$62,750.26	4.96%	N
US1019	ADZI	1,939	$30.24	$58,627.63	4.63%	N
US1024	AFOJ	3,272	$16.16	$52,864.69	4.18%	N
US1026	AGFZ	1,185	$53.52	$63,422.93	5.01%	N
US1028	AHBP	952	$75.26	$71,648.41	5.66%	N
US1029	AHGG	1,065	$58.40	$62,200.87	4.91%	N
US1030	AHJQ	912	$66.27	$60,442.27	4.77%	N
US1033	AIAD	2,094	$31.56	$66,077.87	5.22%	N
US1040	AKMW	1,074	$55.83	$59,965.49	4.74%	N
US1042	AKRY	658	$83.73	$55,091.15	4.35%	N
US1045	AKXI	3,324	$17.23	$57,265.32	4.52%	N
US1046	AKZO	914	$75.79	$69,268.94	5.47%	N
US1049	ALTO	766	$84.74	$64,909.69	5.13%	N
US1050	AMGP	4,760	$16.13	$76,764.02	6.06%	N

The second section of the PCF (Table 5.3) relays information about the individual securities in the basket. In general, the file typically contains security identifiers (such as ISINs, CUSIPs, tickers, etc.); share counts, market values, and weights; prices; lot sizes; and CIL designations. For equity-based portfolios, an estimate of dividends associated with each security in the basket (if the trade date falls on an ex-date for that security) would be included, and for fixed-income portfolios, a number of different pieces of information relating to interest (which we discuss in Chapter 16) would also be included.

Expected Cash Versus Actual Cash

The portfolio-level information in Table 5.2 is mostly self-explanatory, including the NAV, total net assets, etc., but the information on cash management in the table deserves some attention. Recall that the portfolio holdings included cash and that the NAV of the fund consists of security-based value and cash value. The value of the securities in a basket, due to rounding, will almost never exactly equal the total NAV for the creation unit. As a result, cash would have to be included to either increase or decrease the total value exchanging hands to make the transaction fair. The PCF relays the actual amount that would have satisfied a creation or redemption from the prior business day (actual cash) and a number of fields that are used to calculate the amount of cash expected to be part of a transaction on the current business day (estimated cash).

Part of that cash calculation involves "cash in lieu," or CIL. We spend more time on CIL in other sections of the book, but we note here that instead of including a security in the PCF, the sponsor may include a cash equivalent for the security. There are reasons for which the AP might want to use cash in lieu of a security (say, for example, the AP is restricted in transacting in that security). The cash management section of the PCF includes information about CIL and dividends (or interest in the case of a fixed-income basket) that contributes to the overall cash calculation:*

- **Actual CIL:** Exact amount of a cash in lieu from an executed basket from the prior trading day

---

* Though we don't present them as part of the PCF here, note that fees are also included in PCF files, including fixed-dollar creation and redemption fees, which are fees paid to the transfer agent from the AP for the transaction, and variable creation and redemption fees, which are fees paid to the fund from the AP in the event that the creation or redemption is cash-based. These fees are meant to reimburse the fund for the transaction costs it will incur to employ the cash in the fund or sell securities to satisfy a cash redemption.

- **Actual cash:** Actual amount of cash from the basket from the prior day
- **Base MV:** The market value of the securities in the basket
- **Estimated CIL:** Estimated cash in lieu for today's basket
- **Estimated cash:** Estimated cash in today's basket
- **Estimated dividends or interest:** Amount depends on the underlying securities in the basket

By definition, PCFs are forward-looking: they describe a transaction that could take place at the close of trading on the date of a creation or redemption. As such, the information set required to fully specify the trades is unknown, as market prices on the close have not been established at the time the PCF is required to be published. Because the share counts in the file are fixed, the value of those shares fluctuates, as does the NAV of the ETF shares. Rule number one in any creation or redemption is that the basket of securities and cash must equal the value of the ETF shares based on the NAV in the transaction. Fixed shares and fluctuating market values only leave one "degree of freedom" in this equation: cash.

Once market closing prices and the NAV of the ETF are established, it is straightforward to figure out how to even the trade out: simply adjust the amount of cash required in the transaction. The PCF, however, will not have this actual cash level required in the transaction. Instead, it reports the expected cash level based on closing prices and the NAV from the prior business day's close. For the sake of completion, and to document the complete transaction in a creation or redemption, the PCF will also include the cash amount that made the *prior* business day's transaction fair, i.e., value-neutral between the basket of securities and cash on the one hand and the ETF shares (valued at NAV) on the other.

Consider the PCF from Table 5.2. The closing NAV on 1/29/2021 was $25.38. The expected cash for any creation or redemption, based on market closing prices and the NAV from 1/29/2021, was $2,933.53. This figure will include expected dividends since the PCF will use closing prices. Once a security goes ex-dividend, its value will decrease, and cash must accompany the security to make up the difference. The market value of the basket of securities in the PCF will change over the course of the day for which the PCF is in effect, which is 2/1/2021; according to the PCF, the market value (based on 2/1/2021 expected open prices) was $1,266,234.84, but actual closing prices resulted in a market value of $1,265,076.66. The NAV of the shares on 1/29/2021 was $25.38, but the actual NAV on 2/1/2021 was $25.36. As a result, instead of the expected cash amount of $2,933.53, the actual cash in the transaction is $2,879.13 (see Table 5.4). This figure would be highlighted in the next day's PCF. Actual cash and expected cash will generally differ, but the important thing to note is that they are not comparable in the sense that they do not represent cash transacting on the same day.

TABLE 5.4

Actual Cash Differs from Expected Cash

Cash Calculations				
Prior NAV (1/29/2021)	$	25.38	NAV (2/1/2021)	$	25.36
Shares in CU		50,000.00	Shares in CU		50,000.00
NAV per CU		$1,269,168.37	NAV per CU (actual)		$1,267,955.80
MV open (2/1/2021)		$1,266,234.84	MV close (2/1/2021)		$1,265,076.66
Dividends	$	707.10	Dividends	$	707.10
Expected cash	$	2,933.53	Actual cash	$	2,879.13
			Diff in CU	$	1,212.57
			Diff in MV	$	1,158.18
			Diff in cash	$	54.39

Concerns About Holdings-Based PCFs

The approach we have taken so far, namely, to construct the PCF from the holdings in the portfolio, suffers from potential drawbacks. For example, some of the securities in the portfolio may be undergoing corporate actions the following day; perhaps a company is being acquired the following morning. A PM would have to manage the implications of receiving the acquiring company stock or cash in a create. Marking some securities CIL when they are undergoing certain corporate actions is a way PMs can mitigate some of these situations.

More importantly, the portfolio may be about to undergo a rebalance on the close of the following day, the date for which the PCF would be valid. This is problematic if the PCF represents a slice of the *current* portfolio, because upon creation, the portfolio would be misallocated, and upon redemption, the PM may be asked to deliver securities that would no longer reflect the portfolio holdings. Both of these complications can be addressed by using a forward-looking approach to what the portfolio is *expected* to look like on the close of the following day, incorporating corporate actions and any potential rebalancing. As we are about to show in the second method of PCF construction, this forward-looking system of what the portfolio will look like is already established by the index process for an index-based ETF. Index-based ETFs can employ PCFs based on index files and pro forma files, rather than portfolio holdings files.

PCFs from Index Files and Pro Forma Files

Recall from Chapter 3 that there are several files that come from the index calculation agent, including the index open files and pro forma open files. An index open file (IOF) reflects what the index will look like on the open of the following index business day. Importantly, this file differs from the index close file (ICF) by processing corporate actions. As a result, the IOF reflects a portfolio ready for replication in a way that the current portfolio holdings file looks like does not. If a stock is going to split, for example, the IOF would incorporate that, while the portfolio holdings file would not. It is conceivable, then, that a PCF based on holdings would be off for a given security by a multiple of two or three or worse, causing headaches for the PM upon a creation or redemption order.

The IOF fixes that. The procedure for calculating the PCF from an IOF on a non–rebalance day is as follows:

1. Calculate the NAV of a creation unit.
2. Create a vector of shares by multiplying the index weights from the IOF by the NAV of a CU and dividing by the (potentially ex-dividend) price contained in the IOF for each security.
3. Round the number of shares for each security to the number of shares in a lot. Shares may be rounded down to ensure cash is positive.
4. Calculate the value of this set of shares by multiplying the rounded shares by the prices and summing them up.
5. If the value of the basket exceeds the value of the NAV of the CU, then the basket would include expected "negative cash," meaning the AP would require a receipt of cash to accompany the shares of a creation order (and vice versa). If the value of the basket comes in short of the value of the NAV of the CU, then the basket would include expected "positive cash," meaning that the AP would include cash along with the shares for a creation order and would expect cash to accompany shares in a redemption order.

The PCF based on the index open file is presented in Tables 5.5 and 5.6.

TABLE 5.5

SWA PCF Based on Index Files—Portfolio-Level Detail (2/1/2021)

SWA ETF				
Trade date		2/1/2021	Actual CIL	$ —
Settlement		T + 2	Actual cash	$ 649.24
Creation unit		50,000	Base market value	$1,268,765.57
NAV	$	25.38	Basket shares	31,130
NAV per CU		$ 1,269,168.37	Estimated CIL	$ —
Shares O/S		400,000	Estimated cash	$ 402.80
Total net assets		$10,153,346.95	Estimated dividend	$ 708.04

TABLE 5.6

SWA PCF Based on Index Files—Security-Level Detail (2/1/2021)

SWA ETF						
ID	Ticker	Shares	Base Price	Base MV	Weight	CIL
US1001	AABA	757	$79.88	$60,468.21	4.77%	N
US1003	AAQZ	874	$73.91	$64,599.63	5.09%	N
US1004	AAWL	1,027	$60.21	$61,835.60	4.87%	N
US1009	ACBU	993	$64.58	$64,127.42	5.05%	N
US1010	ACGN	1,648	$43.97	$72,459.18	5.71%	N
US1012	ACOP	685	$90.92	$62,280.25	4.91%	N
US1018	ADXK	2,186	$28.77	$62,894.12	4.96%	N
US1019	ADZI	1,943	$30.24	$58,748.58	4.63%	N
US1024	AFOJ	3,279	$16.16	$52,977.79	4.18%	N
US1026	AGFZ	1,188	$53.52	$63,583.49	5.01%	N
US1028	AHBP	954	$75.26	$71,798.93	5.66%	N
US1029	AHGG	1,067	$58.40	$62,317.68	4.91%	N
US1030	AHJQ	913	$66.27	$60,508.55	4.77%	N
US1033	AIAD	2,098	$31.56	$66,204.09	5.22%	N
US1040	AKMW	1,076	$55.83	$60,077.16	4.74%	N
US1042	AKRY	659	$83.73	$55,174.87	4.35%	N
US1045	AKXI	3,331	$17.23	$57,385.91	4.52%	N
US1046	AKZO	916	$75.79	$69,420.52	5.47%	N
US1049	ALTO	767	$84.74	$64,994.43	5.12%	N
US1050	AMGP	4,769	$16.13	$76,909.16	6.06%	N

The procedure is exactly the same on a rebalance day, only this time the IOF is replaced by the pro forma close file, since that file reflects what the portfolio will look like upon being rebalanced on the rebalance day (on the close).

PCF and Halted Securities

Corporate actions that are known in advance can be handled in the PCF, as we describe above in the case of marking some securities CIL. There are instances, however, where news arises that is unexpected by the market, and in the interest of maintaining orderly markets, a security might be halted, meaning it is no longer allowed to be purchased or sold on the exchange. A security halt can last from minutes to multiple trading sessions.

When a security is halted, an AP looking to create a standard basket as prescribed by the PCF may be unable to secure the securities necessary to construct the basket. Similarly, an AP may not wish to receive securities in a redemption that has a halted name in it, since the AP will be unable to sell that security in the marketplace upon redeeming shares of the ETF. Orders for a day in which the PCF is already submitted through the NSCC process but are being processed at day's end are likely to require cash in lieu of the security that is halted.

It is good practice for the PM to track which securities are halted so as to be aware of how orders will impact the weights in the portfolio: if a security is halted and a large creation order comes in with CIL as opposed to a security, then the security will likely be underweight in the portfolio, leading to a temporary misallocation in the fund. The PM must consider how to deploy the cash; she can maintain the cash drag by refraining from securities purchases, or she can invest in other securities that are expected to move directionally with the security in question. We delve more deeply into these questions when we discuss tracking error in Chapter 7 and representative sampling in Chapter 19.

NSCC Timing and File Transmission

In general, the PCF is generated by the ETF sponsor (typically through its custodian) and sent to the NSCC by 12:00 p.m. ET of the trade date associated with that PCF.* Note that not all PCFs can go through the NSCC—they

---

* Generally the initial PCF will be sent the evening prior, and if any changes are required, there is a window to amend the file in the morning before the 12:00 p.m. ET cutoff.

need to have securities that are eligible to go through the clearing corporation.* APs have access to the PCF once it is posted through the NSCC process, allowing the AP to know what the basket will look like.

Order Timing and File Transmission

The noon cutoff for the NSCC process is *not* the same as the order creation cutoff. The order cutoff is the time by which the ETF distributor must receive notification from the AP that the AP seeks to create or redeem. Typically, for in-kind baskets (i.e., made up completely of securities and marginal amounts of cash) and domestic portfolios, this cutoff is synchronous with the end of the trading day: 4:00 p.m. ET. However, for non-in-kind baskets (i.e., having significant levels of CIL) and/or international portfolios, the order cutoff will be much earlier and can even be (and often is for international portfolios) the prior day. Consider a domestic portfolio where CIL baskets are accepted. This means that the AP is going to deliver all cash for creations and receive all cash for redemptions. In either case, to have the portfolio match the index to be tracked, transactions need to take place before the close of business: either securities need to be purchased with the cash from the AP in a creation, or securities need to be sold to generate cash for the redemption. Moving up the order cutoff window prior to the end of the trading day allows this to take place.

When the order window cutoff time precedes the NSCC cutoff time, this raises an interesting question: How does the AP know what will be in the PCF? The short answer is that the AP does not know. Of course, unless there is a rebalance on the date in question, the AP will have a very good idea from the prior day's PCF what the portfolio will look like. This will allow the AP to begin trading earlier, buying the basket of securities necessary in the case of a creation or selling the basket of securities that the AP will receive in the case of a redemption.

CUSTOM IN-KIND BASKETS

There are instances where the ETF PM will want a creation or a redemption to look quite different from the current portfolio or the current construction of the index, or even the expected construction anticipated along with

---

* Note that some securities can be removed from the PCF and that cash can be placed in the PCF instead, allowing otherwise ineligible baskets of securities to be eligible to go through the NSCC.

a rebalance. Creation and redemption activity is one of the main drivers of tax management within the ETF portfolio. In Chapter 9, we will discuss the impact of C/R activity on the cost bases of securities in the portfolio and the effect on capital gains and losses associated with transactions within the portfolio. The construction of "custom baskets," special portfolios that act like creations and redemptions but have significant implications for tax management, is discussed in detail in Chapter 12.

A NOTE ON THE ETF ECOSYSTEM

In Chapter 2, we outlined the role of the portfolio manager within the ETF structure itself, along with the roles of a variety of entities in the larger ETF ecosystem. So many facets of this ecosystem play support roles for the primary market transactions described in this chapter. The NSCC handles the PCFs; the APs create and redeem shares; the ETF agents will post the NAV, which drives the value of the basket and determines cash, and handle custody around new shares coming in or out as a result of the transaction; and on it goes. With so many participating entities, it is remarkable how smoothly the process can feel once an ETF is up and running. While it is generally beyond the scope of the PM to manage all these entities, it is critical that he or she monitor all this activity around the primary market, ensuring that what comes into and goes out of the portfolio is what is expected and that the ecosystem is doing what it is supposed to. This starts even before the first day the fund is listed, and in the next chapter we describe how the PM gets the fund off the ground on day one.

CHAPTER 6

Launching the Fund

A n orchestra is about to start a symphony. The conductor steps up to the podium and raises his or her baton, and the musicians get set to play that very first note once the baton drops. It's a moment of anticipation, a moment of excitement, but most of all it's a moment of coordination: if the violins start before the horns, or the cello misses a beat, the whole piece can be off from the get-go.

It is the same way for the launch of an exchange-traded fund. The launch is a coordinated act, and there is a rhythm to an ETF launch. Several workstreams are coming together at once, involving the exchange, the regulators, the fund administration, the AP/lead market maker, etc.—in other words, the players that we outlined in Chapter 2. The initial launch of an ETF is the most critical (and often the most nerve-wracking) time for an ETF PM. Getting a clean launch is imperative; hiccups at the outset, like an errant downbeat of a symphony, do not bode well for the fund. When it works smoothly, however, the launch culminates in the listing of the fund on the exchange on the launch date.

For our purposes, we focus on the actual fund mechanics surrounding the launch. While important, the rest of the mechanics are of less interest to us. The key questions for the PM are:

1. How will the initial funds be received into the portfolio?
2. How does the fund determine the initial NAV of the fund?
3. What, if any, trading decisions need to take place at launch?

SEED CAPITAL

Seed capital refers to the initial order for shares of the fund. Funds need a minimum amount of initial shares as dictated by the exchange on which the fund lists. This is specified in the exchange's listing requirements.* Since the fund knows that it can only list if it has the minimum amount of capital, it needs to secure the funding for the ETF prior to launch. The fund sponsor can either fund the ETF itself, putting its own capital into the product, or seek to partner with a firm, often an authorized participant for the fund, to "seed" the product with its capital, hence the "seed capital" moniker.

Regardless of who puts up the funds, the initial order must come through an authorized participant, just like all other creation orders for an ETF. If the seed capital is provided by the AP, the AP puts in the order for its own account; otherwise the AP would do so for the fund sponsor or whoever else is responsible for the seed capital.

THE INITIAL ORDER AND THE INITIAL NAV

As we know from Chapter 5, standard creation and redemption orders for an ETF tie back to the PCF, which outlines what is in the basket to be delivered or received in the transaction. To construct the PCF, a few inputs were required. For index-tracking ETFs, most PCFs simply reflect the index composition as dictated by the index files (or pro forma files if a rebalance is in order). The PCF also requires a NAV that reflects the value of a share of the ETF.

There is a catch-22, however: A fund that has not launched does not have a NAV, but to launch, the fund needs a PCF that requires the NAV as one of its inputs. Furthermore, if the intent of the PM is to use the fund holdings as the basis for the PCF, as opposed to the index, there would be no holdings in the portfolio prior to the launch of the fund.

In what follows, we describe three different methods for solving the catch-22, all of which facilitate a smooth launch: the fixed NAV, the floating NAV, and the zero-cash methods. Regardless of the method employed, it is critical for the PM, the fund sponsor, the custodian, and the lead market

---

* See, for example, https://listingcenter.nasdaq.com/assets/ETP_Listing_Guide.pdf. Funds generally launch at a share price of $25 or higher, making the minimum capital often around $2.5 million.

maker (LMM), in its capacity as an AP, to communicate effectively so that all parties understand the methodology employed and know what the PCF will look like and what will be delivered to the fund on day one.

Fixed NAV

The fixed-NAV model starts with the premise that the fund sponsor will dictate what the NAV of the fund will be at the close of the first trading day, which we denote $T(0)$. To do this, the sponsor will set a hypothetical NAV on $T(-1)$, i.e. the prior day, equal to a number of its choosing, say $25. To launch the fund, the sponsor will agree ahead of time with the lead market maker how many units of the ETF it will create to launch the fund. Suppose each unit is 50,000 shares and the fund is launched with 8 units. The fund launch in dollars is $10 million:

$$50,000 \text{ shares} \times 8 \text{ units} \times \$25 = \$10 \text{ million}$$

Each unit is valued at $1.25 million, and a PCF will be calculated for day $T(0)$ based on this unit value.

Recall from Chapter 5 that the PCF specifies the number of shares required for delivery by an AP to create shares of the ETF. The shares are rounded, which means that there is typically a cash component as well. If one valued all the shares using the opening (i.e., corporate action–adjusted closing) prices and then added or subtracted the expected cash figure from the PCF, the value of that basket of securities would exactly equal the value of a unit. In a stylized example, suppose $24 of the $25 worth of NAV is in securities and $1 is in cash (see Figure 6.1).

With this in mind, we can begin to see what the AP will deliver in a fixed-NAV model: at the close on $T(0)$, the AP will deliver the shares specified in the PCF times the number of negotiated units. The value of those shares, however, will not be known until the underlying securities settle and will presumably move over the course of the day. Once closing prices are established, that basket of securities is valued. If the value of the securities is less than the value of the shares of the ETF, the AP delivers the difference in the form of cash to the fund sponsor. If, however, the value of the securities is more than the value of the ETF shares, the fund sponsor delivers cash to the AP (depicted as negative cash in the figure). Either way, the total value transferred from the AP to the fund exactly matches the preestablished value

FIGURE 6.1

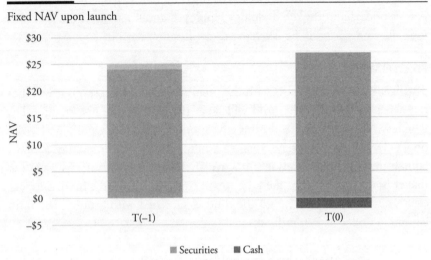

Fixed NAV upon launch

of the launch, which, in this example, is $10 million. By construction, the NAV on T(0) is fixed and is equal to the NAV on T(–1).

The NAV of a fund is published every day from day T(0) onward. Some funds may publish the NAV on T(0) *and* T(–1). If these two values are the same, there is a strong likelihood that the sponsor employed the fixed-NAV method during the fund launch.

Floating NAV

The floating-NAV method is not too different from the fixed-NAV method. The construction kicks off in the same way, by specifying a T(–1) NAV, the number of shares per unit, and the number of units negotiated with the AP. A PCF is calculated with open prices just as described above, and the rounded shares that make up a unit are specified.

The key difference lies in the cash that is transacted at the close on T(0). As mentioned, the PCF specifies the cash expected to be included in a one-unit creation or redemption. In the fixed-NAV method above, the expected cash is not used at all: shares of securities are transferred, and the cash is calculated so that the NAV at T(0) is equal to the NAV at T(–1). In the floating-NAV method, cash is treated as a security. Think of cash as a number of units of a security valued at $1. As such, the PCF includes a complete portfolio that exactly matches the unit value, since partial shares of cash are allowed. Continuing our stylized example, the market value of the securities that make up the basket is $1.2 million, while the value of a unit is $1.25 million. This means that to make the transaction balance, the AP must include $50,000 cash in a create (per unit). Consider this cash 50,000 units of a security valued at $1.

How does this impact the NAV at T(0)? Now the AP knows exactly what to deliver to the fund per unit: the exact number of shares per the PCF and 50,000 units of cash. Once the closing values of the securities are known, the total market value of the basket and cash is computed, and the T(0) NAV of the fund is simply the market value divided by the total number of shares outstanding. In the above example, we mark the securities at $1.35 million; along with the cash, the unit is worth $1.4 million, and the NAV is $28 (see Figure 6.2). Notice unlike the case of the fixed-NAV method, the NAV now floats from day T(−1) to T(0) and will continue to do so going forward.

FIGURE 6.2

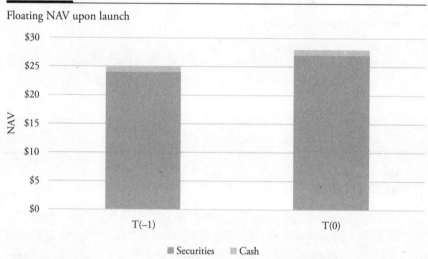

Floating NAV upon launch

Zero-Cash NAV

One way to avoid the intricacies of cash in the initial basket at launch is to employ the zero-cash NAV method. The zero-cash NAV method sounds just like what it is—no cash will change hands between the sponsor and the AP. The process is started by specifying a *temporary* T(−1) NAV, but note up front that this temporary NAV will not be the reported NAV. From this prespecified NAV, the PCF is constructed, and the number of shares of each stock in the basket is specified. Normally, we would then compute the expected cash to get the unit to be valued such that the value of a share precisely equals the NAV. Instead, we zero out the cash and recompute the NAV based solely on the market value of the shares in the PCF. In general, this NAV will not equal the temporary NAV, but this computed value is what would be reported. On the close on T(0), the AP delivers the specified basket (with zero cash, of course), and the NAV at T(0) reflects the T(0) value of the basket, as shown in Figure 6.3.

FIGURE 6.3

Zero cash upon launch

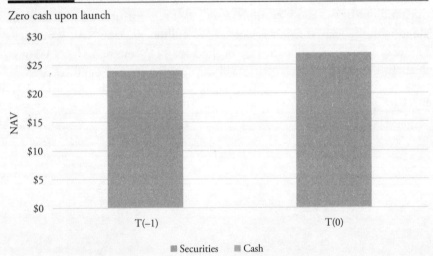

Securities ■ Cash

LAUNCHING SWA

To illustrate the above, we are going to launch the SWA ETF (see Table 6.1). We are going to employ the floating-NAV method and launch our fund on 1/11/2021. For the purposes of exposition, this date is T(0). We have arranged for an 8-unit create on launch, where each unit will equal 50,000 shares of the ETF. The T(−1) NAV is set at $25.

In Table 6.2, we show the opening index file from the SWA Index provider. Recall from Chapter 3 that the index holds the 20 largest stocks whose tickers begin with the letter A. The stocks are equally weighted upon rebalance. Note that the index weights in Table 6.2 are all in the 5% range, as the index inception was 12/31/2020, at which point the stocks in the index were equally weighted.

TABLE 6.1

AAAA ETF Launch Overview

Launch Details	
Launch date	1/11/2021
Number of units	8
NAV construction	Floating
T(−1) NAV	$ 25.00
Underlying index	SWA Index
Fee	50 bps
PCF construction	Index-based

TABLE 6.2

SWA Index Open File

Index	SWA Index
Date	1/11/2021
Index Level	99.7785

ID	Ticker	Base Price	Weight	Index Shares	Index Value
US1001	AABA	$ 85.93	5.19%	0.0602	5.1738
US1003	AAQZ	$ 69.02	4.81%	0.0695	4.7964
US1004	AAWL	$ 60.17	4.92%	0.0816	4.9111
US1009	ACBU	$ 59.42	4.70%	0.0789	4.6893
US1010	ACGN	$ 40.78	5.35%	0.1310	5.3413
US1012	ACOP	$ 89.70	4.89%	0.0544	4.8836
US1018	ADXK	$ 25.89	4.51%	0.1737	4.4980
US1019	ADZI	$ 30.70	4.75%	0.1544	4.7407
US1024	AFOJ	$ 18.07	4.72%	0.2606	4.7085
US1026	AGFZ	$ 50.33	4.76%	0.0944	4.7514
US1028	AHBP	$ 67.30	5.11%	0.0758	5.1018
US1029	AHGG	$ 55.95	4.76%	0.0848	4.7447
US1030	AHJQ	$ 75.97	5.53%	0.0726	5.5165
US1033	AIAD	$ 31.67	5.29%	0.1668	5.2827
US1040	AKMW	$ 55.35	4.74%	0.0855	4.7343
US1042	AKRY	$104.97	5.51%	0.0524	5.4994
US1045	AKXI	$ 17.47	4.64%	0.2647	4.6254
US1046	AKZO	$ 72.95	5.33%	0.0728	5.3132
US1049	ALTO	$ 84.58	5.17%	0.0610	5.1610
US1050	AMGP	$ 14.00	5.32%	0.3790	5.3055

Tables 6.3 and 6.4 show the PCF. Note the rounded shares for each of the constituents. The market value of the basket of shares is equal to $1,249,474.82. Since the NAV of the fund on T(−1) was fixed at $25, and there are 50,000 shares per unit, 1 unit of the fund is expected to be valued at $1.25 million. Since the value of the shares is lower than that, the expected cash of $525.18 would make up the difference.

TABLE 6.3

SWA PCF Based on Index—Portfolio-Level Detail

SWA ETF				
Trade date		1/11/2021	Actual CIL	$ —
Settlement		T + 2	Actual cash	$1,250,000.00
Creation unit		50,000	Base market value	$1,249,474.82
NAV	$	25.00	Basket shares	30,988
NAV per CU	$	1,250,000.00	Estimated CIL	$ —
Shares O/S		400,000	Estimated cash	$ 525.18
Total net assets		$10,000,000.00	Estimated dividend	$ —

TABLE 6.4

SWA PCF Based on Index—Security-Level Detail (1/11/2021)

ID	Ticker	Shares	Base Price	Base MV	Weight	CIL
US1001	AABA	754	$85.93	$64,791.47	5.19%	N
US1003	AAQZ	870	$69.02	$60,048.47	4.81%	N
US1004	AAWL	1,022	$60.17	$61,493.33	4.92%	N
US1009	ACBU	988	$59.42	$58,707.90	4.70%	N
US1010	ACGN	1,640	$40.78	$66,878.77	5.35%	N
US1012	ACOP	682	$89.70	$61,176.13	4.90%	N
US1018	ADXK	2,176	$25.89	$56,338.76	4.51%	N
US1019	ADZI	1,934	$30.70	$59,371.88	4.75%	N
US1024	AFOJ	3,264	$18.07	$58,975.92	4.72%	N
US1026	AGFZ	1,182	$50.33	$59,490.76	4.76%	N
US1028	AHBP	949	$67.30	$63,866.39	5.11%	N
US1029	AHGG	1,062	$55.95	$59,418.73	4.76%	N

(continued on next page)

TABLE 6.4

SWA PCF Based on Index—Security-Level Detail (1/11/2021) *(continued)*

ID	Ticker	Shares	Base Price	Base MV	Weight	CIL
US1030	AHJQ	909	$75.97	$69,053.57	5.53%	N
US1033	AIAD	2,089	$31.67	$66,168.69	5.30%	N
US1040	AKMW	1,071	$55.35	$59,283.62	4.74%	N
US1042	AKRY	656	$104.97	$68,858.42	5.51%	N
US1045	AKXI	3,316	$17.47	$57,937.57	4.64%	N
US1046	AKZO	912	$72.95	$66,534.62	5.33%	N
US1049	ALTO	764	$84.58	$64,621.72	5.17%	N
US1050	AMGP	4,748	$14.00	$66,458.10	5.32%	N

As described above, the floating-NAV method treats the cash as its own security. In this case, our basket includes 525.18 "shares" of cash, valued at $1. With this approach, our basket is fully specified.

What does our portfolio look like on the close of T(0)? The LMM has delivered eight units, which means that we receive eight times the amount of shares specified in the ETF and eight times the amount of cash specified as "expected cash" from the PCF (subject to rounding). Our portfolio is presented in Table 6.5. Using the closing values on T(0) for each of the securities, the value of the portfolio is $9,946,901.00, which translates to a NAV (dividing by 400,000 shares) of $24.87.

The resulting portfolio will generally be quite close to the desired composition, as dictated by the index files. Could we be closer to the desired number of shares? Perhaps. By "truing up" the portfolio the following morning, the PM could bring some of the share counts further in line with the desired portfolio as dictated by the index files. Maybe a stock traded ex-dividend and the cash portion was higher and needs to be reinvested. Misallocations at this point are primarily driven by the market movements during the launch day as well as the rounding of the shares in the PCF, which gets magnified with the multiunit create.

TABLE 6.5

SWA Portfolio Holdings on the Close

Date   1/11/2021
NAV $24.87
Shares OS   400,000
AUM $9,946,901.00

Ticker	Shares	Local Price	Market Value	Portfolio Weight
CASH	4,201.42	$ 1.00	$ 4,201.42	0.04%
Accrued	—	$ 1.00	$ —	0.00%
AABA	6,032	$ 81.63	$492,393.56	4.95%
AAQZ	6,960	$ 67.31	$468,456.88	4.71%
AAWL	8,176	$ 58.10	$475,060.18	4.78%
ACBU	7,904	$ 61.58	$486,758.44	4.89%
ACGN	13,120	$ 40.88	$536,306.63	5.39%
ACOP	5,456	$ 91.66	$500,120.51	5.03%
ADXK	17,408	$ 25.48	$443,552.50	4.46%
ADZI	15,472	$ 30.41	$470,569.17	4.73%
AFOJ	26,112	$ 18.40	$480,578.32	4.83%
AGFZ	9,456	$ 51.10	$483,194.72	4.86%
AHBP	7,592	$ 67.18	$510,035.89	5.13%
AHGG	8,496	$ 55.67	$472,970.56	4.76%
AHJQ	7,272	$ 76.75	$558,138.07	5.61%
AIAD	16,712	$ 32.13	$536,929.16	5.40%
AKMW	8,568	$ 53.76	$460,656.36	4.63%
AKRY	5,248	$103.81	$544,811.89	5.48%
AKXI	26,528	$ 17.60	$466,808.91	4.69%
AKZO	7,296	$ 74.40	$542,831.90	5.46%
ALTO	6,112	$ 79.95	$488,653.15	4.91%
AMGP	37,984	$ 13.79	$523,872.74	5.27%

FINAL THOUGHTS ON LAUNCH

A few final points on the launch bear mention. First, while we address corporate actions and dividends in a later chapter, please note that the PM should consider how these might impact the launch process. It is a good idea to start receiving index files and corporate action files several days prior to launch, so that any notifications from the index provider are processed and prepared for launch day.

Second, Murphy's law is part of the nature of the launch process. What can go wrong, will. Therefore, planning the launch midweek (and not before a holiday) is wise; being able to address any hiccups in short order the following day is important, and if, in a worst-case scenario, the launch has to be pushed back, it is possible to simply push back just one day as opposed to several.

Third, the LMM is a critical partner in the launch. The exchange will load the product into its systems the night before launch, and it will show up pre-market as a live security in a state of halt. The exchange will unhalt the security shortly after the open when the LMM shows a two-sided market. It is therefore imperative to make sure the LMM is ready to quote before launch, and unsuccessful launches have been attributed to LMMs rather than the fund sponsors, investment advisors, etc.

Finally, you may decide to ask the exchange where you are listing the ETF to ring the bell the morning of the launch. Don't do that. If there is an unforeseen problem that pushes the launch back, that will add to your woes. Instead ask for the bell a couple of days out past the launch when the coast is clear.

PART IV

The Three Ts and the Three Cs

We devote the next three chapters to the three objectives of managing ETFs:

- Minimizing tracking error
- Minimizing transaction costs
- Minimizing taxes on capital gains

Each of these objectives deserves detailed attention individually, but what the PM needs to keep in mind throughout the discussion of each is that the three are intimately entwined. One cannot consider a transaction to minimize tracking error without considering the impact on the portfolio of transaction costs. Tracking an index to minimize tracking error at the expense of all else may result in large capital gains to the fund, while managing the fund to minimize—or defer—taxes may result in a higher tracking error to the index. Any ETF PM would agree that the biggest challenge is managing all three of these objectives effectively and knowing when to prioritize one objective over the other. In what follows we provide a deeper context for each of the objectives, giving the PM the framework for making decisions that serve the shareholders' best interests.*

---

* Note that because these topics are so intertwined, it is impossible to discuss one without referencing the other two. As a result, some of the topics introduced in one chapter might be covered again in a subsequent chapter, which is done deliberately to give the reader enough context to handle the present topic of discussion.

We then turn our attention to the Three Cs:

- Cash
- Corporate actions
- Custom in-kind baskets

It is impossible to master the Three Ts without thinking about the Three Cs. Cash, covered in Chapter 10, plays an important role in every transaction, and understanding when cash comes into and how cash goes out of a portfolio is critical to portfolio management. Corporate actions, covered in Chapter 11, are exogenous events that can have serious implications for the portfolio and that can also impact all the Three Ts, especially tracking error and tax management. In Chapter 12, we cover custom in-kind baskets, or CIBs, primary market transactions that can have profound effects on the tax efficiency of ETFs.

Given the emphasis on rebalancing throughout Chapters 7 to 12, we devote the final chapter in Part IV to the portfolio rebalancing process. While we covered index rebalancing in Chapter 4, in Chapter 13 we draw an important distinction between how an index theoretically rebalances a portfolio—indices do not actually hold securities—and how the ETF portfolio manager must rebalance his or her portfolio. The emphasis will be on process—how and when the ETF PM analyzes his or her information set to construct the rebalance trade efficiently—and this process will be dependent on the Three Ts and Three Cs.

CHAPTER 7

Tracking Error

Your favorite chef posts her most famous recipe online, and you decide you want to make it for dinner. A quick scan of the ingredients, however, reveals that one of the items is not only absent from your cupboard but difficult to get at your local grocery store. No worries, you say to yourself; you will simply leave it out. Then you notice that the recipe requires a particular piece of equipment—say, a sieve—that you do not have. No worries, again: you will use a cheesecloth instead. And so it is that you proceed with the recipe, only to find that your finished meal is *very close* to what you get at your favorite restaurant, but it just isn't quite the same.

This is what it is like to manage an index-based ETF. The goal of the (passive ETF) PM is to provide the investor with the returns of the index he or she is tracking, less fees. Ideally, each day the PM's portfolio has exactly the same construction in terms of weights as the index itself. Since the index weights, i.e., the "ingredients," are made public on a daily basis, in theory this should not be a difficult task. The challenges, however, just like those for a budding chef, are quite daunting. They range from the relatively simple (e.g., indices typically use closing prices, whereas PMs transact at the bid and ask prices) to the more complex, including how corporate actions are handled in the index relative to in the portfolio. It would be impossible to list all the things that could potentially move the portfolio construction away from the index construction, but a keen understanding of where the differences lie and how to measure them is an important part of ETF portfolio management.

A review of index performance versus portfolio performance is actually quite straightforward and is often referred to as a tracking error (TE). Bear in mind that TE is not only a measurement, but something the ETF PM can manage but not eliminate.

In this chapter we continue to maintain our focus on index-based products. We will address active management and a tracking error "equivalent" in Chapter 15.

Depending on the context, tracking error can mean one of two things:

1. The difference in performance over a specific time period between a portfolio and the index it seeks to track.

    Or

2. The standard deviation or volatility of the daily differences in performance between a portfolio and the index it seeks to track.

We recognize that most of the time that a tracking error is quoted, it is typically referring to the standard deviation of the daily differences between a portfolio and index. One obvious difference between the two different definitions is that in the first instance, the figure can be positive or negative, whereas in the second instance it can only be positive. To differentiate in our usage, we refer to the first case above by using the terms "underperformance" and "overperformance," reserving the term "tracking error" for the second case only.

NAV OR CLOSING PRICE?

Tracking error or performance differentials must rely on a measure of value for the portfolio in order to compare returns of a portfolio to returns on its associated underlying index. For ETFs, closing prices and closing net asset values are available. Recall that closing prices reflect secondary market values, whereas NAVs are meant to reflect the value of the basket of securities held in the portfolio. With this in mind, the PM can only control one of these two values: the NAV. If a trade goes off a considerable way away from NAV at the close, a performance analysis based on closing prices would obviously skew the metrics. For our purposes, we restrict the discussion of performance differentials and tracking error to the NAV of the ETF relative to the underlying index.

AN EXAMPLE

In Figure 7.1 and Table 7.1, we show the NAV and index returns for the SWA ETF and SWA Index, respectively, for the month of January 2021. On a daily basis, the returns are very close to each other, and that also manifests itself in a similar monthly performance.

FIGURE 7.1

Daily overperformance or underperformance (January 2021)

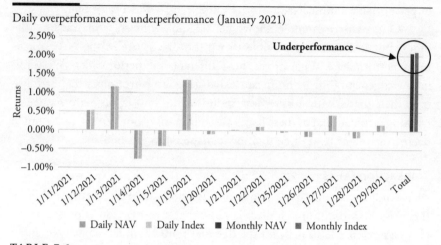

■ Daily NAV ■ Daily Index ■ Monthly NAV ■ Monthly Index

TABLE 7.1

Overperformance or Underperformance Versus Tracking Error (January 2021)

Date	NAV	Index Level	NAV Return	Index Return	Performance Differential
1/11/2021	24.87	99.25			
1/12/2021	25.00	99.78	0.529%	0.531%	−0.002%
1/13/2021	25.29	100.93	1.156%	1.159%	−0.003%
1/14/2021	25.09	100.16	−0.766%	−0.765%	−0.001%
1/15/2021	24.99	99.73	−0.426%	−0.424%	−0.001%
1/19/2021	25.32	101.07	1.338%	1.343%	−0.006%
1/20/2021	25.30	100.98	−0.096%	−0.094%	−0.001%
1/21/2021	25.30	101.00	0.024%	0.025%	−0.001%
1/22/2021	25.33	101.11	0.104%	0.105%	−0.001%
1/25/2021	25.32	101.08	−0.038%	−0.034%	−0.004%
1/26/2021	25.28	100.93	−0.150%	−0.149%	−0.001%
1/27/2021	25.39	101.35	0.418%	0.420%	−0.002%
1/28/2021	25.34	101.17	−0.175%	−0.174%	−0.001%
1/29/2021	25.38	101.34	0.159%	0.160%	−0.002%
Total return	2.075%	2.104%		Annualized TE	0.021%
Underperformance		0.028%		Zero-Mean TE	0.041%

Figures in this table and other tables throughout the book may appear not to precisely compute due to rounding.

The data shows that the portfolio returned 2.075% over the period, while the index returned 2.104%. The portfolio *underperformed* its index by approximately 3 basis points. The standard deviation of the daily differences in performance (annualized)—the tracking error—is 2.1 basis points.*

Our stylized example shows considerable efficiency in tracking the index, but it is certainly possible to witness divergence in the NAV versus index performance. What drives these differences in performance? What follows is a general (but by no means exhaustive) list of reasons why portfolios miss their mark, with a brief description of the impact on performance or tracking error. Several of these issues are important enough to warrant a much deeper treatment (and often their own chapters) in this book.

Transaction Costs

Many indices assume that a transaction is priced at "mid," or the middle of the bid-ask spread. Some indices assume that a transaction is priced at the closing price of the security on the day that transaction takes place. In either case, there is no difference in the price, depending on whether the intended transaction is a purchase or a sale. In reality, purchases are often nearer to the ask price, and sales are often effected at the bid price. Furthermore, transactions generally require commission fees to be paid to brokers, so that additional costs are incurred whether there is a purchase or a sale of a security.

When bid-ask spreads and commissions are ignored in the context of an index, the index effectively trades at a zero cost, and any attempt to mimic the portfolio in the index is subject to that cost. As a result, the portfolio underperforms the index. While there are a few indices that incorporate transaction costs into the indices themselves, these are less common. Minimizing transaction costs (discussed in Chapter 8) is an important goal for any ETF PM, primarily because it reduces tracking error and improves performance.

Fees

ETFs charge fees that accrue daily and serve as a reduction in daily performance. Indices typically do not have fees built into them. An ETF that perfectly tracks an index in every other way but charges a fee of 25 basis points per year can be expected to underperform that index by a similar amount.

---

* In the appendix to this chapter we discuss different methods of computing tracking error depending on whether or not the mean of the series is set to zero. In Table 7.1, we report both metrics.

Generally, fees are calculated on a daily basis by applying 1/365 of the fee to the performance of the fund each day (accruing three days' worth over the typical weekend); as a result, if an index is consistently rising over the course of a year, the accrued fees on the ETF will be lower as a function of the closing value of the product than the stated fee, and vice versa for an ETF that tracks an index that consistently declines over the course of the year.

Securities Lending

Securities lending (sec lending or stock loan) is the process by which a portfolio lends its securities for the purposes of another investor effecting a short sale in the security. The key for the ETF PM is that if the ETF trust allows for securities lending, the investor who borrows the security would provide a fee to the fund. The fee can range from a few basis points per annum to hundreds of basis points per annum and varies on a security-by-security basis.

Now imagine that the ETF portfolio has several names in it that are "hard-to-borrow" names, i.e., securities for which the price to borrow is quite high. This can yield a significant stream of income to the portfolio in terms of securities lending revenue. Securities lending revenue may be enough to offset, for example, the annual fee on the ETF. Securities lending is a net positive for the fund and, all else equal, results in one of the rare instances of overperformance relative to an index that a passive ETF tracks.

Taxes

We will devote a chapter to tax management, as it is a significant part of the ETF PM's job. Here, though, we highlight the idea that so long as an index does not reflect the tax implications of its holdings and transactions, any portfolio that tracks the index will be sure to underperform. In addition, ETF PMs may also transact in a way that optimizes tax implications for the end investor but might deviate from the way the index evolves (e.g., tax-loss harvesting). These strategies contribute to the tracking error of the ETF.

Round Lots

Index weights tend to be specified to extremely precise levels, often to the eighth decimal place. For a tracking portfolio, it is impossible to get this type of precision, as prices are generally quoted to two decimal places. Even if the portfolio manager is able to transact in single-share lot sizes, there will be some cash left over if there is full investment of the portfolio. Sometimes to round the shares there might be a slight overinvestment corresponding to a short cash position. There are securities, however, that are only available for trading in round lots, say sets of 100 shares or 1,000 shares, for example. As a result, it is more challenging for the portfolio manager to match the weights of the index.

Consider the SWA ETF. Instead of allowing single-share lots, we have gone back and increased the lot sizes for all the shares in the portfolio. In Figure 7.2, we compare the resulting NAVs of the fund against the index for the period 1/11/2021 to 3/31/2021 for a range of lot sizes. Clearly, the increased lot-size restriction constrains the PM's ability to closely track the index.

FIGURE 7.2

Larger lot-size constraints increase the tracking error (Q1 2021).

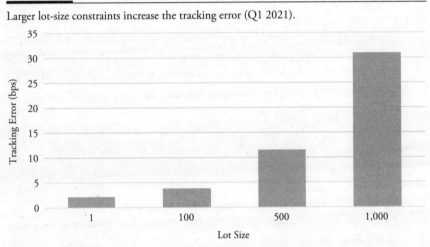

Cash Management

Cash is one of the Three Cs, a significant part of managing an ETF portfolio, as we will see in Chapter 10. ETF portfolios always have cash positions. At the most basic level, as discussed above, the index weights rarely correspond to exact share counts, and so the portfolio is either slightly over or slightly under on cash. Add in fees, dividends, coupon payments, accruals, foreign exchange for international portfolios, etc., and it is no wonder that cash contributes to some deviation on the part of the portfolio to the performance of the index.

Dividend Reinvestment

Indices will generally assume instant reinvestment of dividends. Typical speci-
fications include where the dividend is instantaneously reinvested in the issuing company or where the dividend is instantaneously reinvested across the
entire portfolio. Either way, the real-time reinvestment of dividends diverges
from reality, where PMs are subject to a lag in receiving dividends from a
company and/or where precise reinvestment across a whole range of securities
is impractical or impossible. While the portfolio will accrue the dividend as
part of its valuation, the reinvestment of the dividend and the delay in receipt
will contribute to portfolio tracking error.

Corporate Actions

While many corporate actions (the focus of Chapter 11) are not impactful,
some may have repercussions that increase the tracking error of the ETF.

No Lag Between the Calculation Date and the Rebalance Date

When an index sponsor allows for a lag between the calculation date and the
rebalance date of an index, it gives a portfolio manager an opportunity to
prepare for what is to come by allowing him or her an opportunity to receive
pro forma files that dictate how the index will evolve on the rebalance date.
However, some indices do not allow for a lag between the two dates: calculations for the rebalance are performed after the close on the rebalance date and
implemented immediately. Because the index does not actually hold or trade
securities, the new index constituents or weights can be incorporated into the
index when the market is closed.

For a PM, however, this can be a challenge—the PM needs to know
what to do as the market is nearing the end of a trading day, and he or she
must try to get as close to the perceived goal as possible. In some contexts, this
is called "hitting the close." We will see this play out in leveraged and inverse
funds, which we discuss in Chapter 17; it also plays out in funds tracking
equally weighted indices without a rebalancing lag. For these indices, as long
as the constituents are known, then simply knowing the rebalance date tells
the PM that at the end of the trading day, the securities ought to be equally
weighted; a pro forma doesn't add much to the information set required for
action. Still, any inability to hit the close will result in some tracking error.

Trading Halts and Pricing Discrepancies

Trading halts can happen for a variety of reasons: significant news regarding a security may be forthcoming, or a marketwide halt may occur due to a circuit breaker. We already saw that trading halts can impact the PCF (in Chapter 5); here we note that trading halts allow for the possibility that the PM cannot engage in transactions, while the index will assume that transactions are, in fact, possible.

It is also possible for the NAV of a fund to use a different price than that used by the index sponsor. Whereas the index sponsor will typically use a last-trade price or last-close price, ETF sponsors often have pricing committees that dictate what they believe to be the "fair value" of a security. Discrepancies in these prices may result in a spurious overperformance or underperformance on a particular day (which can often offset in the ensuing days if and when prices realign), since the ETF sponsor price will be used for NAV calculations.

We provide a more detailed example of the impact of trading halts and pricing discrepancies in our discussion of corporate actions in Chapter 11.

Concentration Limits

There may be firm or regulatory/exchange limits on how much of a given listing the portfolio may hold.* If the position for the fund is a significant part of the overall valuation of the underlying security, the portfolio may be limited in how much of that security it may hold. Any difference from the index weight as a result of this limitation will be a source of tracking error.

Obviously, that is quite a list, and it is not exhaustive. The PM may intentionally decide to deviate from the index over a period of time to manage taxes, rebalances, etc. Several examples of this behavior are described in this book.

ATTRIBUTION: UNLOCKING THE SECRETS OF UNDERPERFORMANCE AND OVERPERFORMANCE

Tracking an index is a lot harder than it would appear to be at first glance. Mastering how to guard against these deviations is where the ETF PM earns

----

* Often indices are constructed with these constraints in mind.

his or her money. By utilizing information available over time, the ETF PM can paint a far more detailed picture of tracking error and identify where, potentially, there is room to improve. This is what is known as attribution.

Right off the bat we can ask a few simple questions:

1. How much was removed from the portfolio for ETF fees for the ETF sponsor?
2. How much of the underperformance was due to transaction costs (in basis points)?
3. How much did the ETF sponsor receive in securities lending fees?

These categories of underperformance and overperformance are relatively straightforward both to understand and to calculate. Fees are typically taken out of performance on a daily basis as discussed above, transaction costs should be captured by fund accounting or the order management system utilized by the PM, and securities lending (if applicable) is captured by the custodian (and reported to the fund sponsor by the institution responsible for the lending program, typically an investment bank).

There are other sources of tracking error that require a bit more explanation—in particular, cash drag and misallocation.

Cash Drag

Cash drag is the positive or negative impact on the portfolio as a result of holding cash relative to apportioning that cash pro rata over the rest of the portfolio's holdings or index. The assumption underlying cash drag is that 100% of the portfolio's assets should be invested in accordance with the index, to the extent possible. When the PM holds cash (or is short cash), the (positive or negative) cash position could be employed in the same manner as the invested assets. To calculate cash drag on a particular day, we take the cash position as a percentage of fund AUM, and multiply it by the difference between the performance of the portfolio or index and the performance of the cash.

For example, imagine an ETF with 400,000 shares outstanding with a NAV of $25. The fund is worth $10 million. The ETF PM has a cash position of 10 basis points, or $10,000. Cash earns a risk-free rate of 2% per annum, so for a particular day, the cash earns

$$Cash\ Return = \frac{.02}{365} \times \$10,000 = \$0.55$$

Suppose the remaining invested position of $9.99 million returns 20 basis points for the day. Had the cash been invested along with the rest of the portfolio, the cash would have earned

$$Invested\ Cash\ Return = .20\% \times \$10,000 = \$20$$

By not investing the cash, the drag to the portfolio is $19.45, or 0.0001945%. This may not seem like a large amount, but if the cash drag were equal to this amount every day, the cash drag impact on fund performance would be significant.

Misallocation

Having accounted for the cash drag and several other categories of tracking error sources, we leave the most significant one for last: misallocation. Every day, the PM seeks to exactly mimic the allocations of the index in his or her portfolio. One of the central themes of this book is that this goal is lofty and impossible to achieve. Whether it's round lots, rounded prices, corporate actions, rebalances, or any of the other items listed above in this chapter, the portfolio weights are going to differ from the index weights. What is the impact on tracking error when the portfolio cannot hold the desired weights in the portfolio?

Deviation from the prescribed index weights is commonly called "misallocation." Misallocations are the PM's overweights and underweights relative to the index, and a misallocation or "over/under" report is critical for the index-based ETF PM. By definition, the misallocations must sum to zero, and therefore there are always positive and negative misallocations that will give the PM insight into his or her performance vis-à-vis tracking the index.*

Table 7.2 shows misallocations for the SWA portfolio versus the SWA Index on 3/31/2021 for the aforementioned case where lot sizes were increased (in this example to 100). The misallocations here are not too big—on the order of a few basis points rather than a few percentage points. They would be even smaller if we used our standard lot size of one, but the broader point is that if a misallocation is larger than a few basis points, this is cause for investigation (and potential correction) on the part of the PM.

---

* This assumes, of course, that cash is a misallocation as well. If a portfolio has all underweights, then by definition it is underinvested with positive cash; if a portfolio has all overweights, it is overinvested with short cash.

TABLE 7.2

Misallocations for the SWA Portfolio Relative to the Index

Index   SWA Index
Portfolio   SWA ETF Portfolio
Date   3/31/2021

ID	Ticker	Port Weight	Index Weight	O/U
CASH	CASH	0.13%	0.00%	0.13%
Accrued	Accrued	0.07%	0.00%	0.07%
US1001	AABA	5.88%	5.88%	0.00%
US1003	AAQZ	4.46%	4.48%	−0.02%
US1004	AAWL	4.40%	4.44%	−0.04%
US1009	ACBU	6.61%	6.61%	0.01%
US1010	ACGN	5.33%	5.35%	−0.03%
US1012	ACOP	5.17%	5.18%	−0.01%
US1018	ADXK	4.28%	4.28%	0.00%
US1019	ADZI	5.06%	5.07%	−0.01%
US1024	AFOJ	5.57%	5.59%	−0.02%
US1026	AGFZ	4.29%	4.32%	−0.03%
US1028	AHBP	5.79%	5.77%	0.02%
US1029	AHGG	4.77%	4.77%	0.01%
US1030	AHJQ	5.05%	5.09%	−0.04%
US1033	AIAD	4.79%	4.82%	−0.03%
US1040	AKMW	2.79%	2.81%	−0.02%
US1042	AKRY	3.93%	3.93%	0.00%
US1045	AKXI	4.49%	4.50%	−0.02%
US1046	AKZO	5.80%	5.78%	0.02%
US1049	ALTO	6.44%	6.42%	0.02%
US1050	AMGP	4.89%	4.90%	−0.01%

Consider the impact of a misallocation on the portfolio; if those assets that are underallocated overperform, then the portfolio will lag the index, and vice versa. As we noted in the discussion on cash drags, a one-day differential may not be worthy of much attention, but if the magnitude of the difference occurred on a daily basis, the resulting underperformance and tracking error could be significant.

In the appendix to this chapter, we describe the mathematics that go into attributing overperformance and underperformance to cash drag, misallocation, and other categories.

PUTTING IT ALL TOGETHER

Over a period of time, the PM can begin to see patterns of behavior that he or she may not even realize are occurring on a more frequent basis. If a PM were told that the cash drag was less than 1/10 of a basis point for a particular day, we'd be fairly confident the PM wouldn't spend much time worrying about it. However, if that same PM were told that cash drag resulted in underperformance for the year of 25 basis points, that PM would be more concerned. Therefore, best practice in portfolio management is to aggregate the attribution on a somewhat frequent basis, perhaps quarterly or even monthly. Aggregating across periods of time and categorizing the various forms of underperformance and overperformance described above is the best way for PMs to see how the portfolio is doing.*

In Table 7.3, we present a quarterly attribution report for SWA for the first quarter of 2021. We begin with the understanding that we *expect* the portfolio to underperform: fees on the product automatically put the product at a disadvantage relative to the index, and we haven't included securities lending as a source of income for the portfolio. On a 50–basis point product, one would naturally expect a shortfall of approximately 12.5 basis points per quarter.†

TABLE 7.3

Attribution Report for the SWA Portfolio

Fund	SWA ETF
Start date	1/11/2021
End date	3/31/2021
Index return	−1.5600%
Fees	−0.1113%
Transaction costs	−0.0003%
Misallocation	0.0027%
Cash drag	0.0016%
Linearity/rounding	−0.0001%
NAV return	−1.6673%

---

* As a minor point, the more mathematically inclined reader will recognize that aggregating these categories may result in a bit of rounding error in the calculations.

† We also note that the transaction costs are quite low due to the fact that there was no rebalance in the first quarter of 2021.

APPENDIX

In this chapter we discussed elements of tracking error in a largely nonmathematical framework. Here we add some mathematical rigor to the exercise for those readers wishing to take a more analytical approach.

Define the performance on the index for a given day as

$$r_t^I = \sum_i w_{it}^I r_{it},$$

Define the performance for the portfolio on a given day as

$$r_t^P = \sum_i w_{it}^P r_{it} + (1 - w_{it}^{*P}) r_t^f + \varepsilon_t,$$

And define the outperformance for a given day, α_t, as the difference:

$$\alpha_t = \sum_i w_{it}^P r_{it} + (1 - w_{it}^{*P}) r_t^f - \sum_i w_{it}^I r_{it} + \varepsilon_t$$

where

w_{it}^P = the weight of security i in the portfolio at time t

r_{it} = the return to security at time t

w_{it}^{*P} = the sum of the weights in the portfolio (which may not sum to 100% due to cash)

r_t^f = the return to cash at time t

w_{it}^I = the weight of security i in the index at time t

$\varepsilon_t = -fee_t + SL_t - TC_t$; i.e., the daily fee, the securities lending income, and transaction costs (all in basis points)

and

   i ∈ M, which represents the securities in the index

Normalizing the portfolio weights on the securities to add up to 100%, we have

$$\alpha_t = w_{it}^{*P} \sum_i \frac{w_{it}^P}{w_{it}^{*P}} r_{it} + (1 - w_{it}^{*P}) r_t^f - \sum_i w_{it}^I r_{it} + \varepsilon_t$$

or, replacing $\dfrac{w_{it}^{P}}{w_{it}^{*P}}$ with $\tilde{w}_{it}^{P}$,

$$\alpha_t = w_{it}^{*P} \sum_i \tilde{w}_{it}^{P} r_{it} + (1 - w_{it}^{*P}) r_t^f - \sum_i w_{it}^{I} r_{it} + \varepsilon_t$$

Since

$$w_{it}^{*P} \sum_i \tilde{w}_{it}^{P} r_{it} = \sum_i \tilde{w}_{it}^{P} r_{it} - (1 - w_{it}^{*P}) \sum_i \tilde{w}_{it}^{P} r_{it}$$

we have

$$\alpha_t = \sum_i \tilde{w}_{it}^{P} r_{it} - (1 - w_{it}^{*P}) \sum_i \tilde{w}_{it}^{P} r_{it} + (1 - w_{it}^{*P}) r_t^f - \sum_i w_{it}^{I} r_{it} + \varepsilon_t$$

Combining terms yields

$$\alpha_t = \sum_i \tilde{w}_{it}^{P} r_{it} + (1 - w_{it}^{*P}) \left[r_t^f - \sum_i \tilde{w}_{it}^{P} r_{it} \right] - \sum_i w_{it}^{I} r_{it} + \varepsilon_t$$

and rearranging results in

$$\alpha_t = \sum_i \tilde{w}_{it}^{P} r_{it} - \sum_i w_{it}^{I} r_{it} + (1 - w_{it}^{*P}) \left[r_t^f - \sum_i \tilde{w}_{it}^{P} r_{it} \right] + \varepsilon_t$$

or

$$\alpha_t = \sum_i (\tilde{w}_{it}^{P} - w_{it}^{I}) r_{it} + (1 - w_{it}^{*P}) \left[r_t^f - \sum_i \tilde{w}_{it}^{P} r_{it} \right] + \varepsilon_t$$

The first term is misallocation, while the second term is cash drag. Note that the second term is a function of the performance of the risk-free rate relative to the portfolio weights, not the index weights. Alternatively, we can proceed as follows:

$$\alpha_t = w_{it}^{*P} \sum_i \tilde{w}_{it}^{P} r_{it} + (1 - w_{it}^{*P}) r_t^f - \sum_i w_{it}^{I} r_{it} + \varepsilon_t$$

$$\alpha_t = w_{it}^{*P} \sum_i \tilde{w}_{it}^{P} r_{it} + (1 - w_{it}^{*P}) r_t^f - (1 - w_{it}^{*P}) \sum_i w_{it}^{I} r_{it} - w_{it}^{*P} \sum_i w_{it}^{I} r_{it} + \varepsilon_t$$

or

$$\alpha_t = w_{it}^{*P}\left[\sum_i (\tilde{w}_{it}^P - w_{it}^I)r_{it}\right] + (1 - w_{it}^{*P})\left[r_t^f - \sum_i w_{it}^I r_{it}\right] + \varepsilon_t$$

Put another way, outperformance is a weighted combination of misallocation to the index and the cash drag to the index.

Expected daily outperformance would be $E[\alpha_t]$, though typically outperformance is aggregated over the number of days in a trading period.

Tracking error, under this construct, would be the standard deviation of the outperformance, which is annualized by multiplying by the square root of 252 (since variance scales linearly). Tracking error may also be calculated by assuming a zero mean. A portfolio that consistently underperforms an index by 1bp every day has a standard deviation of outperformance of zero, since it is always the same. It is clear, however, that most would consider such a portfolio to have a tracking error; replacing the mean with zero achieves this effect.

CHAPTER 8

Transaction Costs

When my son was younger and first learning about money, he asked me if he could purchase a special football trading card online. I asked him if he had researched what the card was worth and found the best price. He proudly said that he had, told me that the card cost $12, and asked if he could use some of his allowance money to purchase it. I said yes, and we went to the website to make the transaction. There the card was, priced at $12, but when we put it in the cart for purchase, we learned that the shipping charge was $20(!), for a sum total of $32. And so it was that my son learned—the hard way—about transaction costs.

Transaction costs are a necessary evil for any portfolio manager, and the intent of this chapter is to discuss their impact on the portfolio and the desire to minimize those costs for the most efficient portfolio. We mentioned at the outset that ETFs already bring with them a level of cost-efficiency, and one specific area where that happens is transaction costs—many of the transactions that occur inside the construct of the fund are addressed in the primary market through AP activity, whereas in a mutual fund much of the activity would be completed within the fund. This is like "free shipping" when purchasing trading cards. Nevertheless, for those transactions remaining within the fund construct, the ETF PM seeks to minimize transaction costs to the extent possible.

A passive ETF PM is responsible for tracking an index, but when the index changes its composition, the portfolio composition does not change unless the PM takes action. That action costs money, in the form of commissions and spreads, and as a result, the performance of the fund lags relative to the index performance. An active ETF portfolio manager (discussed in more detail in Chapter 15) will undoubtedly update the composition of his or her portfolio and in the course of doing so will pay commissions and spreads as well. Unlike other contributors to tracking error such as misallocation or cash drag, transaction costs are generally a one-way street: they can only lead to underperformance, not overperformance. An exception is when an index explicitly incorporates transaction costs, and the PM can transact more efficiently.*

If transaction costs are necessary, then to a large extent the most a PM can do to manage transaction costs is seek to get the best execution and trade as little as possible. Both tactics can lead to improved performance at the margins. As we will see, the PM can, in fact, decide whether to transact at all, weighing the "cost" of not transacting versus the cost of executing a trade.

BEST EXECUTION AND MARKET IMPACT

According to the SEC:

> The Advisers Act [of 1940] establishes a federal fiduciary standard for investment advisers. As a fiduciary, when an adviser has the responsibility to select broker-dealers and execute client trades, the adviser has an obligation to seek to obtain "best execution" of client transactions, taking into consideration the circumstances of the particular transaction. An adviser must execute securities transactions for clients in such a manner that the client's total costs or proceeds in each transaction are the most favorable under the circumstances."[1]

This might seem like an obvious standard—surely trading should be done in a manner that is best for the stakeholder in the transaction—but getting best execution is not as simple as it might seem.

Best execution is not just about minimizing the cost of a trade; it's also about designing the trade to help minimize the market impact of the transaction. Market impact is the effect on the price of an asset that results from an order to buy or sell that asset. Consider two stocks, both currently trading at $100 per share. Stock A is incredibly liquid; millions of shares trade every day at a tight bid-ask spread. Stock B is incredibly illiquid; some days no stock

---

* Indices that incorporate transaction costs are the exception, not the norm.

trades at all. A PM holds both stocks in a portfolio and wishes to add 100 shares to each of his or her positions. Which stock's price is likely to move as a result of the order? Clearly, it is stock B. As a result, the execution desk working with the PM might seek to spread the order over a couple of days or seek out pockets of liquidity with particular brokers. In general, larger orders will have greater market impact, and securities with lower average daily volumes will have greater market impact.

It is important to establish exactly how best execution and market impact apply to an index-based ETF. Recall from Chapter 7 that index-based PMs try to minimize tracking error, and given the headwinds that cause underperformance to an index as a rule (e.g., fees, corporate actions, etc.), when PMs outperform an index as a result of misallocation or cash drag, that may seem to be a positive for the PM. However, transacting in a way that minimizes tracking error to the index but does not benefit the shareholder runs counter to the notion of best execution and fiduciary responsibility.

Consider a portfolio that needs to increase a position in a somewhat illiquid security on the close to reduce a misallocation to the index. The execution desk's models show that the execution desk can potentially reduce market impact by trading earlier than the close, "working" the order through the end of the day. The alternative, of course, is putting in a market-on-close (MOC) order that guarantees (absent transaction costs) that the price of the transaction is the closing price of the security, which, coincidentally, is the price that the index uses when valuing the index shares. Given the security's illiquidity, this will likely push the closing price higher. If the PM wants to reduce tracking error, then transacting on the close will accomplish this. But if there's an opportunity to allow the shareholder to purchase shares at a lower price, then that is in the best interest of the fund, even if it means additional tracking error. Improving performance relative to the index at the expense of lower performance overall is not a trade-off a portfolio manager should make. Rather, he or she should welcome the better execution even if it means that the tracking error is higher.

TRADING FREQUENCY AND OPTIMIZATION

A typical index to be tracked by an ETF PM might be rebalanced quarterly. During the rebalance, a percentage of the holdings will be removed from the index while those holdings get replaced by new holdings in the index.

The amount that is changed in the index (and subsequently, the portfolio) is typically called the "turnover" in the index. To be clear, we often differentiate "one-way turnover," the percentage of the portfolio that changes, from "two-way turnover," which is twice that amount but reflects the amount of trading necessary (incorporating buys and sells) to rebalance the portfolio.

In Table 4.7, we depicted the index "trade" for the SWA Index. Assume for the moment that the portfolio exactly mimics the index. In this case, we can add up all the buys, where weights in the index were increased, and all the sells, where weights in the index were decreased. As Table 8.1 shows, two-way turnover for this rebalance was 28.03%.* If this were reflective of the rebalancing expected each quarter, annual two-way turnover would be at least 112%, though other trading activity (due to corporate actions, cash reinvestments, etc.) would increase this figure.

Turnover can be specified for a particular rebalance or can be aggregated over the course of time, typically benchmarked to one year. It is common practice for funds to report portfolio turnover for the fiscal year of the fund, as this can give an indication to investors (and potential investors) how much activity (and by extension, transaction costs) the fund experiences over the course of a year. Some funds' annual turnover can be as low as single digits, while some funds have an annual turnover over 100%, meaning that on average the fund changes the entire portfolio more than once throughout the course of the year.

The kind of rebalancing activity within the index and the frequency of the rebalance will determine the turnover for the index and tracking portfolio. A market capitalization–weighted index may not have too much turnover if company market capitalizations do not wildly fluctuate quarter to quarter. On the other hand, a fundamentally weighted index, a volatility-weighted index, or an equally weighted index with volatile constituents may exhibit significant turnover on an annual basis. If the cost of transactions is, for example, 1 basis point for each transaction, then—all else equal—a portfolio whose annual (two-way) turnover is 200% will underperform by 2 basis points, while a fund whose turnover is 25% will only underperform the index by a quarter of a basis point.

---

*Pro formas are used, as turnover is usually calculated before the rebalance as an indicator for the portfolio manager. Ex-post turnover can be calculated as well.

TABLE 8.1

Two-Way Turnover Calculation

Index   SWA Index
Date   4/8/2021
Index Level   97.4188

Ticker	Index Shares	Index "Trade"	Closing Price	Change in Weight
AABA	0.1044	−0.01751	$42.22	−0.76%
AAQZ	0.0790	0.00873	$62.20	0.56%
AAWL	0.0000	−0.08260	$56.90	−4.82%
AAXX	0.1548	0.15480	$29.35	4.66%
ACBU	0.0609	−0.01901	$88.24	−1.72%
ACGN	0.1247	−0.00788	$38.15	−0.31%
ACOP	0.0535	−0.00158	$84.52	−0.14%
ADXK	0.2067	0.03087	$24.89	0.79%
ADZI	0.1552	−0.00108	$29.65	−0.03%
AFOJ	0.2373	−0.02636	$20.92	−0.57%
AGFZ	0.1114	0.01591	$47.20	0.77%
AHBP	0.0669	−0.00978	$70.16	−0.70%
AHGG	0.0907	0.00484	$57.94	0.29%
AHJQ	0.0727	−0.00083	$69.32	−0.06%
AIAD	0.1764	0.00763	$27.65	0.22%
AKEK	0.0509	0.05091	$95.35	4.98%
AKMW	0.0000	−0.08655	$31.11	−2.76%
AKRY	0.0679	0.01486	$72.47	1.11%
AKXI	0.2994	0.03153	$15.89	0.51%
AKZO	0.0642	−0.00954	$74.32	−0.73%
ALTO	0.0484	−0.01331	$103.41	−1.41%
AMGP	0.3940	0.01044	$12.09	0.13%
			Sum buys	14.02%
			Sum sells	−14.02%
			Two way	28.03%

PERFECT REPLICATION VERSUS TRANSACTION COSTS

If perfect replication at every instant is the goal, then there is really very little left to this discussion: the index provider signals index changes, and the PM does his or her best to mimic the portfolio composition on a daily basis. But what if perfect replication isn't the optimal strategy?

Consider the following example, which follows a hypothetical acquisition. We cover corporate actions in Chapter 11, but for our purposes here, an acquisition can be instructive in describing an instance when a PM should not necessarily track the index due to transaction costs. The SWA Index is set to rebalance on 4/8/2021. The calculation is completed on 3/31/2021, and pro formas are sent to subscribers indicating a 5% position in AKEK as of the close of 4/8/2021. On 4/6/2021, AKEK announces an all-cash acquisition, whereby AKEK will be acquired by BDAC at the close of 4/9/2021. The board has already approved the transaction. As we know from the index methodology for SWA (see Chapter 3), once a ticker is acquired by a constituent that is not in the index, that ticker's weight is removed from the index, and the weight is redistributed over the remaining constituents in the index. Until the next rebalance, the SWA Index, normally a 20-stock index, would hold only 19 constituents.

AKEK is *not* a current holding on this date (and neither is BDAC, of course). The PM now has a decision to make. He or she can purchase shares of AKEK as part of the index rebalance on 4/8/2021 and then turn around and sell all those shares on the close of 4/9/2021 to finance the purchase of the remaining securities as part of the redistribution of the acquired company's assets, or the PM can refrain from purchasing AKEK on 4/8/2021, thereby obviating the need to sell out of those shares just one business day later and simply use the cash from the rebalance (i.e., the cash that was not put to use to buy AKEK) to purchase the additional shares in the remaining stocks on the close of 4/9/2021.

What should the PM do?

In the first case, the PM is going to incur a round-trip cost to the AKEK position. He or she would purchase on the close (presumably an MOC order) on 4/8/2021 and sell on the close (again, MOC) on 4/9/2021. According to the pro forma files, and considering the size of the fund, the PM would be purchasing 5,076 shares. If the cost per share in commissions/spread is 1 cent per share, then the total cost to the round trip is $101.52. With just two days before the acquisition, it is possible that the stock is already trading at the deal price, so there may be no expected appreciation in the position.

In the second case, the PM simply holds cash. No transaction costs are paid (since there are no transactions in AKEK). In fact, the PM can potentially earn a return on the cash, though with low rates and a very short horizon, cash earnings are of little consequence.

In this stylized example, it is clear that absent any deal risk and with the prices given, the PM's best strategy is to deviate from holding what the index holds. Fewer transactions result in tighter performance to the index. There are instances where this could be more nuanced. What if the board had not yet approved the deal, the approval was expected to be granted on 4/9/2021, and the deal close was pushed back to 4/12/2021? In that scenario, it is possible that the price of the stock could be trading below the acquisition price if there was some risk that the deal would fall apart and any premium involved in the deal would evaporate. Being in the stock during that period could mean appreciation in the stock that the index, by definition, would participate in but a PM that chose to hold cash instead of AKEK would not. That appreciation, however, comes with potential risk to a considerable position in the portfolio: if the deal were rejected by the board, the stock could move considerably.

A NOTE ON MARKET-ON-CLOSE TRANSACTIONS

When executing trades for the portfolio, the PM (or the execution desk) often utilizes a market-on-close order type. Unlike a market order that seeks execution at the time of the order at the best available price, the MOC order is designed to be executed at the closing price of the security. Because indices are often calculated using the closing prices for the constituents, portfolio managers often utilize MOC orders to track the indices more closely. Remember, however, that portfolios are not like indices—PMs need to place orders before the close in order to get the close, whereas indices simply update with closing prices. As a result, while MOC orders guarantee the closing price for the transaction (absent transaction costs), the required position size might not exactly line up by using the MOC construct. One could imagine a scenario where the equity market moves considerably lower from 3:45 p.m. ET to 4:00 p.m. ET, for example, but because an order is placed for MOC at 3:40 p.m., the number of shares of a security to be purchased is underestimated based on the closing print. In this situation, the PM may require a true-up trade in the morning to move the position closer to the desired holdings. While this would not be a "cost" in the traditional sense of transaction costs (although commissions would be, of course), there is an implicit cost to transactional friction like that described here: misallocation and tracking error in the period following the transaction.

Note

1. https://www.sec.gov/files/OCIE%20Risk%20Alert%20-%20IA%20Best%20Execution.pdf.

CHAPTER 9

Taxes

In the previous two chapters, we discussed tracking error and transaction costs, two of the Three Ts of ETF portfolio management. In this chapter, we turn our attention to taxes, the final T. It was Ben Franklin who said that nothing is certain except death and taxes. When it comes to taxes in investing, the general principle is that investors pay taxes on securities that appreciate in value. This leads to a bit of a paradox—investors want their securities to appreciate, but they want to minimize their tax bills. It's like rooting for your favorite football team: you want your team to do well and win the Super Bowl, but if it does, it's going to get the last pick in next year's draft. When your team does poorly, you accept its performance by focusing on what a great draft pick the team is going to get. Smart tax management can help investors achieve performance and defer taxes until they sell their ETFs; it is like winning the Super Bowl and drafting well at the same time.

On the surface, sales of a security at a price higher than the purchase price result in gains—which are taxed by the government—and sales at a lower price than the purchase price result in losses, which can offset gains (and therefore taxes by the government). When it comes to taxes as they relate to ETFs, though, there are a surprising number of conditions that can move a transaction from the simple to the sophisticated in terms of tax calculations, and understanding each of these conditions can be the difference between reporting gains and reporting losses for the ETF at the end of the fiscal year. We discuss some of those considerations in this chapter. It is nearly impossible to overstate the importance of diligent tax management in an ETF portfolio.

THE PORTFOLIO MANAGER'S DISCLAIMER

While it is incumbent upon the ETF PM to understand the broad basics (and some of the advance topics) of tax management, it is important to recognize that it is also *not* the job of the ETF PM to be a tax expert; that is where the accountants come in.* As we saw in Chapter 2, the fund accounting function is part of the fund administration infrastructure that supports the smooth operation of the ETF. PMs should never take on the accounting responsibility of the fund they manage, and before taking action (or no action) that has tax consequences, it is strongly advised to communicate with tax experts if any uncertainty is present.† It is also important to recognize that some ETFs may be held in nontaxable accounts; we assume the PM manages the fund as if there are investors who hold the products in taxable accounts.

BASIC DEFINITIONS

The basics of tax management are fairly straightforward. Securities are purchased at a price on a particular date, which is formally known as the "cost basis" and the "basis date," respectively, for that transaction. Any transaction costs incurred in the purchase are included in the cost basis. It is possible for the cost basis and the basis date to be adjusted, however, and we'll outline certain instances of adjustments below. But in general, you can think of the cost basis and basis date as what the government will perceive as the price you paid for a security and the date you purchased the security for the purposes of calculating taxes.

At some point, a security may be sold. The amount received in that sale (after transaction costs) is the "sale proceeds," which are received on the date of sale (or agreed to and paid at a later date). The difference between the sale proceeds and the cost basis for a security will determine whether or not there is a capital gain or a capital loss: if the proceeds exceed the cost basis, there is a capital gain, and if the cost basis exceeds the proceeds, there is a capital loss. Because tax rates change depending on the holding period, capital gains and losses are defined as short term if the time between the basis date and the date of sale is one year or less. Otherwise, the gains or losses are considered long term.

---

* This could be fund accounting, internal tax accountants, or other tax experts.
† The author is not an accountant either, and the material in this chapter is not intended to constitute tax advice. Readers managing portfolios should consult their accountants before engaging in any transactions.

Gains and losses are only realized in the portfolio when a security is sold. If a security is purchased for $100 and that security is currently trading at $80, the purchaser has not incurred any *realized* capital loss—yet. The holder has to complete the transaction before the loss is realized. The holder does have, however, an *unrealized* loss in that position: were he or she to sell the security at its current price, the holder would realize a loss of $20. As a result, the unrealized loss for this position is $20. This important distinction between realized and unrealized gains and losses drives a lot of portfolio optimization decisions on the part of the ETF PM, as we will see shortly.

TAX FILES

Every time a PM purchases a security, a record of that transaction is created and housed at the custodian for the ETF. Just like the index files, pro forma files and corporate action files serve as the information superhighway for the ETF PM tracking an index; tax files are the lifeblood of tax management for the ETF, regardless of whether the fund is index-based or actively managed.

Tax files can come in different forms, so here we focus on two sets of information that are critical to the ETF PM. The first set of information is a complete description of the portfolio as it is presently constructed from a tax perspective. We typically call this a "tax lot" file. A tax lot is essentially a unique identification that ties all the securities purchased in a particular transaction to each other. An ETF PM may hold 1,000 shares of a particular equity, for example, but 500 might have been purchased on January 7 for $10 per share, and another 500 may have been purchased on July 25 for $8 per share. Clearly, those shares have to be treated differently for tax purposes. Securities that are acquired for a particular price on a particular date are grouped together in what is called a "lot," and each share of that lot is assigned the same identifier that is associated with that share until it is sold.

The tax lot file may have a large number of fields, but the key elements are:

- Identifiers for the security in the transaction
- The lot number of the transaction
- The number of shares in the lot
- The cost basis of the transaction
- The basis date of the transaction
- Current unrealized gains/losses in the lot

Table 9.1 presents a portion of the hypothetical tax lot file for the SWA portfolio on 4/15/2021. Recall that while there are generally 20 securities in the portfolio, securities come into the portfolio at different times—through purchases, rebalances, creations, etc.—and as a result, there are typically multiple entries for a given security in the tax lot file.

TABLE 9.1

Tax Lot File for the SWA Portfolio (4/15/2021)

Ticker	Lot	Shares	Basis	Basis Date	Price	Unrealized
AABA	AABA1001	10,341	$40.82	1/11/2021	$38.48	$(24,153.32)
AABA	AABA1002	34	$39.42	1/14/2021	$38.48	$ (31.96)
AABA	AABA1003	30	$40.02	2/3/2021	$38.48	$ (46.27)
AABA	AABA1004	26	$43.24	2/22/2021	$38.48	$ (123.68)
AABA	AABA1006	14	$42.23	4/9/2021	$38.48	$ (52.56)
AABA	AABA1007	28	$39.33	4/15/2021	$38.48	$ (23.69)
AAQZ	AAQZ1001	6,960	$67.31	1/11/2021	$54.62	$(88,314.63)
AAQZ	AAQZ1002	22	$67.88	1/14/2021	$54.62	$ (291.84)
AAQZ	AAQZ1003	17	$71.24	2/3/2021	$54.62	$ (282.51)
AAQZ	AAQZ1004	14	$68.40	2/22/2021	$54.62	$ (192.90)
AAQZ	AAQZ1005	18	$72.49	3/24/2021	$54.62	$ (321.77)
AAQZ	AAQZ1006	851	$62.21	4/8/2021	$54.62	$ (6,464.30)
AAQZ	AAQZ1007	30	$62.21	4/9/2021	$54.62	$ (227.88)
AAQZ	AAQZ1008	22	$55.73	4/15/2021	$54.62	$ (24.53)

The table shows that there are over $24,000 in unrealized losses in AABA and over $96,000 in unrealized losses in AAQZ; note that the respective closing prices on 4/15/2021, $38.48 and $54.62, are below all the prices for which the respective stocks were purchased.

REALIZED GAINS/LOSSES

In addition to the tax lot file, the fund administrator might provide a second set of information regarding realized gains and losses, which will include two kinds of files: one is a transaction file telling the PM which lots have been sold and what the realized gains and losses on those lots were, and the other is an overview file that will break down the portfolio's short-term and long-term realized gains and losses accrued in any tax year. One of the central tenets of tax management is that losses offset gains in a given fiscal year. In addition, losses from previous fiscal years can carry over into the present fiscal year to offset gains incurred during the year. Because of these rules, every PM should be in command of the taxable position of the fund, not just from transactions performed in the current fiscal year, but from any loss carryovers. This is why the loss carryover is reported by the fund administrator.

CREATION/REDEMPTION ACTIVITY AND THE IMPACT ON TAXES

Armed with the tax files, the PM is ready to understand the impact of any transaction on taxes for the fund. However, not all transactions are treated equally. In particular, creations and redemptions—primary market transactions—are treated differently than are secondary market transactions for the purposes of tax management for an ETF. When shares of the ETF are created, the securities that are received from the AP in the in-kind transaction come into the portfolio with a cost basis equal to the closing price on the trade date. When redemption orders come in, securities removed from the portfolio by being included in the redemption on an in-kind basis are not considered sold for the purposes of capital gains and losses calculation. They are removed from the portfolio without tax consequence to the fund.*

Think about that for a moment. If a PM sells a security, the fund incurs the tax consequence of the secondary market transaction. If, however, the PM includes that security in the basket for a redemption, that is considered a primary market transaction, and regardless of the price at which the security is removed in the redemption, there is no consequence to the fund regarding taxes.

This is one of the key reasons why ETFs are more tax-efficient than mutual funds. When a mutual fund receives redemption orders, it generally sells a slice of the portfolio *in the secondary market*, thereby incurring gains or losses that accrue to all holders of the mutual fund (see Figure 9.1). Mutual funds do not have access to APs to handle primary market transactions, and as a result, they are constantly transacting in the secondary market to fulfill orders. They may transact in kind with a large shareholder to facilitate a redemption, but this is not the standard course of business for most transac-

---

* More specifically, gain exclusion falls under Section 852(b)(6) of the tax code, and loss exclusion falls under Section 311(a).

tions. An ETF PM running a portfolio that has no corporate actions and no rebalances may not be required to make any secondary market transactions despite consistent creation and redemption activity and also because they trade "in-kind" securities through the AP, and the sales of those securities are not taxable events to the fund (see Figure 9.2).

FIGURE 9.1

Mutual fund redemption

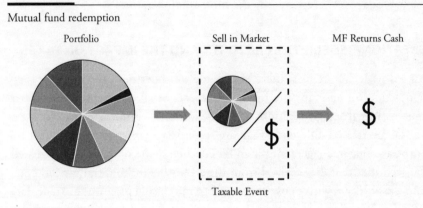

FIGURE 9.2

ETF redemption

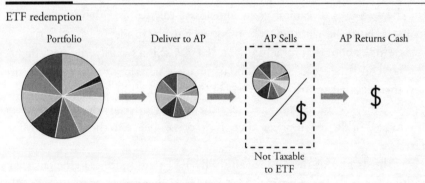

Furthermore, when redemption orders come into the fund, the custodian will include lots in the redemption basket that have the *lowest* cost bases. This means that lots with the largest unrealized gains get taken out of the portfolio *without having to realize those gains*. When sales occur in the secondary market in the normal course of business for the ETF PM, the custodian will include lots of a security with the *highest* cost basis, allowing the PM to realize the greatest amount of losses for a given security. Table 9.2

shows the tax lot file on 4/15/2021 as it pertains to holdings in ACBU. Lots ACBU1001 and ACBU1007 are in gains, while lot ACBU1006 is in losses.

TABLE 9.2

Cost Basis and ETF Redemption

Ticker	Lot	Shares	Basis	Basis Date	Price	Unrealized	Per Share
ACBU	ACBU1001	6,068	$61.58	1/11/2021	$87.14	$155,088.55	$ 25.56
ACBU	ACBU1006	23	$88.25	4/9/2021	$87.14	$ (25.45)	$(1.11)
ACBU	ACBU1007	17	$86.28	4/15/2021	$87.14	$ 14.65	$ 0.86

Were a market sale to take place,* the fund would capture losses by selling the shares from lot ACBU1006 first. If a redemption were to take place, shares would be taken from lot ACBU1001.

These accounting methods are advantageous to ETFs, and it should not take long to realize the impact of increasing amounts of creation and redemption activity. Table 9.3 depicts the phenomenon by showing how "recycling" securities through creation and redemption activity in the SWA portfolio leads to increasingly more unrealized losses in the portfolio or the reduction of unrealized gains as a whole relative to a fund that has no C/R activity. The table shows the impact on one security, assuming one share per lot and per unit. Even without any price movement, after a creation on T + 1 and a redemption on T + 2, we see that on T + 2, the unrealized gains for the portfolio as they pertain to that security fall as a result of the primary market activity.

TABLE 9.3

The Impact of C/R Activity on Unrealized Gains/Losses

Date	T	Date	T + 1	Date	T + 2
Price	$100	Price	$100	Price	$100
Lot	**Cost Basis**	**Lot**	**Cost Basis**	**Lot**	**Cost Basis**
1001	$90	1001	$90	➤ Lowest cost basis removed	
1002	$95	1002	$95	1002	$95
		1003	$100	1003	$100
Unrealized	$1,500	Unrealized	$1,500	Unrealized	$500

---

* We ignore wash-sale considerations for the moment, though we cover the subject later in this chapter.

In Figures 9.3 and 9.4, we show the aggregate effect of this recycling activity. We present the SWA portfolio with no C/R activity after the initial launch and compare it with a scenario in which one unit is created on odd days and one unit is redeemed on even days. Shares outstanding for the fund are shown in Figure 9.3, and we see that shares rise and fall day in and day out with our C/R scenario. In Figure 9.4, we show the unrealized gains/losses in

FIGURE 9.3

Shares outstanding fluctuate with C/R activity

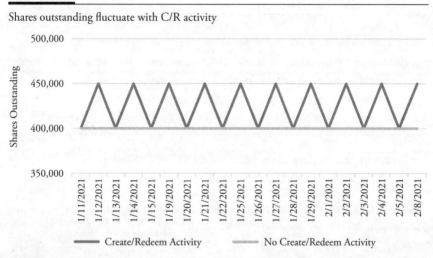

FIGURE 9.4

The impact of C/R activity on gains/losses

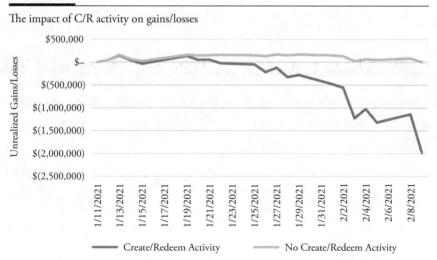

each scenario. By design, the increased C/R activity manages to create more unrealized losses (or reduce more unrealized gains) than the no-C/R scenario. Even in a generally rising market environment, C/R activity can keep a portfolio in negative territory from a capital gains and losses perspective. It is no wonder that, according to Bloomberg Intelligence, 6% of ETFs pay capital gains versus 55% of mutual funds.[1]

CIL AND TAX MANAGEMENT

In Chapter 5 we noted that the portfolio manager can mark securities "cash in lieu" (or "CIL") in the PCF. This instructs the APs that they are to deliver (in the case of a creation) or receive (in the case of a redemption) cash instead of the security in kind. Marking securities CIL can be a tax-advantageous strategy.

Imagine a fund has a considerable position in one security. All the shares of this security were purchased for the same price, and over time this security has built up considerable unrealized losses. By including the security in the PCF, the PM is at risk for having those losses come off the books of the portfolio without being realized, since these transactions are pushed off to the AP through the in-kind mechanism. Often a security will have some lots in gains and some in losses, so this may not be an issue, but in this example, all the shares have suffered the same price decline. If the PM were to mark the security as CIL in the PCF, however, then he or she would need to deliver the cash equivalent of the value of that security in the portfolio. This is desirable for the PM, since selling the security in the marketplace will turn the unrealized losses into realized losses (subject to wash sales). If a creation happens to come in, then the security will need to be purchased by the PM to deploy cash. This is the trade-off the PM makes when marking these securities CIL.

BASIS ADJUSTMENT: A SIMPLE EXAMPLE

While the cost basis and basis date are originally the price and date at which a security is acquired, they are actually subject to change for the purposes of the government's tax calculations. Consider a simple stock split. Suppose you purchased 100 shares of stock XYZ on January 19 for $100 per share. You paid a commission of $10 on the transaction, so the total cost basis for the shares is $10,010, or $100.10 per share. On January 21, the stock appreciates by 10%, closing at $110. You seek to sell half of your position on the close of the 21st, and your sell order includes a $10 transaction fee. You receive $5,490 for 50 shares, or $109.80 per share. Your capital gain on the transaction (short term) is $9.70 per share, or a total of $485.

Now suppose that XYZ had declared a two-to-one stock split effective January 20. Now each share is worth (assuming no price movement) $50 per share, and a holder of the stock receives an additional share for every share held. On January 21, just as it did in the prior example, the stock appreciates by 10%, closing at $55 per share. You seek to sell half of your position (now 100 shares) on the close of the 21st, and your sell order includes a $10 transaction fee. You receive $5,490, or $54.90 per share. What are your gains or losses from this transaction?

Your original cost basis is $100.10 per share, but surely the stock split cannot result in a capital loss of $45.20 per share ($100.10 – $54.90). Stock splits have no direct economic value implication: you don't lose or gain money on the split alone. The cost basis needs to be adjusted to reflect the split, so instead of a cost basis of $100.10 per share, the cost basis for a split gets adjusted by the split ratio, resulting in a new cost basis of $50.05. This new adjusted cost basis will be reflected in the tax lot file. In fact, after a stock split, every lot of the stock held in the portfolio is adjusted to reflect the exchange of shares for a different number of shares and the offsetting price adjustment. Now it is straightforward to see that what appeared to be a capital loss in the unadjusted case becomes a capital gain of $4.85 per share, or a total gain of $485, the same figure we computed in the case without the split in XYZ.

Back in Chapter 3 we introduced the corporate action file, and there we saw that AAQZ had a three-for-one stock split with an ex-date of 4/19/2021. In Table 9.4, we show the tax lots for the close on 4/16/2021 and the open on 4/19/2021. Note how the share counts in all the lots have tripled, while the cost basis is one-third of the original cost basis and the total cost remains constant.

TABLE 9.4

Basis Updating for Stock Split (4/19/2021)

Lot	4/16/2021 Close			4/19/2021 Open		
	Shares	Cost Basis	Total Cost	Shares	Cost Basis	Total Cost
AAQZ1001	6960	$67.31	$468,456.88	20,880	$22.44	$468,456.88
AAQZ1002	22	$67.88	$ 1,493.44	66	$22.63	$ 1,493.44
AAQZ1003	17	$71.24	$ 1,211.02	51	$23.75	$ 1,211.02
AAQZ1004	14	$68.40	$ 957.56	42	$22.80	$ 957.56
AAQZ1005	18	$72.49	$ 1,304.90	54	$24.16	$ 1,304.90
AAQZ1006	851	$62.21	$ 52,944.33	2,553	$20.74	$ 52,944.33
AAQZ1007	30	$62.21	$ 1,866.43	90	$20.74	$ 1,866.43
AAQZ1008	22	$55.73	$ 1,226.12	66	$18.58	$ 1,226.12

The basis date for a transaction can also change, as we will show in the following section on wash sales.

WASH SALES

Wash-sale regulations guard against investors seeking to lock in unrealized losses by selling securities to lock in the realized loss and then buying the security right back to hold in the portfolio. In a similar vein, investors can purchase new shares of a security prior to selling previously owned shares with unrealized losses so that when they sell the old shares, they still maintain their desired exposure. These types of transactions are called "wash sales," allowing investors to create a tax benefit (realizing the loss) without substantially changing the portfolio. The US Tax Code addresses these transactions under the "Wash-Sale Rule."[2]

On the surface, the wash-sale rule appears to be straightforward. Under the code:

A wash sale occurs when a taxpayer sells or trades stock or securities at a loss, and within 30 days before or after the sale:

1. Buys substantially identical stock or securities,
2. Acquires substantially identical stock or securities in a fully taxable trade,
3. Acquires a contract or option to buy substantially identical stock or securities, or
4. Acquires substantially identical stock for an individual retirement account (IRA).

Without delving into what "substantially identical" means, the short story is this: an investor cannot replace a security sold for a loss within 30 days before or after the sale. Sounds simple. It is remarkable, then, that a rule that can be summarized in under 20 words can be so challenging to implement or interpret. Volumes can be written on the intricacies of the wash-sale rule. Here we try to hit a couple of highlights that give the PM an idea of how it can impact his or her portfolio.

Wash-sale rules are important to the ETF portfolio manager. One of the most value-enhancing things an ETF PM can do for his or her investors is to provide a product that does not distribute any capital gains to those investors while the investors hold the product, deferring their tax bills until they dispose of their shares. If ETFs distribute capital gains, then even if the investor hasn't sold his or her shares, the investor is responsible for a tax bill. That could require the investor to be forced to sell other securities (or the ETF) to pay the tax bill, an argument consistently made for why ETFs are structured to the investor's advantage vis-à-vis mutual funds.

ETF PMs do not have to sell securities if they utilize in-kind transactions, but corporate actions and rebalancing activities often force the PM to sell securities in the market. If some of these transactions generate gains, then the PM needs offsetting transactions that generate losses before the fiscal year of the fund concludes. However, if the offsetting transactions that generate losses are subject to the wash-sale rule, thereby deferring the loss, then the offset to the gains may not apply, and the ETF will end up having to declare gains.

Guarding against this situation is primarily a function of two things: knowing the wash-sale rule and its implications for each transaction in and out and avoiding—whenever possible—trading within the wash-sale window. Avoiding the window is fairly easy: If the PM has sold a security for a loss, that security should be flagged for future purposes over the course of the next 30 days. The PM could decide to trade within the window, but he or she should know the impact. If a security has been purchased, then a desire to sell the security within 30 days of the purchase for a loss could potentially have wash-sale implications, and the PM could hold off on sales until the window has passed.

Knowing and/or interpreting the rule, however, can be quite challenging. There are three important principles for the PM to understand with respect to the wash-sale rule:

1. Realized losses that are subject to the wash-sale rule do not disappear. Rather, they are deferred.
2. To capture the deferral, every transaction (potentially) updates the cost basis for a security on a lot-by-lot basis and the basis date for a security on a lot-by-lot basis. We provide an example below.
3. Transactions for losses subject to the wash rule must have remaining shares to "attach" to that were purchased during the wash-sale window.

The first two points here are fairly straightforward. If a loss is captured but is in violation of the wash-sale rule, the portfolio still has an opportunity to capture that loss, just at a later date that falls outside the wash-rule window. To maintain the proper accounting for that loss, accountants adjust the cost basis and basis date for the transaction.

For example, on 4/15/2021, the SWA ETF requires a true-up trade, as cash has crept up due to dividends. As a result, the PM purchases 14 shares of ACOP (see Table 9.5). On 4/8/2021, however, the PM had sold shares of ACOP for a loss as part of the rebalance. The loss on the 147-share sale on 4/8/2021 was $901.08. Because the purchase on 4/15/2021 occurs within 30 days of the sale for a loss, the purchase violates the wash-sale rule. As a result, there will be a basis adjustment. First, note that if there were no basis adjustment, the weighted average basis for the shares in the ACOP1001 and the new shares would be $91.6468 (5,330 shares at $91.6644 and 14 shares at $84.9401). However, 10.2% of the shares that were sold on 4/8/2021 are being bought back, so 9.5% of the loss is washed out. The loss does not disappear, though; it gets added back to the cost basis. The $85.82 worth of losses in ACOP gets added to the cost basis of the newly purchased shares, raising their cost basis from an unadjusted $84.94 to an adjusted $91.07 and raising the average from an unadjusted $91.6468 to an adjusted $91.6628. When the shares are sold outside of the wash-sale window, the losses would once again be realized. That is why this is a tax deferral.

TABLE 9.5

Basis Updating as a Result of Wash-Sale Rule (4/15/2021)

ACOP	
Cost basis for existing shares in ACOP1001	$ 91.6644
Number of existing shares in ACOP1001	5,330
Shares to buy on 4/15/2021	14
Purchase price on 4/15/2021	$ 84.9401
Shares sold on 4/8/2021 (in wash-sale window)	147
Proportion of shares sold	9.5%
Losses on shares sold on 4/8/2021	$(901.08)
Losses to revert to basis	$ (85.82)
New share count for ACOP1001	5,344
New basis for ACOP1001	$ 91.6628
New basis without wash sale (weighted average basis)	$ 91.6468

In addition, the basis date for the shares reverts to the initial purchase date for lot ACOP1001, which in this case is 1/11/2021 (part of the initial basket). This could have implications if the sale of the securities takes place between January 11 and April 15 of 2022: the sale would be considered a long-term sale, since the initial shares' basis date is 1/11/2021.

The third point regarding "attachment" deserves more explanation. Because the wash-sale rules are designed to guard against purchases and sales in close proximity to capture losses, one of the key elements of calculating the impact of wash sales is finding remaining shares to "assign" the realized losses back to; in other words, if the PM has generated realized losses from unrealized losses, and those realized losses get washed, they have to turn back into unrealized losses. But to do so, they have to be unrealized for particular shares that still exist in the portfolio. The now-unrealized losses are "attached" to those shares.

In practice, many situations are not quite as clean as some of the examples here. There may be multiple lots with different cost bases. There is a whole host of scenarios to consider with every transaction, underscoring the need for strong fund accounting.

The final point to make regarding wash sales is that capital gains, losses, and basis information for each position in a portfolio may come to the PM on a delayed basis, much to the PM's frustration. Building a wash-sale system in-house as part of the portfolio management process and/or investing in a more real-time system is well worth it for the meticulous PM.

Wash-Sale Rule Exemption

In addition to the advantage bestowed upon ETFs through in-kind creation and redemption, a consequence of this activity manifests itself in a wash-sale rule exemption. Imagine the ETF recently sold a portion of shares of a particular constituent for a loss and then within 30 days a creation order comes in. If the fund received cash for the creation, the PM would have to purchase shares of each name in the portfolio, including shares of the stock he or she just recently sold. This would trigger a wash-sale violation, delaying the loss on the recently sold shares. This could, in theory, send the fund into positive territory with respect to capital gains and losses without any recourse for the PM other than taking on tracking error by delaying the purchase of that particular constituent beyond the wash-sale window.

This is less than ideal. Creation orders are what PMs live for: more AUM. These orders should not create uncertainty with respect to taxes at any moment in time. In-kind creation orders solve this problem. In an in-kind transaction, as we have discussed in Chapter 5, the basket of securities is delivered to the portfolio as new shares are issued to the AP, and AP-delivered shares *do not count* as purchases when it comes to attaching losses in the wash-sale tax code.

WHY TAX MINIMIZATION IS NOT TAX AVOIDANCE

So far, we have used the terminology of "minimizing" taxes, much like we have used the term "minimize" when describing our efforts around tracking error and transaction cost. Tax "minimization" isn't exactly the right term to use, however. Taxes are largely unavoidable, but it is worth drilling down on what tax minimization means in the context of ETF portfolio management.

Consider an ETF investor for a moment. On 3/15/2020, she buys shares of an ETF for $25 per share on the first day of the fund's existence. There are no capital gains or losses in the fund, and the fund's fiscal year ends on March 29. On that day on the close, the fund rebalances, and every single security in the fund happens to have increased in value by 10% (there are no dividends), and the ETF closes at $27.50. The portfolio manager turns over 20% of the portfolio in the market, resulting in capital gains for the portfolio of $0.50. The following business day, April 1, the price drops from $27.50 back to $25, with every security in the portfolio dropping approximately 9.1% (a loss of $2.50 on $27.50) and remaining at those prices for the rest of the year. At the end of the year, the investor sells her shares.

The investor in our example bought the ETF and sold the ETF at the same price: $25. Because, however, the fund made secondary market transactions at a capital gain for the fiscal year, the ETF investor is required to pay capital gains taxes.

Consider a counterexample whereby all the shares take losses first and then recover in value. In that case, the first rebalance would capture a loss in the fund, and the fund would declare zero in capital gains. In the following year, the fund would incur gains, but those gains would be offset by carryover losses in the first year, nullifying those gains. As a result, the investor in the fund would pay no capital gains taxes (assuming no further price movements): none through the fund and none through the sale of her shares, since the sale's proceeds (ignoring transaction costs) would exactly match the cost basis.

When we say that the portfolio manager is "minimizing capital gains," what we mean is that the fund's capital gains taxes are minimized and potentially deferred, irrespective of what transactions the ETF investor makes. There are, of course, other examples of tax deferral in financial products, such as retirement accounts.

There are several ways for the portfolio manager to minimize what taxes show up in the form of the fund's taxable position. Three of them bear specific mention. First, we already alluded to how the cost basis is adjusted depending on whether a transaction occurs in the secondary market or through an AP transaction during a creation or redemption. Second, PMs can "harvest" tax losses, the subject of the following section. Third, the PM can use custom in-kind baskets, the subject of Chapter 12.

TAX-LOSS HARVESTING

Investors do not want to pay taxes related to their holdings in an ETF, especially if the investors have not sold out of their position. As mentioned, managing the capital gains to zero is a service that an ETF PM can provide that defers the tax an investor pays on the appreciation of his or her position when the position is exited. Using the information in the tax files, an astute PM can recognize positions that have accrued a considerable amount of unrealized losses, and the PM may sell those positions to realize the loss at the expense of transaction costs and tracking error. This is called "tax-loss harvesting."

Formally, tax-loss harvesting is when a PM recognizes that the sale of a position in the portfolio would result in a capital loss, which would then decrease or render negative the capital gains account for the fund. Imagine a fund had $100,000 in capital gains, but it had a position in the portfolio worth $1 million that was purchased for a cost basis of $1.1 million. If the position were sold (absent transaction costs), then the portfolio would recognize a realized loss of $100,000, exactly offsetting the capital gains that had accrued to that point.

This sale has serious implications for the portfolio: in addition to incurring transaction costs, in all likelihood there was a reason that the portfolio held that $1 million position—an index weight to be tracked for an index-based fund or a desired holding for an actively managed fund—and having sold the position, the portfolio becomes underallocated to the intended holding for that security. As a result, the PM is intentionally misallocating the fund; the question for the PM is whether or not that is in the best interests of the ETF shareholder. Several things go into that decision in addition to the cost of the transaction—namely, the alternative position for the cash proceeds from the sale, the tax implications of the sale, and the timing.

Redeploying Cash Proceeds

Balancing the tax-deferring interests of the investor against these costs can be an intricate process, one that tends to rely on quantitative models to weigh the cost-benefit analysis. One of the key inputs to the process is what the PM plans to do with the funds that become available as a result of the sale. Imagine a portfolio where virtually all the securities are very highly correlated and share similar volatility characteristics. The PM holds one position with a considerable loss and others with gains; perhaps the PM entered this position at a different time than some of the other positions, or perhaps the position's timing differed as a result of an index rebalance. Either way, once the PM sells the position at a loss, he or she can reinvest the proceeds into one or more of the assets; and because of the similar risk profile of these assets, the tracking error imposed on the portfolio is likely to be quite low.

Now imagine that the portfolio has a small number of highly *uncorrelated* assets. What is the PM to do with the funds from the liquidated position? None of the options in the portfolio will likely provide a price path similar to what he or she would expect from the tax-loss harvested position. The PM may consider other names that are not in the portfolio, depending on whether or not the PM is using representative sampling techniques (see Chapter 19). However, if the PM is constrained to hold only those securities that appear in an index in the case of the index-based ETF, then the choice set is a lot less appealing with respect to tracking error than in the aforementioned case of highly correlated alternatives. On 4/15/2021, the tax lot file also included the position in AKRY shown in Table 9.6.

TABLE 9.6

Tax Lot File Entry for AKRY (4/15/2021)

Ticker	Lot	Shares	Basis	Basis Date	Price	Unrealized
AKRY	AKRY1001	5,248	$103.81	1/11/21	$70.19	$(176,438.14)

AKRY has an unrealized loss of $176,438.14 in AKRY1001. Consider the correlations between AKRY and other names in the portfolio shown in Table 9.7. Clearly, redeploying assets into ACBU and ACGN might be more advantageous from a tracking perspective than redeploying assets into AKXI or AKZO.

TABLE 9.7

Correlations Between AKRY and Other Stocks

ACBU	93%
ACGN	87%
AGFZ	42%
AKXI	−10%
AKZO	−20%

Tax Implications—Bang for the Buck

Another consideration for the PM is which positions to liquidate to take advantage of the tax-loss harvesting opportunity. On 4/15/2021, the tax lot file shows that AKRY has the largest unrealized loss position in the portfolio at over $176,000. What is more pertinent though is how much in losses is connected to each dollar invested in that position. In other words, if we were to sell $1 of that lot, how much in losses would we realize? The answer to that question is the "bang for the buck," or in the case of lot AKRY1001, $0.48 (see Table 9.8). If we rank every lot by this metric, we see that not all of the AKRY

TABLE 9.8

Bang for the Buck (4/15/2021)

Ticker	Lot	Shares	Basis	Basis Date	Price	Unrealized	Position Value	BfB
AKRY	AKRY1001	5,248	$103.81	1/11/2021	$70.19	$(176,438.14)	$368,373.75	$(0.48)
AKRY	AKRY1002	16	$ 96.75	1/14/2021	$70.19	$ (424.83)	$ 1,123.09	$(0.38)
AAQZ	AAQZ1005	18	$ 72.49	3/24/2021	$54.62	$ (321.77)	$ 983.13	$(0.33)
AGFZ	AGFZ1004	20	$ 53.71	2/22/2021	$40.88	$ (256.66)	$ 817.54	$(0.31)
AAQZ	AAQZ1003	17	$ 71.24	2/3/2021	$54.62	$ (282.51)	$ 928.51	$(0.30)
AGFZ	AGFZ1003	23	$ 53.19	2/3/2021	$40.88	$ (283.28)	$ 940.17	$(0.30)
AMGP	AMGP1003	93	$ 15.82	2/3/2021	$12.17	$ (338.95)	$ 1,132.26	$(0.30)
AGFZ	AGFZ1002	29	$ 52.00	1/14/2021	$40.88	$ (322.55)	$ 1,185.43	$(0.27)
AAQZ	AAQZ1004	14	$ 68.40	2/22/2021	$54.62	$ (192.90)	$ 764.65	$(0.25)
AGFZ	AGFZ1001	9,456	$ 51.10	1/11/2021	$40.88	$ (96,661.98)	$386,532.74	$(0.25)

123

lots are the most efficient to sell in terms of capturing loss. After AKRY1001 and AKRY1002, the next lot in terms of efficiency is AAQZ1005. Were the PM to consider harvesting losses, the most efficient lots would be the place to start. Inefficient lots result in selling more of the portfolio than is necessary, resulting in undue tracking error. (We return to this bang-for-the-buck concept in Chapter 12 when we discuss how to construct custom baskets.)

Timing Risk

Tax-loss harvesting can introduce unintended consequences into a portfolio if the PM is not careful. Two particular notes of risk relate to timing. The first is something we have already discussed in this chapter: wash sales. It is important that the PM understand exactly when and for how long to implement a tax-loss harvesting trade. Missing a wash-sale deadline can easily mean the difference between reporting capital gains on the fund for the fiscal year and declaring none at all.

The second timing risk regards rebalancing in index-based ETFs. If a rebalance is coming up within the next 30 days, then the ability to sell the position and maintain flexibility for the upcoming rebalance is compromised. It is possible that the upcoming index rebalance requires an increase in the security that the PM reduced in size to harvest losses; this means that whatever risk analysis preceded the decision to harvest that particular name no longer applies. The PM may choose to ride out the harvested position a bit past the rebalance if it is deemed not too significant, but this requires further analysis of the risk-reward tolerance. Buying back into the position too soon will wash out any losses. Of course, the other side of the coin is that the rebalance may, in fact, work out in the PM's favor: if the harvested security has a lower weight in the upcoming index reconstitution, then having sold the security ahead of time means that this turned out to be directionally part of the upcoming rebalance anyway.

Most ETF PMs will apply some form of quantitative analysis to integrate all these considerations into the tax-loss harvesting decision. How much tracking error is likely to occur is a matter of looking at volatilities and correlations among alternative holdings. The benefit in terms of capital gain deferral might be assumed to be the full amount or some function of the expected holding period for an investor. There is no standard analysis that comes with tax-loss harvesting—the standard is making judgments that the PM feels are in the best interests of the shareholder.

Notes

1. "Non-Transparent ETFs May Trail in Tax Efficiency," Bloomberg Intelligence, May 28, 2020.
2. Section 26 USC § 1091.

CHAPTER 10

Cash

The old saying is that "Cash is king," an expression meant to stress the importance of cash flow in business or the flexibility that comes with having cash to fund short-term business operations. In the ETF portfolio management business, the goal is actually to minimize the magnitude of the portfolio's cash position, getting the cash allocation as close to zero as possible, while still maintaining the ability to fund certain transactions when necessary.

The ETF PM must have complete transparency into his or her cash position at any time, just as the ETF PM should know the portfolio composition and overallocations and underallocations at any time for an index-based fund. Whether the fund is passive or active, cash transparency comes from understanding how cash comes into the portfolio and goes out of the portfolio, and it leads to improved index tracking on behalf of the fund for index-based products and improved allocations for active products. In what follows, we focus on index-based products as we have done so far, and we will address cash in the active product space in Chapter 15.

IMPACT OF CASH ON THE PORTFOLIO

Why does having a position in cash matter to the ETF PM? In short, if the underlying index to be tracked does not have cash, then the ETF PM should not want to hold any cash either. Any deviation from the zero-cash position effectively results in tracking error to the fund. Tracking error as a result of a cash position is known as "cash drag," a term introduced in Chapter 7. In this standard vernacular, cash is seen as contributing to negative performance of the portfolio relative to the index to be tracked, given the assumption that the index to be tracked is meant to outperform the borrow rate. In reality, this is not always the case, of course, as cash often outperforms the index to be tracked over certain periods of time.

For our purposes, we are going to define cash drag as we did earlier: the positive or negative impact on the portfolio as a result of holding cash relative to apportioning that cash pro rata over the rest of its holdings. In other words, if x% of a portfolio is held in cash, the assumption underlying cash drag is in theory that cash could be redistributed over the remaining $(1 - x)$% of the portfolio, resulting in a portfolio with 100% invested. Note that this definition does *not* assume that the cash is invested in the underlying index, but rather across the portfolio holdings; but as we did in the appendix to Chapter 7, we can alternatively define the drag relative to the index performance.

SOURCES OF CASH INFLOW AND MANAGING CASH IN

Several transactions can lead to an increase in cash in the PM's portfolio, including:

- Sales of securities
- Acquisitions of securities with a cash component in the deal terms, e.g., a deal in which a security is acquired for part stock and part cash
- Securities lending fees
- Interest payments on existing cash positions
- Cash in lieu in creates
- Tax reclaims
- Dividend payments from stocks held in the portfolio
- Creates where there is a cash component that is positive

CASH VERSUS ACCRUALS

The events listed above represent instances where cash comes into the portfolio. In certain cases, however, cash does not immediately make its way into the cash holdings of the portfolio. Rather, cash is "accrued," meaning it is due to be received, but not received yet.

As an example, consider the case of a cash dividend paid by a stock held in a portfolio. When the stock goes ex-dividend (trades without the rights to the dividend), the dividend per share is not immediately received by the shareholder of record. The payout date that is specified with each dividend is often a few days after the stock goes ex and may even be weeks out from the ex-dividend date. During this time, the stock trades at the post-dividend adjusted price (lower than it would trade otherwise). If the investor were to value his or her position in the stock, it would appear artificially low due to the price drop. To make up the difference, the investor is owed the dividend on the payout date. In the interim, the dividend is accounted for as an accrual, a payment that is going to convert to cash on the payout date. Figure 10.1 depicts this process, assuming no underlying price variation from the ex-dividend date through the payment date.

FIGURE 10.1

Dividends first become accruals, then payments to the fund.

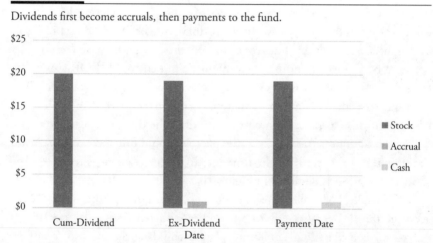

Accruals can lead to short cash positions in the portfolio. Consider a stock that declares a dividend on January 13. The stock goes ex-dividend on January 20, and the dividend is payable on January 27. An index with that stock as a constituent *immediately* reinvests the proceeds of the dividend payment so that on the open of the 20th, the index is fully invested (assuming the index does not hold cash). The portfolio, however, does not have the cash since the payable date is still a week away.

What does the ETF PM do in this case? There are two options:

1. Do nothing, and allow the dividend payment to sit in the accrual account and contribute to the NAV of the fund, but remain uninvested.

    Or

2. Invest the amount in a manner identical to that which is prescribed by the underlying index methodology.

In the first case, the fund will incur tracking error, because the index is fully allocated with no cash position while the portfolio has accrued cash from the impending dividend payment. In the second case, assuming the portfolio was fully invested at the close of January 19, a reinvestment means purchasing stocks without having the cash to settle the trades. This results in the fund having to borrow the cash to fund the purchases, leaving the fund "short" cash. While cash in a portfolio can be invested (typically in overnight repos or other short-term instruments), negative cash (or borrow) needs to be funded. Funding costs might be linked to a LIBOR-based rate (e.g., LIBOR + 50 basis points) on negative cash balances, facilitated by the fund custodian. As a result, there is a cost to negative cash, which can be thought of as a transaction cost for funding the dividend accrual period. Stock transactions settle T + 2, so the borrow would only be necessary from the time the stocks settle to the time the dividend payment is received. The short cash option is depicted in Figure 10.2.

Generally, PMs follow both options at different times. For small dividend accruals, the PM may decide to not bother with reinvestment, especially as other cash considerations come into play. It could be the case, for example, that an impending rebalance would require a redistribution of assets that differs from the current portfolio constitution. If that were the case, then the portfolio manager might wait to invest the cash, avoiding round-trip transaction costs to get into a set of securities and then sell out of them. Alternatively, it could also be the case that the fund is preparing to declare its own distribution. At that point, the fund takes cash from the portfolio (typically from dividend or coupon income) and returns it to the shareholders (as we discuss in more detail below). Depending on the timing of the disbursement relative to the receipt of cash from one of the fund's holdings, it may be the case that the PM chooses to defer purchases in light of the need to fund other cash requirements.

FIGURE 10.2

Accruals can lead to short cash positions

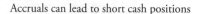

Dividend Declared for Stock A: January 13

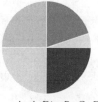

■A ■A–Div ■B ■C ■D

Fund Becomes Short to Reinvest: January 20

Accrued: $5
Cash: –$5

■A ■B ■C ■D

Dividend Accrued (Ex-Dividend): January 20

Accrued: $5
Cash: $0

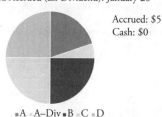

■A ■A–Div ■B ■C ■D

Dividend Gets Paid: January 27

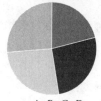

■A ■B ■C ■D

REPORTING CASH INFLOW

Every ETF PM must be intimately familiar with his or her positioning; cash reporting is an important tool for doing so efficiently. While individual PMs and ETF sponsors likely develop their own tools for cash management, there are two categories that are important to cover when it comes to managing cash entering (unexpectedly) into the portfolio: one is a cash and accrual reporting system, and the other is a dividend (for equities) or coupon (for fixed income) reporting system. Timely information is critical. The PM's reporting system should yield certain information on a daily basis to ensure as much transparency as possible.

Cash and Accrual Reporting

Cash and accrual reporting tells the ETF PM what percentage of each portfolio is in cash. A typical report would present not only how much of the portfolio was actually in cash but also what percentage of the portfolio value was in cash accruals, i.e., cash expected to be received. A solid portfolio management system would alert the PM if these figures netted to a cash position that significantly differed from zero, prompting the necessary response on the part of the PM.

A second feature of this report would provide the accrual schedule in terms of expected receipt. Accruals that amount to 25 basis points of the portfolio expected to be received in 2 business days is different from accruals expected to be received in 20 business days. For large positions in the portfolio with large accruals (a special dividend on a stock, for example), investing the accrual as described above might require a greater overdraft than would be typical day to day. Internal compliance functions would likely monitor this activity and communicate with the PM about mitigating excess borrowing relative to predefined parameters.

Forward-Looking Dividend/Dividend Payment Reporting

Dividend reporting for equity portfolios is closely linked to accruals, as these will often be the lion's share of the accrual total. As a result, there can be significant overlap, and some may choose to blend these types of reports together. There is no right and wrong per se, provided that any reporting gives the PM a clear view of what is to come. For dividends, the key questions are "When do we expect stocks to go ex?," "What is the expected cash impact of each dividend event?," and "When do we expect accruals to move to the cash account?"

Understanding when stocks are expected to go ex-dividend is critical for the PM. The morning a stock in an index trades ex-dividend, the index has reallocated those dollars in a manner described in the index methodology. This is like a mini index rebalance. The PM must have a clear understanding of when this will happen and how much of the portfolio is impacted. For some portfolios and some dividends, this is of marginal impact at best. For others, say a dividend-tilted fund or a high-yield fund, these mini rebalances are happening constantly and serve as alerts for the PM to reinvest funds on a more frequent basis. A typical dividend report might look like the one shown in Table 10.1.

For fixed-income portfolios, dividends are no longer relevant, but coupon payments are. Consider a 5% weight in a particular bond issue as part of a fixed-income portfolio. The coupon on the bond is 8% and pays semiannually. As a result, the PM can expect a 4% semiannual coupon on a 5% position, which amounts to a cash coupon of 20 basis points every six months. This movement from position to cash is just like the movement from position to cash when holding an equity that goes ex-dividend. The index will likely reinvest the cash into that security or the portfolio of securities, requiring similar action on the part of the PM.

TABLE 10.1

Dividend Report for SWA Portfolio (1/11/2021)

Ticker	Shares	Ex-Date	Payable Date	Dividends per Share	Dividend
AKZO	7,296	1/12/2021	1/20/2021	$0.81	$5,873.68
AHGG	8,496	1/13/2021	1/21/2021	$0.45	$3,783.27
ACOP	5,456	1/14/2021	1/22/2021	$1.40	$7,660.63
AKRY	5,248	1/14/2021	1/22/2021	$1.55	$8,130.45

SOURCES OF CASH OUTFLOW AND MANAGING CASH OUT

Cash coming into the portfolio through the sources listed above generally results in the need for the PM to put that cash to work: purchasing securities and/or some rebalancing is the likely outcome. On the other hand, there are instances where cash leaves the portfolio, often requiring the sale of securities to fund the outflow. Some examples are:

- Purchases of securities
- Interest on short cash positions (borrowing fees)
- Creates where there is a cash component that is negative
- CIL components in a redemption
- Fees
- Fund distributions

The last of these deserves particular attention. ETFs pass along distributions that the fund receives through to the end investor. This means that when an equity fund receives a dividend from a stock in its portfolio, the dividend ultimately goes to the ETF shareholder, who "owns" that dividend through his or her proxy ownership in the ETF. This also holds for bond portfolios, where coupon payments get passed along to the end investor in a similar fashion.

Consider the quarterly distribution to the SWA Fund. As shown in Table 10.2, the total dollars received (not accrued, but actually paid) in dividends over the period was \$105,932.92. The total AUM in the fund at the end of the quarter was \$9,781,054.75. If the fund were to distribute all the dividends received, it would disburse 1.08%, and given the NAV of \$24.45, it would declare a \$0.26 dividend. The ETF would go ex on the agreed-upon ex-date, say 4/1/2021, and would pay out the funds shortly thereafter.*

TABLE 10.2

Quarterly Distribution of the SWA ETF (Q1 2021)

Total dividends received	\$ 105,932.92
Total AUM 3/31/2021	\$9,781,054.75
Distribution as percent of fund	1.08%
NAV 3/31/2021	\$ 24.45
Distribution per share	\$ 0.26
Fees	\$ 10,885.71
Net	\$ 95,047.21
Net distribution as percent of fund	0.97%
Net distribution per share	\$ 0.24

Distributions, however, generally get passed along to the investors in the fund net of expenses because investors can net them out against distributions when getting taxed for income. In Table 10.2, we outline a net distribution considering fees.†

Fund distributions are subject to delays between the ex-date and the payment date, just like distributions from a security. The NAV of the fund will drop on the ex-date, but the PM's systems might still show the cash in the portfolio until the cash is removed for payment. The PM must be on top of this situation and position accordingly, so that the cash is not mistakenly invested, leading to overallocation to securities in the portfolio. We illustrate this in a stylized example in Figure 10.3, where we show that for a \$25 NAV fund with a \$2 distribution, the portfolio may *appear* to have the \$2 after the ex-date, but the PM must know that this \$2 is set to be distributed several days hence.

* Some smoothing over the course of the fiscal year may take place.
† Other expenses may also be considered.

FIGURE 10.3

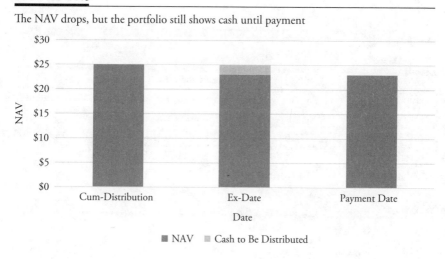

The NAV drops, but the portfolio still shows cash until payment

MANAGING CASH IN LIEU: AN INFLOW OR AN OUTFLOW

In Chapter 5, we discussed how certain securities can be marked "CIL" in the PCF. If a create comes in and a security is marked CIL in the PCF, then instead of delivering the security to the fund, the AP delivers the cash equivalent of that security. For a redemption, the fund delivers the cash-equivalent value to the AP in lieu of delivering the security. Marking certain securities that have unrealized losses as CIL would mean that the PM would sell the securities in the instance of a redemption in the market, rather than pass along the unrealized losses to the AP. In Chapter 11, we will go through examples of why this might be a valuable tool for the PM in managing corporate actions as well.

For the purposes of cash management, CIL should be tackled much like some of the other areas we've addressed in this chapter. The goal is to keep cash drag to a minimum, and so the PM should do his or her best to manage the cash component of orders effectively.

Consider the case where the SWA Fund has a creation order that came in on 3/1/2021. The PCF for 3/1/2021 marked the security ACBU CIL (see Table 10.3). This means that the PM should expect, along with the basket of securities from the AP, a cash component of over $75,000 (in addition to the standard expected cash calculation). Furthermore, no shares of ACBU will be in the basket. The PM's job is to put that cash to work effectively to manage to the index.

TABLE 10.3

PCF with Cash in Lieu (3/1/2021)

SWA ETF

Trade Date		3/1/21	Actual CIL	$	–
Settlement		T + 2	Actual cash		$645.93
Creation unit		50,000	Base market value		$1,188,308.04
NAV	$	25.29	Basket shares		30,207
NAV per CU	$ 1,264,611.36		Estimated CIL	$	75,657.39
Shares O/S		400,000	Estimated cash	$	76,303.32
Total net assets	$10,116,890.86		Estimated dividend	$	–

ID	Ticker	Shares	Base Price	Base MV	Weight	CIL
US1001	AABA	759	95.67	72,613.43	5.7449%	N
US1003	AAQZ	876	72.48	63,491.88	5.0232%	N
US1004	AAWL	1,029	57.58	59,246.41	4.6873%	N
US1009	ACBU	995	76.04	75,657.39	5.9857%	Y
US1010	ACGN	1,652	38.43	63,488.05	5.0229%	N
US1012	ACOP	686	103.91	71,278.90	5.6393%	N

. . .

PUTTING IT ALL TOGETHER: CASH MAPPING

All these forward-looking reports have one thing in common: they are all estimates. Payments can move around, and any report based on basis points or percentages relative to the fund will change simply because the value of the fund will be moving over time as well. Nevertheless, the best portfolio management systems will aggregate cash movements both in and out of the portfolio so that the PM has the most insight into the composition of the fund and can make the necessary decisions to manage the fund based on current estimates. Not only does mapping cash assist in managing distributions and cash drag, but cash is a critical input to creations and redemptions: an all-cash redemption for a fixed-income portfolio, for example, might require a substantial cash buffer in the portfolio or planned liquidity management for when redemption orders arise. Mapping out cash is critical for ETFs of all kinds.

CHAPTER 11

Corporate Actions

Corporations are dynamic entities, and the securities issued by corporations are dynamic as well: what the holder of a security is entitled to can change over time, and the actions of a corporation can have significant impact on the valuation of a security and any portfolio that holds that security. For the index-based ETF PM, the index file process provides a lot of insight into corporate actions and guides the actions of the PM. In the active ETF case, covered in more detail in Chapter 15, this is not so, but active PMs may subscribe to a service tracking corporate actions or handle that process in-house.

In this chapter, we continue to focus on index-based equity ETFs and present several corporate actions—from simple events like dividends to more complex events like rights offerings—along with a discussion of not only what a PM should come to expect in the index files and pro forma files in each case, but also what actions to take as a result. We comment on fixed-income–related corporate actions in Chapter 16.

CASH DIVIDENDS

A dividend payment from a stock is usually a cash payment to shareholders, but dividends can come in a variety of forms. For example, besides cash, dividends can be paid in stock; and while the schedule of dividend declarations, ex-dates, and payment dates is typically announced well ahead of time, "special" dividends can be paid off-cycle.

We've covered dividends in a number of chapters already, with the key points being how the dividends are handled in the index files and PCF files and how PMs ought to think about the timing of cash flows as they relate to dividends.

In the case where dividends are received in stock instead of cash, the impact on the index is generally different (unless otherwise stated in an index methodology): instead of a declining weight in the dividend-paying stock, the weight remains constant. This generally means that there is no pro rata investment across the remaining names in the index. For the ETF PM, this is a nonevent: the weight remains unchanged in the portfolio as well, and therefore no action is required.

MERGERS AND ACQUISITIONS

Mergers and acquisitions (M&A) occur either when two companies come together to form a new, larger entity (merge) or when one company buys another company and folds the business into its existing infrastructure. When a proposed merger or acquisition is announced, the terms of the proposed deal are generally announced as well. Acquisitions are often made for a combination of acquiror stock and/or cash, though a wide array of structures is possible. For publicly traded stocks, board approval is required, a process that could take a significant amount of time. During this time, stock prices can fluctuate wildly, depending on whether or not the market believes the deal will be accepted, how the deal is structured (all-cash deals expected to close will have less volatility post-announcement), or even if another deal will come along that will be preferable to the board. When a deal is in play, a lot could happen with a stock.

Consider a deal we introduced in Chapter 3 in our discussion of corporate action files. On 4/29/2021 it is announced that AAQZ has agreed to purchase AABA in a stock and cash deal (see Table 11.1). Each shareholder of AABA would receive 1.27 shares of AAQZ and $24.53 cash. Prior to the announcement, AAQZ was trading at $18.18; by the close of 4/29/2021, that price was $19.28. The deal was to be approved by the board on 5/5/2021 and to be delisted and go ex on 5/6/2021. Because of the premium built into the deal, the stock price of AABA jumped on the announcement news and closed at $49.07 on 4/29/2021. In Figure 11.1, we plot the price movements for the two stocks. Note how the price of AABA moved in line with AAQZ post-announcement; for a stock-based deal, this is standard for deals that are expected to close.

TABLE 11.1

Deal Summary for AAQZ Acquisition of AABA

Announcement date	4/29/2021
Nature of bid	Friendly
Payment type	Cash + stock
Cash terms per share	$24.53
Stock terms (acquiror shares per target share)	1.2728

FIGURE 11.1

Price action for AAQZ and AABA during proposed acquisition

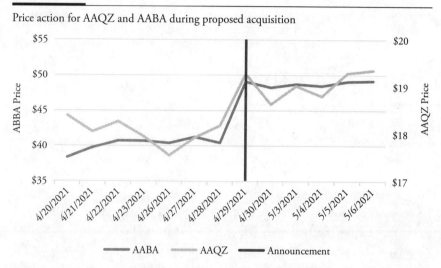

While an active ETF PM would be keenly interested and likely quite aware of the nuances surrounding a particular deal, much of this detail is of no concern to the index-based ETF PM. The index-based ETF PM's goal is to track the index, and so as long as the portfolio weight is roughly in line with the index weight during the period prior to the deal closing, there may be little or nothing for the PM to do. As always, the index methodology is the PM's best friend: well-documented indices will very clearly articulate what will happen in the event of a merger or acquisition.

Deals are structured in all kinds of ways as mentioned earlier. Here we will consider six important cases, as illustrated in Table 11.2, depending on the makeup of the index and the structure of the deal.

TABLE 11.2

M&A Matrix

	All Cash	Cash + Stock	All Stock
Acquiror in Index	Cash reinvestment	Cash reinvestment	No action
Acquiror Not in Index	Sell target/wait for cash + cash reinvestment	Sell target + cash reinvestment	Sell prior to delisting

For the makeup of the index, there are two cases pertaining to the acquiror:

1. Both the acquiror and the target are in the index.
2. Only the target is in the index.

For the structure of the deal, there are three cases:

1. All cash
2. Cash plus stock
3. All stock

In the case where both acquiror and target are in the index, there may be no action required on the part of the ETF PM if the transaction is for all stock: if the index methodology allows for the increased weight in the acquiror vis-à-vis the acquisition of the target shares, then the PM simply waits for the deal to close, and his or her shares are automatically converted through the custodian and will show up as acquiror shares after the deal closes. If there is a cash component in the deal, however, that cash must be reinvested in accordance with the index methodology. There is also the possibility that the acquiror weight is not allowed to grow as specified in the index methodology; in this case, the weight of the target must be redistributed.

In the case where the acquiror is *not* in the index, the target is removed from the index, and its weight must be redistributed across the remaining constituents of the index. This requires activity on the part of the PM, dependent on the structure of the deal:

1. For an all-cash deal, the PM can wait for the deal to process and then reinvest received cash, or the PM can sell the stock prior to the deal closing and reinvest along with the index.

2. For a hybrid stock-cash deal, if the PM waits for the deal closing, he or she will receive acquiror stock, which is not in the index and is therefore sold. Along with any cash, the PM would reinvest the proceeds.
3. For an all-stock deal, if the PM waits for the deal closing, as in a hybrid deal, he or she will receive acquiror stock, which is not in the index and is therefore sold. Along with any cash, the PM would reinvest the proceeds. PMs generally sell prior to the delisting of the target stock to avoid holding acquiror shares.

On the surface, such a replacement may seem relatively straightforward, as it is almost like an index rebalance where one name is removed and weights are adjusted in other names. Several index issues arise, however, as the approval process draws near. In particular, the stock could stop trading unexpectedly, or a rebalance could take place around the time of the deal close.

Typically, the market will be expecting the stock to stop trading on a particular day; trading might be halted during the board meeting for approval or shortly thereafter prior to the deal closing. However, trading might stop early, and when that happens, the PM will no longer be able to exit his or her position if necessary. Importantly, standard index methodologies typically assign a price to a halted stock as its last closing price, subject to the index committee stepping in to amend this to account for unusual circumstances.

Consider a real-life example. On 10/3/2018, Cloudera (CLDR) announced a deal to acquire Hortonworks (HDP) (see Table 11.3). Shareholders of HDP would receive 1.305 shares of CLDR in an all-stock deal (i.e., no cash). The deal was approved by HDR shareholders on 12/28/2018. Closing was expected on or about 1/3/2019, and it was anticipated that shares of HDP would be delisted on 1/4/2019. An ETF PM tracking this index would have to sell out of his or her position on the close on January 3 and reinvest pro rata if CLDR was not also in the index to be tracked.

TABLE 11.3

Deal Summary for CLDR Acquisition of HDP

Announcement date	10/3/2018
Nature of bid	Friendly
Payment type	Stock
Stock terms (acquiror shares per target share)	1.305

As with most corporate actions, the index sponsor would announce treatment a couple of days prior to implementation, ostensibly to give the PMs a chance to track the index seamlessly. On 12/31/2018, suppose an index sponsor announces that HDR would be removed from the index on January 3 (close) at its last traded price. The weight in the index, say 5%, would be redistributed for the open on January 4. So far, so good.

Unexpectedly, however, shares of HDP were halted on the exchange prematurely on 1/2/2019. The last price of the stock was $14.68. The acquiring company, CLDR, continued to trade, and since the deal was all stock, one could compute the fair value of HDP shares as a function of the price of CLDR on the January 3 close, which was actually $13.53.* The index would likely use the last close to value HDP, which would be at a considerable premium to the implied value according to the terms of the deal.

It is a different story in a tracking portfolio. Instead of a value of $14.68, the value of the shares becomes $13.53. It is as if the index's hypothetical portfolio got a price-per-share premium of $1.15. As a result, any tracking portfolio would suffer underperformance due to the corporate action. In Table 11.4, we show the impact on the portfolio relative to the index on the open on January 4. A portfolio with a 5% weight in HDP would underperform this hypothetical index by 39 basis points due to the valuation of the CLDR shares at a lower price. It is situations like this that keep ETF portfolio managers up at night—without warning of a corporate action, the ETF PM's options to address that action become limited.

TABLE 11.4

Underperformance of the Portfolio due to HDP Trading Halt

Price of HDR (last close)	$14.68
Conversion post–deal close	$13.53
Loss in dollars relative to last close	$ 1.15
Loss in % relative to last close	−7.83%
Weight in index	5.00%
Underperformance to index	−0.39%

---

* CLDR closed at $10.37 on 1/3/2019. With the deal terms set at 1.305 shares of CLDR per share of HDP, this works out to a fair value of 1.305 × $10.37 = $13.53.

A second way an acquisition could impact an index is if the index rebalances around the deal close. Imagine an index that rebalances quarterly—calculating on quarter-end and rebalancing five business days later—and selects stocks based on their three-month realized volatilities, overweighting the lower-volatility stocks in the eligible universe. On the morning of March 31, before the open, a company in the eligible universe discloses that it has agreed to be acquired in an all-cash deal with a 20% premium with a closing date expected on or about July 12, subject to the board's approval at its July 9 meeting. What happens in the June rebalance, where the calculation date is June 30 and the rebalance date is July 8?

For starters, we know that if the market perceives the deal will in fact close, then the price of the stock will jump on March 31 (see Figure 11.2). For all the subsequent days between March 31 and July 12, the stock would be expected to trade at a very slight discount to the deal price, accounting for the time value of money and any slight deal risk (that the deal would fall apart).

FIGURE 11.2

Deal impact on volatility: reduced volatility after deal announcement

The problem is that the stock, whose realized volatility was somewhere around 20% prior to the deal, would be measured as minuscule on June 30, when three-month realized volatility is required as an input to the index methodology. The overweight in this stock would be enormous (or at the very least, significantly higher than it would be had the deal not been announced), and the PM would, under normal circumstances, follow the index methodology and increase holdings in the rebalance.* If he or she does so, however, then the position would have to be sold on the following day. So the PM has a choice:

1. Buy into the stock during the rebalance.

   Or

2. Hold cash into the deal close and reinvest on July 12.

The potential for tracking error in this situation comes from the possibility that if the PM holds cash and the deal is voted down, the stock would likely gap (probably down, but potentially up if the deal is turned down because a better deal arises). The gap would be reflected in the index but not in the portfolio. On the other hand, the PM would be incurring a round-trip transaction cost for buying and then promptly selling the same stock when it will, in all likelihood, not deviate much in price, acting similarly to a cash position. This is where the PM needs to be in tune with the deal and the news surrounding the deal. If the gap risk is to the downside (i.e., no other deals seem likely), then the tracking error potentially created by holding cash would accrue to the end investor positively relative to the index. That might push the PM into option 2 above.

Every merger or acquisition event is different. It is incumbent upon the ETF PM to be aware of the index methodology and to be in touch with the index sponsor if questions arise as the event draws near.

TENDER OFFERS

Tender offers are like acquisitions, but they proceed toward the culminating event (the takeover) in a different manner: shareholders are invited to sell, or "tender," their shares for a prespecified price, which is typically higher than the current market price. The deal, however, is often contingent upon enough shareholders accepting the proposal, so that the acquiror can gain enough of the shares outstanding to control the company after the tender is completed.

Understanding all the nuances around tender offers is beyond the scope of this book, but it is important for our purposes to note that tender offers have an element of game theory associated with them: each shareholder must

---

* An index committee might address this situation prior to rebalance.

consider what other shareholders would do as they consider their own decision to tender or not to tender their shares, and it may not be clear that a particular tender offer will succeed. This introduces uncertainty into the portfolio management process. The index sponsor may wait to decide about removing a stock from an index, for example, depending on whether or not the offer is successful. That might be fine for the index, but it is likely that a shareholder (in this case, the ETF PM) must decide well before that what he or she is going to do.

One important contributing factor to the "game" that is played during a tender is that if the tender offer is accepted, then the remaining shares are often bought out at the tender price (though that isn't necessarily the case). The PM can accept the tender offer if he or she believes the deal will close, and will, in all likelihood, remain in line with the index, likely resulting in redistributing proceeds from the tender offer. If the offer does not get enough takers ("undersubscribed"), then the index and the ETF would still hold the shares, so that works from a tracking error perspective. Taking no action or rejecting the offer may avail the PM of the opportunity to sell the shares at the time the index sponsor makes the announcement on how the tender offer is being handled, but that would result in incurring transaction costs and accepting the additional risk of price fluctuation after the tender closes.

RIGHTS OFFERINGS

A rights offering (sometimes called a rights issue) is when a company allows existing shareholders to buy more shares at a reduced price. The offering is a source of cash for the company: an offer of shares for an infusion of capital. Rights offerings are generally treated as tax-free dividends to the existing shareholders to which the rights are offered.*

The amount of shares a company allows an existing shareholder to purchase is based on the shareholder's present holdings. A typical rights offering is structured as follows: A company will offer the option to purchase number of shares for each share held, e.g., two shares for every five shares held, or "two for five," and will specify the share price, or "subscription price" at which the company will issue the additional shares. The company will specify the window of dates for which the offer is valid as part of the deal.

Rights are effectively call options. If the share price during the allowing purchase window falls below the offering price, then the rights holder will

---

* Fund accountants should be consulted for any tax advice.

not exercise the rights: he or she would clearly be better off purchasing in the marketplace than agreeing to pay the prespecified subscription price. Options have value, and therefore when an investor is given the rights through a rights offering, there is value to those rights. Unlike exchange-listed options, however, some rights are not "renounceable," which means one cannot trade the rights in the market; investors may only exercise the rights or let them expire worthless.

What is the the impact of the rights offering (renounceable and nonrenounceable)? Consider the impact on the following:

1. The stock price and market capitalization
2. The index
3. The portfolio

Stock Price

Stock prices generally fall with rights offerings because the subscription price is typically below the market price of the stock. The dilution that comes from the additional shares is offset to the shareholder by the value of the opportunity to purchase shares at a discount.

The expected price of the stock upon a rights offering becomes a weighted average of the market price and the subscription price. See the appendix at the end of the chapter for an exact calculation.

Index

What about the impact on an index? When an index assumes participation in the rights offering, the weight in the index will generally go up. This is because by "participating" in the offering (there is no real holding, of course), the index is effectively purchasing more of the underlying security. It does so in a value-neutral way, so there is a slight decline in other weights. As for the security in question, the number of shares will increase by the ratio in the offering, and the price will decline as shown above. Just like the market cap of the company, the weight in the index will increase. However, with this increase in position, all the positions must be scaled back so that the weights as a whole continue to sum to 100%. The important takeaway is that the weight of the offering security will increase in the index, *but not by quite as much as the increase in market value.*

To see this in action, in Tables 11.5 and 11.6 we present the ICF and the IOF for 4/28/2021 and 4/29/2021, respectively, for the SWA Index, reflecting the AFOJ rights offering that went ex on 4/29/2021. AFOJ offered rights at a ratio of two per five at a price of $15. The shares closed at $21.90 on 4/28/2021. The percentage weight in AFOJ goes from 5.46% to 6.86% (note there are no other corporate actions in the portfolio to be processed on this date, so the figures are pure with respect to the rights offering). This is an increase of 25.64%, which is lower than the increase of 27.40% in the market value of AFOJ.

TABLE 11.5

SWA Index Close File Pre–Rights Offering

Index	SWA Index
Date	4/28/2021
Index Level	95.5622

ID	Ticker	Base Price	Weight	Index Shares	Index Value
US1001	AABA	$ 40.44	4.44%	0.1048	4.2389
US1003	AAQZ	$ 18.18	4.53%	0.2382	4.3314
US1005	AAXX	$ 28.57	4.65%	0.1555	4.4422
US1009	ACBU	$ 78.37	5.01%	0.0611	4.7907
US1010	ACGN	$ 37.58	4.92%	0.1252	4.7061
US1012	ACOP	$ 84.02	4.73%	0.0538	4.5169
US1018	ADXK	$ 25.34	5.50%	0.2076	5.2598
US1019	ADZI	$ 32.79	5.35%	0.1559	5.1119
US1024	AFOJ	$ 21.90	5.46%	0.2384	5.2216
US1026	AGFZ	$ 40.44	4.74%	0.1120	4.5276
US1028	AHBP	$ 66.56	4.68%	0.0672	4.4755
US1029	AHGG	$ 55.70	5.31%	0.0911	5.0721
US1030	AHJQ	$ 79.18	6.05%	0.0730	5.7786
US1033	AIAD	$ 25.29	4.69%	0.1772	4.4808
US1038	AKEK	$ 88.48	4.73%	0.0511	4.5245
US1042	AKRY	$ 67.58	4.82%	0.0682	4.6079
US1045	AKXI	$ 15.54	4.89%	0.3008	4.6744
US1046	AKZO	$ 76.11	5.13%	0.0644	4.9050
US1049	ALTO	$103.12	5.25%	0.0487	5.0175
US1050	AMGP	$ 12.33	5.11%	0.3958	4.8787

TABLE 11.6

SWA Index Open File Post–Rights Offering

Index	SWA Index
Date	4/29/2021
Index Level	95.5622

ID	Ticker	Base Price	Weight	Index Shares	Index Value
US1001	AABA	$ 40.44	4.37%	0.1033	4.1764
US1003	AAQZ	$ 18.18	4.47%	0.2347	4.2675
US1005	AAXX	$ 28.57	4.58%	0.1532	4.3767
US1009	ACBU	$ 78.37	4.94%	0.0602	4.7201
US1010	ACGN	$ 37.58	4.85%	0.1234	4.6367
US1012	ACOP	$ 84.02	4.66%	0.0530	4.4503
US1018	ADXK	$ 25.34	5.42%	0.2046	5.1822
US1019	ADZI	$ 32.79	5.27%	0.1536	5.0366
US1024	AFOJ	$ 19.93	6.86%	0.3289	6.5540
US1026	AGFZ	$ 40.44	4.67%	0.1103	4.4608
US1028	AHBP	$ 66.56	4.61%	0.0662	4.4095
US1029	AHGG	$ 55.70	5.23%	0.0897	4.9973
US1030	AHJQ	$ 79.18	5.96%	0.0719	5.6934
US1033	AIAD	$ 25.29	4.62%	0.1746	4.4147
US1038	AKEK	$ 88.48	4.66%	0.0504	4.4577
US1042	AKRY	$ 67.58	4.75%	0.0672	4.5400
US1045	AKXI	$ 15.54	4.82%	0.2963	4.6055
US1046	AKZO	$ 76.11	5.06%	0.0635	4.8326
US1049	ALTO	$103.12	5.17%	0.0479	4.9435
US1050	AMGP	$ 12.33	5.03%	0.3900	4.8068

Portfolio

The ETF PM, of course, needs to track the index performance through the rights offering. We learned from the index open file that the percentage weight in the issuing name will go up, but as a result, all the other weights have to decline. This is because when rights are exercised, they require an investor to pay for additional shares. In an index, the corporate actions cannot change the value of the index, so in this case, shares of other holdings must be reduced to reflect the larger holding in the issuing stock.

Immediate exercise of the rights would require cash to purchase the additional shares—cash that would need to be borrowed, leaving the portfolio overinvested, or leveraged. Selling a slice of the portfolio (including shares of the issuing stock) for enough cash to offset the purchase correctly aligns the portfolio. This is just like what the index does: it increases the shares of the issuing stock by exercising the rights, but then pares down *all* the positions to account for the cost of exercising those rights.*

An alternative course of action for the ETF PM would be to sell the rights and use the cash obtained from the sale along with the cash obtained from selling a slice of the nonissuing stocks to top up the holdings in the issuing stock. It is worth noting that because the rights are being sold, that is a taxable event (a realized gain), whereas when the rights are exercised, gains in the purchased shares (which accrue immediately) are unrealized and only result in taxable gains when the shares are sold (if they are eventually sold above the subscription price).†

The offering, however, is going to impose some tracking error for three obvious reasons:§

1. Transaction costs
2. Taxes
3. Timing

---

* Note that if the PM sells some of the rights offering security prior to the ex-date, then those shares are obviously no longer participating in the rights offering in the portfolio. This creates a circularity, complicating the math ever so slightly. The easiest thing to do is to sell the other names into the ex-date. This might lead to a very slight misallocation that can easily be trued up the following day if necessary.

† As we have stated before, fund accountants should be consulted for any tax advice.

§ A more nuanced reason for tracking error is that there are some situations in which the ETF may not be entitled to receive the rights being issued by the company. This is typically the case when the rights are issued in a country where the offering is made to domestic shareholders. Unless the index methodology specifically ignores these instances (and that is generally not the case), then the value typically inherent in the rights offering and accrued to the ETF portfolio to offset the dilution effect is no longer received. This becomes a value loss to the ETF relative to the index. On the other hand, it is possible for a rights offering to be ignored by the index methodology because rights are being given to purchase a different security as opposed to the security in the index; this means that the portfolio receiving the value of the rights will grow relative to the index. Both cases result in tracking error, but clearly one is value-enhancing to the shareholder, while the other is value-destroying.

Transaction costs and taxes are straightforward, but what about that nasty lag? The index may assume immediate investment, but oftentimes the rights offering itself specifies a window for subscription, meaning that the actual exercise of the rights can be delayed. In this case, two important steps must take place:

1. The portfolio needs to ensure that the rights themselves are being valued and incorporated into the NAV of the fund.
2. The shares of the nonissuing stocks that were sold to raise cash for the purchase involved in the rights exercise ought to be sold on the close prior to the ex-date.

The first of these two might seem obvious: the portfolio "owns" something, so it should be valued as part of the NAV. The second point, though, deserves a bit more detail. The key question for the ETF PM is "How can I ensure that my portfolio tracks the index, even though I can't exercise the rights I've been given?" The answer is that as long as the PM holds the cash and the rights, his or her exposure will mimic the index exposure provided the stock trades above the subscription price. Note that the valuation of the rights, much like any holding in a portfolio, must be updated continually to get a proper accounting of the NAV.

In one final twist with respect to rights offerings, companies often declare dividends (and stocks go ex-dividend) on the same date as the rights offering goes ex. This means that adjustments are required not only because of the rights offering but also due to the price adjustment that occurs ex-dividend. For indices that redistribute dividend payments across assets rather than back into the asset that went ex-dividend, this adds a layer of complexity to the calculations above.*

STOCK SPLITS AND REVERSE SPLITS

Occasionally when a stock trades at a price deemed too high per share or too low per share by the company, the company may elect to split or reverse-split the shares. In a standard stock split, for every share of stock a shareholder

---

* See the appendix at the end of the chapter for an accounting of the scenario in which rights and the dividend go ex on the same date.

owns, the shareholder receives additional shares, and the price of the shares adjusts accordingly so that the economic value of the transaction is zero. In a reverse split, the shareholder gives shares back to the company, while the price of the remaining shares is adjusted up so that the economic value of the transaction is zero.

Consider a company whose stock is trading at $9.00. The company announces a three-for-one split. A shareholder who owns 100 shares would receive an additional 200 shares, so that the new amount he or she holds is 300 shares. The price drops from $9.00 to $3.00, so that the overall value of the original 100 shares of $900.00 is now reflected in the overall value of the new 300 shares at $3.00 apiece, or $900.00.

Now suppose the same company declared a one-for-two reverse split. This means that for every two shares a shareholder owns, he or she would hold one after the event. Someone holding 100 shares would now hold only 50 shares, but the price (and basis) adjustment would be a multiple of a factor of 2. In the example above, the price would adjust to $18.00.

It is possible for the split to be uneven with respect to shares. Imagine instead of holding 100 shares, an investor held 99. In this case, the 99 shares would typically be surrendered in exchange for 49 shares, and the remaining share would be processed with a cash-in-lieu transaction, where the shareholder would receive cash instead of shares.

SPINOFFS

Spinoffs are, in effect, the opposite of mergers: instead of two companies becoming one, one company becomes two. A particular subset of a business is separated from the original entity to form a new entity, and ownership of the new entity is returned to the original entity's shareholders in the form of a special dividend. An ETF that holds a security that spins off a new entity could end up with shares of both the original company and the new company. Index-tracking ETFs would, of course, look through to the index methodology to establish what, if any, actions take place in this scenario, but it is quite possible that no action is required on the part of the PM, unless the index removes the spun off entity. Other related corporate actions, like split-offs (where shareholders are offered a choice to hold the original company's or the new company's shares) and carve-outs (where the new company's shares are sold to the public rather than granted to existing shareholders), would almost certainly require action on the part of the PM to reflect how the index handles such events.

CORPORATE ACTIONS AND CASH IN LIEU

Marking a security CIL can assist a PM during a corporate action event. For example, say that a stock announces it will be acquired in an all-cash deal on 1/29/2021 and that shares will be delisted the following morning. The last opportunity to trade the stock on the exchange will be at the close of the 29th. Suppose the news is only made public on the 29th, leaving no time to handle the situation in the index without any notification.* The index calculation agent sends out a notification on behalf of the index sponsor that the stock will be removed from the index, but not until the close of 2/2/2021 (two days after the stock is eligible to be traded on the exchange), and the weight from the stock will be reinvested on the close in the remaining stocks in the index pro rata.

In this case, the PM expects to sell the stock and reinvest the proceeds into the remaining stocks in the index, but because of the lag, the reinvestment will not take place until two days after the position is closed out. The index files, however, will still reflect a holding in this position, and as a result, the PCF, if based on the index, will also reflect a position in the stock. The PM, rather than expose the portfolio to the risk of receiving shares that have been delisted and might only trade OTC, sells all of the position in the stock on the close of January 31.

What happens, though, if a create or redeem comes in on February 1? The stock is still technically in the index, but (a) the PM no longer holds the stock for a redeem, and (b) the PM does not want more shares of the stock coming in due to liquidity concerns. This is where CIL comes in. The PM can mark the security CIL, ensuring that the weight associated with the stock in the basket is exchanged in cash as opposed to shares (see Table 11.7). Marking the security CIL also changes the amount of cash that is exchanged in the transaction.

---

* It is not uncommon for an index to lag certain changes in the index by a number of days to allow those tracking the index to make portfolio adjustments.

TABLE 11.7

Marking a Security CIL During a Corporate Action

Date	Actions
January 29	Corporate action announced
	Index announces February 2 removal
	PM sells position
February 1	PM marks security CIL
February 2 (close)	Index removes security
	PM reinvests sale proceeds

Another example with similar implications is when an index constituent is being acquired by a company outside the index in a deal that consists of the acquiror's stock. Upon announcement (and assuming the deal is approved and/or seems certain to be approved), the stock to be acquired will move in lockstep with the acquiror's stock but will continue to trade until the transaction closes. On the day the transaction is completed, the weight from the acquired stock will be redistributed across the holdings in the index, which will require the PM to sell this stock on the close and purchase other index constituents. In case an order happens to come in on this day, the PM can mark the stock as CIL. The CIL indication, however, would require the PM to either invest incoming cash or refrain from investing all the proceeds from the sale of the stock in question to provide cash in case of a redemption. An even better option for the PM is to reweight the PCF to reflect the end-of-day post–corporate action weights in the index, treating the action like an index rebalance and marking the PCF off what would effectively feel like a pro forma.

MULTIPLE CORPORATE ACTIONS ON THE SAME DAY

Many corporate actions overlap—in a large portfolio of holdings, it is almost certain that a PM will encounter situations where multiple corporate actions need to be processed on the same day. This is not as complex as it sounds. The key to the PM is not trading more than is necessary. One corporate action might result in cash coming into the portfolio (or an accrual, as in a dividend), while another might require cash (as in the rights offering). PMs should account for all the possible actions in response to each corporate action individually and then ensure that the most efficient path to the post–corporate action portfolio is taken.

APPENDIX

As we mentioned earlier, a rights offering will have an impact on a company's share price and shares outstanding. The corporate action will also have an impact on an index holding the shares, which will generally require action on the part of the ETF PM. In this appendix, we provide some mathematical context for how prices, shares, and index weights are adjusted.

Consider a stock for which rights are offered at a ratio of one per N, meaning a holder of N shares of the stock has the right to purchase one additional share for the subscription price of X, while the shares trade at P_T. The company also may declare a dividend of D (which can be zero if no dividend is declared). The stock trades ex the dividend and the rights on day $T + 1$. Shares outstanding are S_T, and the total market capitalization for the company is MC_T.

We expect the rights-adjusted price $\tilde{P}_T$ to be

$$\tilde{P}_T = \frac{P_T + XR}{1 + R}$$

where

$$R = \frac{1}{N}$$

This can be seen from calculating the weighted average price of new and old shares, where new shares are simply $R \times S_T$ and the rights-adjusted shares $\tilde{S}_T$ are

$$\tilde{S}_T = S_T + R \times S_T = S_T(1 + R)$$

Therefore,

$$\tilde{P}_T = \frac{S_T \times P_T + R \times S_T \times X}{\tilde{S}_T} = \frac{P_T + XR}{1 + R}$$

The new market cap is simply $\tilde{S}_T \tilde{P}_T$.

With respect to a dividend, often in overseas cases, taxes are withheld from dividends. We assume a withholding rate of δ. Therefore the post–withholding adjusted dividend $\tilde{D}$ becomes:

$$\tilde{D} = \frac{D \times (1 - \delta)}{1 + R}$$

The opening price on the ex-date is then

$$P_{T+1} = \tilde{P}_T - \tilde{D}$$

The market capitalization for the company is now

$$MC_{T+1} = \tilde{S}_T \times P_{T+1}$$

As for the weight in the index, the position will also grow just like the market capitalization for the company did. With a fixed portfolio value, however, the growth of the position in the company issuing rights must be offset across the entire portfolio to fund the rights purchase.

The index shares before the processing of the rights are defined as IS_T, and the index shares after the rights are processed as $\tilde{IS}_T$. The price post-rights and dividends (expected) is P_{T+1}. The position has grown by a factor of

$$\gamma = \frac{\tilde{IS}_T P_{T+1}}{IS_T P_T}$$

Denoting the preprocessed closing weight in the stock as w^*, each position in the portfolio (including the stock offering the rights) is scaled down by a factor of $1 + \gamma w^*$, which will achieve the equivalence in value of the portfolio before and after the rights processing.

CHAPTER 12

Custom In-Kind Baskets

Custom in-kind baskets (CIBs) are so important to ETF portfolio management that their own chapter is very much warranted. Effectively, a CIB is a tax-deferral tool that the ETF PM can use to manage capital gains and losses in the portfolio. By working with an AP to customize the construction of a creation or redemption basket (or both), the PM can tax-manage the portfolio more efficiently. CIBs can be challenging to master, so let's begin with an analogy to set the scene.

Imagine you run a store that sells widgets. Each week your widget supplier sells you widgets by the set, which includes equal amounts of widgets in red, blue, and green. Occasionally, an order comes in and you're overstocked, so your supplier lets you return the complete set in full for a refund. Deliveries come in on Wednesdays, and returned sets are picked up on Fridays.

One week you notice that your blue widgets aren't selling, and you're starting to build up an inventory of them that you don't want. You'd like to return the items, but returns are in sets, just as they are delivered. Plus, if you return all the blue widgets, your shelves will look bare.

You come up with a plan, though: you call your supplier and ask for an additional delivery this Wednesday so you can remove the extra blue widgets and maintain a full selection. Then you ask your supplier if rather than you return a standard set on Friday, you can return only blue widgets instead. As a thank you for taking on the custom return, you agree to place the supplier's products at the front of the aisle. You clear your blue inventory, solve your shelf-space concern, and provide the supplier with valuable shelf space. Everyone wins.

This, in a nutshell, is the transaction at the heart of the CIB. Standard PCFs dictate what a creation or redemption basket normally looks like (see Chapter 5). But under certain conditions the PM can specify a different, "custom," basket—the "all-blue widgets" basket—that has weights that don't correspond pro rata to the underlying index or holdings, and the PM will ask an AP to create or redeem shares using this special basket. In this chapter, we will walk through the process of constructing that basket and discuss the implications the custom basket has for the fund.

A NOTE ON THE NEW CIB VERSUS THE OLD CIB

Until the ETF Rule was passed, the term "CIB" commonly referred to any basket that did not look like the underlying holdings and was used for tax management purposes. The ETF Rule, however, has redefined what a custom basket means as opposed to a standard basket, and the definitions do not neatly line up to what used to be used in the vernacular. For example, a basket with one or more names marked CIL would not have traditionally been considered custom, but it falls in the "custom" category under the new rule. Formally, custom baskets include those that do not reflect "(i) a pro rata representation of the ETF's portfolio holdings; (ii) a representative sampling of the ETF's portfolio holdings; or (iii) changes due to a rebalancing or reconstitution of the ETF's securities market index, if applicable."[1] On the Street, our expectation is that the term "CIB" will continue its pre-ETF Rule meaning, and as a result, that is how we employ the term going forward. We also note that active ETFs (discussed in more depth in Chapter 15) may use CIBs under the ETF Rule. Here, as we've done so far, we focus on the index-based products, but the principles are similar.

CUSTOM IN-KIND BASKETS: KEY PRINCIPLES

The foundation of the creation/redemption mechanism is the value equivalence of the ETF shares and the in-kind basket that are exchanged. Assuming perfect liquidity among all securities in a basket, one could imagine that the AP should be indifferent to which stocks are received in a redemption basket or which stocks would be required for purchase for a creation basket. As long as the value of the securities equals the value of the unit, the AP is made whole in the transaction. The fund sponsor and PM, however, are far from indifferent; three key principles drive the process:

1. **CIB Principle 1:** Sales of securities in the market are done in order of the highest cost basis first, to minimize the realized gain per transaction.
2. **CIB Principle 2:** "Sales" of securities through redemptions by an AP do not result in capital gains or losses to the fund.
3. **CIB Principle 3:** The number of units created equals the number of units redeemed.

These principles lead to a natural preference ordering when disposing of securities in a portfolio: it is better that a security with unrealized losses is sold by the PM in the market than redeemed by an AP. Conversely, the PM would prefer that securities with unrealized gains are redeemed as opposed sold in the market for the benefit of the investor. And whatever the creation and redemption baskets look like, the size of the fund in units is designed to remain constant when the process is completed (absent organic C/R activity).

CIB 1: STANDARD CREATION FOLLOWED BY CUSTOM REDEMPTION

CIBs are complicated, so an in-depth example will prove instructive. Consider the following scenario: The SWA portfolio has a rebalance on 10/7/2021. The calculation day is on 9/30/2021 (quarter-end), and pro forma files are already being constructed. Some summary information regarding the expected trade upon calculation is presented in Table 12.1.

Some tickers are removed (e.g., AAXX), some are added (e.g., AABD), and some positions already held are adjusted (e.g., AAQZ). To help set the scene even further, let's drill down for a particular security; in Table 12.2, we show portfolio holdings for AAQZ by lot, ordered by descending cost basis. Based on CIB Principle 1, if we sold AAQZ in the market, we would want to sell the *highest* cost basis lots first. The rebalance requires a sale of 8,801 shares, so if we performed the whole trade in the secondary market, we would sell all of lots AAQZ1013, AAQZ1012, and AAQZ1001 as well as some shares of lot AAQZ1006. This results in a capital gain of $160,357.09. If we proceeded in this fashion for all the tickers to be sold in the rebalance,

TABLE 12.1

SWA Portfolio Rebalance (9/30/2021)

Tickers to be Removed			Tickers to be Added	
Ticker	Shares Held	Unrealized G/L	Ticker	Target Shares
AAXX	13,952	$ 166,692.15	AABD	5,339
ADPQ	7,639	$ 68,381.02	AFDA	7,153
AGFZ	12,145	$(26,867.54)	AIAD	19,967
AHOR	17,237	$ 122,062.51	AIYO	5,371
ALTO	5,493	$ 75,277.14	AKXI	31,833

Tickers to be Adjusted			
Ticker	Shares Held	Target Shares	Trade
AAQZ	24,612	15,811	(8,801)
ACBU	6,596	6,213	(383)
...			

Current Realized Gains/Losses:	$ (596,364.67)
Projected Market Trade Gains:	$ 695,574.98
Projected Realized Gains/Losses:	$ 99,210.31

NAV	$ 1.97
NAV per CU	$1,598,609.50

the resulting increase in capital gains would be $695,574.98. Given a realized capital *loss* position of $596,364.67 to date, this would push the portfolio into net gains prior to the end of the fiscal year on 12/31/2021 in the amount of $99,210.31 (see Table 12.1). Unless the PM can harvest losses (see Chapter 9), the PM is likely in a bind to avoid capital gains for the year.

In our first iteration of a CIB, we show how to redirect securities with unrealized gains to baskets that will go to the AP, using the SWA Index rebalance. Think of these unwanted market transactions as our blue widgets. To return the blue widgets in our analogy, we had to receive a standard order of red, blue, and green first. The same principle applies here: to customize the redemption basket, we receive a standard basket first, as depicted in Figure 12.1. The typical creation usually occurs two business days prior to a rebalance day, based on the standard PCF.

TABLE 12.2

AAQZ Lots Sorted by Cost Basis (9/30/2021)

Lot	Shares	Basis	Price	Unrealized	Trade Lot	Realized
AAQZ1013	56	$27.75	$40.44	$ 710.85	56	$ 710.85
AAQZ1012	55	$23.60	$40.44	$ 926.56	55	$ 926.56
AAQZ1001	7,491	$22.41	$40.44	$135,093.10	7,491	$135,093.10
AAQZ1006	2,553	$20.74	$40.44	$ 50,307.49	1,199	$ 23,626.59
AAQZ1007	90	$20.74	$40.44	$ 1,773.47	—	$ —
AAQZ1010	123	$19.00	$40.44	$ 2,637.10	—	$ —
AAQZ1009	14,095	$18.81	$40.44	$304,909.42	—	$ —
AAQZ1008	66	$18.58	$40.44	$ 1,443.14	—	$ —
AAQZ1011	83	$16.59	$40.44	$ 1,979.98	—	$ —
Total	24,612			$499,781.11	8,801	$160,357.09

FIGURE 12.1

Standard creation followed by custom redemption

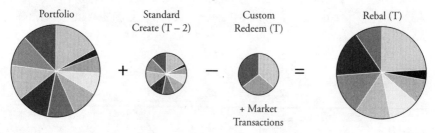

So which securities go into the redemption basket? We start by assuming a number of units in the CIB (and we can iterate over any number of them). For the sake of this analysis, we assume a one-unit CIB. Looking back at Table 12.2, we see that lots that we didn't include in the market-based transactions have greater gains per dollar of the position due to their lower cost basis. We discussed this notion before of gains or losses per dollar position when we discussed tax-loss harvesting: this is the bang-for-the-buck statistic. For tax-loss harvesting, we were seeking positions with large losses per dollar of the position held to minimize misallocation. Here we seek lots with the highest gains per dollar of position held.

By ordering all the lots irrespective of security that could potentially be sold in the rebalance by their bang for the buck, we would see what lots would be most efficient to dispose of through the redemption basket, since these transactions would not impose capital gains on the fund (CIB Principle 2). A selection of lots is shown in Table 12.3. (Though they do not appear in the table, we note that the lots that would come in with the create would appear in this table as well.)

TABLE 12.3

Lots Ordered by "Bang for the Buck" (9/30/2021)

Lot	Shares	Basis	Price	Unrealized	BFB	Basket
AAQZ1011	83	$16.59	$ 40.44	$ 1,979.98	$0.59	(83)
AAQZ1008	66	$18.58	$ 40.44	$ 1,443.14	$0.54	(66)
AAQZ1009	14,095	$18.81	$ 40.44	$304,909.42	$0.53	(11,732)
AAQZ1010	123	$19.00	$ 40.44	$ 2,637.10	$0.53	—
AAQZ1006	2,553	$20.74	$ 40.44	$ 50,307.49	$0.49	—
AAQZ1007	90	$20.74	$ 40.44	$ 1,773.47	$0.49	—
AAQZ1001	7,491	$22.41	$ 40.44	$135,093.10	$0.45	—
AAQZ1012	55	$23.60	$ 40.44	$ 926.56	$0.42	—
ACGN1005	33	$33.27	$ 56.91	$ 779.98	$0.42	—
ACBU1001	6,001	$61.58	$102.93	$248,090.33	$0.40	(1,208)
AAXX1004	418	$27.20	$ 41.27	$ 5,881.52	$0.34	(418)
ACBU1014	14	$68.04	$102.93	$ 488.33	$0.34	—
AAXX1002	11	$27.97	$ 41.27	$ 146.25	$0.32	(11)
AAXX1003	42	$28.22	$ 41.27	$ 547.80	$0.32	(42)
AAQZ1013	56	$27.75	$ 40.44	$ 710.85	$0.31	—
ACGN1002	40	$39.60	$ 56.91	$ 692.13	$0.30	—
AAXX1001	13,339	$29.35	$ 41.27	$158,970.17	$0.29	(1,608)
ACGN1001	9,735	$40.95	$ 56.91	$155,355.24	$0.28	—

It turns out that AAQZ is at the top of the list. By placing shares of AAQZ in the redemption basket, a sizable amount of capital gains can be avoided; including lots AAQZ1011, AAQZ1008, and AAQZ1009 in the basket means we no longer need to sell lots AAQZ1013, AAQZ1012, AAQZ1001, and AAQZ1006 in the market, avoiding the $160,357.09 capital gain we discussed earlier. Note that the number of AAQZ shares going into the redemption basket has increased: since the PCF* included 3,080 shares of AAQZ and the net trade needs to be a sale of 8,801, the total share count to dispose of is 11,881.

* Not shown.

The rest of the exercise is pretty straightforward. With the closing NAV on 9/30/2021 at approximately $31.97, the value of a redemption basket is $1,598,609.50. We proceed to fill the basket with the most impactful bang-for-the-buck lots for securities whose gains would be realized without the CIB (up to the amount required to sell per lot). Typically, the basket has a small amount of cash to maintain value equivalence, but there are a couple of additional points to consider. The first is that if there aren't enough lots in gains to fill a unit, the PM is better off selling securities in the market and placing more cash in the basket to round off a unit rather than place loss-generating lots in a basket. Second, a PM might consider including securities that have large gains but do not need to be sold specifically for the rebalance to round out the basket; in this case the PM would need to consider the implications to the portfolio, as he or she would be underweight in certain names that would likely require purchases in the secondary market to correct.

Once the securities that will be included in the CIB are selected, it will be incumbent upon the PM to trade the rest of the transactions in the secondary market, so that the sum total of the transactions net out to achieving a rebalanced portfolio at the close of the rebalance day. Some securities may be in the basket, some may be in the market, and some may be in both (if lots have different cost bases). Assuming the 9/30/2021 closing prices hold, if the one-unit CIB is performed, the realized gain from the market transactions is now only $362,373.24, which results in year-to-date realized *losses* of $233,991.43—still negative.

As mentioned, any number of units can be constructed: the more units in and out, the more impactful the CIB is to the portfolio.

CIB 2: CUSTOM CREATE FOLLOWED BY STANDARD REDEEM

The overwhelming majority of CIB activity starts with a standard create and a custom redeem. For a passive portfolio, the CIB is part of the index rebalance and can have a substantial impact on the gains/losses profile of the fund. The fund transfers lots with unrealized gains to the AP through the CIB, leaving market transactions that largely (or completely) result in losses.

Consider a scenario, however, where the fund has net unrealized losses. An index rebalance is about to occur just before the end of the tax year for the fund, and the fund has realized gains for the year. The index rebalance is an opportunity for the fund to sell securities for losses to offset gains.

The problem, however, is that the pro forma portfolio is generated, and it turns out that the securities that have unrealized losses are not being sold in the index rebalance. A CIB as described above would allow the fund to avoid further realized gains to add to the tax year's total, but it would not assist in getting the realized tax position to zero or negative.

Tax-loss harvesting is an option, but this is also where a custom *creation* basket might come in. Instead of a process whereby the create is standard and the redeem is custom, the situation is reversed: the creation basket is custom and the redemption basket is standard, as depicted in Figure 12.2. How does this work, and why is this advantageous to the ETF investor?

FIGURE 12.2

Custom creation followed by standard redemption

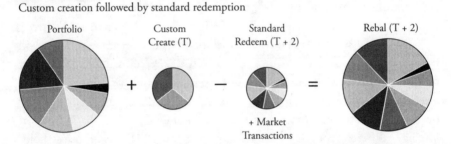

Suppose a fund comprising 100 securities had losses concentrated in four of those securities—A, B, C, and D. Each of those securities is worth $200,000, and each has unrealized losses of $62,500 (see Table 12.4). There are 1 million shares of the ETF outstanding, and a unit consists of 100,000 shares. The ETF NAV is $25, and therefore the total NAV is $25 million. A rebalance is taking place that will take the portfolio to equal weight, meaning each of A, B, C, and D will require a net *increase* in position value of $50,000, so that each position is worth $250,000. A market rebalance would result in no change in unrealized or realized gains or losses.

The custom create process works as follows: At the close on the rebalance date (T), the $800,000 already held in A, B, C, and D is sold in the market and redistributed pro rata across the rest of the securities according to the pro forma, realizing the $250,000 loss. A one-unit create is structured; it is worth $2.5 million, and the create is customized so that $1.1 million of it is in the four securities of interest in equal weight ($275,000 each). The rest of the basket is in line with the pro forma weights pro rata. After the create, the

TABLE 12.4

Custom Creation Followed by Standard Redemption

Ticker	Initial Holding	Unrealized	Market TX	1 CU Create	Position (T)	1 CU Redeem	Position (T + 2)
A	$ 200,000	$ (62,500)	$(200,000)	$ 275,000	$ 275,000	$ (25,000)	$ 250,000
B	$ 200,000	$ (62,500)	$(200,000)	$ 275,000	$ 275,000	$ (25,000)	$ 250,000
C	$ 200,000	$ (62,500)	$(200,000)	$ 275,000	$ 275,000	$ (25,000)	$ 250,000
D	$ 200,000	$ (62,500)	$(200,000)	$ 275,000	$ 275,000	$ (25,000)	$ 250,000
Rest	$24,200,000	$ —	$ 800,000	$1,400,000	$26,400,000	$(2,400,000)	$24,000,000
Total	$25,000,000	$(250,000)	$ —	$2,500,000	$27,500,000	$(2,500,000)	$25,000,000

fund is worth $27.5 million, and $1.1 million is in the four securities—still 4%. At this point, the portfolio is completely rebalanced.* On the back end, a redemption offsets the AP's exposure, only this time, the redemption is standard, corresponding to the index file post the rebalance to reflect the newly reformulated portfolio that was in place with the assistance of the custom create. The portfolio is rebalanced, the size of the fund (absent any interim C/R activity) is the same, and the fund has realized losses.

CIB 3: CUSTOM CREATE FOLLOWED BY CUSTOM REDEEM

While not as traditional as the first CIB we discussed, another possibility using CIBs would be to have a CIB upon both creation and redemption. This would not generally apply to an index-based product for rebalance because one leg of the transaction tends to match the index either prior to the rebalance or upon the rebalance.

In an active portfolio, however, CIBs might be used to alter the profile of the fund with securities going out of the portfolio (custom redemption) and new portfolios coming into the portfolio (custom creation). Because there is no index in the active case, both ends of the transaction can be customized (with a standard lag between them) to effect a "rebalance" without having a formal rebalance as an index would.

THE CIB PROCESS

It is critical for the ETF PM to figure out the need for a CIB and communicate with the capital markets team about finding an AP to assist in the CIB order. CIBs do not just happen automatically on their own; they are negotiated, and it requires strong partnerships with APs to make the process happen—and happen smoothly—as it requires capital allocation on the part of the AP. Often the AP will handle the transactions associated with the secondary market as part of the rebalance, taking in commission income as part of the process. For a passive product, discussions with APs around CIBs do not take place until the index rebalance is made public.

---

* One question this raises is whether or not the transactions wash out the loss capture, but as we stated in Chapter 9, AP transactions (i.e., baskets both custom and standard) are usually considered outside of market transactions for tax accounting purposes. And please remember, a tax professional should be consulted.

A staggered CIB requires that the orders come in at least a day prior to the index rebalance date. For a two-day stagger with a custom redemption, the creation order will come in T – 2 (where T is the index rebalance date), and the redemption order will come in on day T. Working with the AP to agree to do the CIB will likely take a day or two, so in essence the PM needs to get to work on a CIB about four days before the index rebalance date. Settlement for the transactions may be altered such that the two legs of the transaction settle on the same day. For example, with a one-day stagger, the first leg could settle normal cycle (T + 2), and the back end could settle short (T + 1), which, because the transaction took place one day after, would align settlement against the first leg of the CIB.

The best way, in our view, to think about the CIB, or any other standard basket for that matter, is simply as a trade. Securities come into or go out of the portfolio. If a CIB is employed alongside standard market transactions, the "sum" of those two procedures will "equal" the total transactions that the PM would like to effect in the portfolio. The composition of the CIB will impact the transactions that occur in the secondary market.

WHEN A CIB IS APPROPRIATE

It is important to point out that CIBs are only to be used when it is in the best interest of the shareholders of the fund. Historically, many fund sponsors and PMs (though not all) of index-based funds have had their use of CIBs restricted to align with the rebalancing activity of the fund, availing themselves of the tax-efficiency properties of the transaction. If this weren't the case, PMs would use this process far more often: in theory, if there were no costs to the CIB and an AP had enough appetite for the transactions, instead of trading in the market, PMs would use CIBs every time they wanted to readjust the portfolio in any way, resetting the cost bases for the securities in the portfolio on an almost continuous basis. In addition to rebalancing events, ETFs might employ CIBs for large corporate actions that act like rebalances, where a constituent may leave the index and where the weight assigned to that constituent is redistributed across remaining assets. This looks and feels like an index rebalance.

With the adoption of the ETF Rule, fund sponsors must outline custom basket policies and procedures as a requirement, demonstrating that the CIB is in the best interest of the shareholders of the fund. Furthermore, the

SEC requires that the investment advisor must specify who specifically is responsible for ensuring that the procedures outlined are strictly followed.

Note

1. http://www.sec.gov/rules/final/2019/33-10695.pdf.

CHAPTER 13

Portfolio Rebalance

Nothing is more important for an index-tracking ETF than to track the index, but by design, indices change: they are updated typically on a calendar basis, and corporate actions often impact the evolution of an index and its constituents. It is the job of the ETF PM to match the holdings to the index in the most efficient way possible.

We covered index rebalancing in Chapter 4, but portfolio rebalancing is different from index rebalancing. The index is a stylized, hypothetical portfolio of securities. The portfolio that the ETF PM manages is real, and real transactions need to take place to achieve the index-tracking mandate. Armed with our understanding of the Three Ts and the Three Cs, in this chapter we walk through the complete *portfolio* rebalance process. Figure 13.1 maps out this process. Note that this is a broad generalization; there might be nuances in a particular ETF that are not covered here, but the large majority of ETFs fall under a process similar to that illustrated in Figure 13.1. It is important to recognize that a lot of the issues covered in this chapter are covered in other chapters, and where appropriate, we allude to those references. This chapter is more about *process*, and about making sure that it becomes clear how all these issues converge as the PM makes decisions regarding how to rebalance the ETF portfolio.

FIGURE 13.1

Portfolio rebalance process

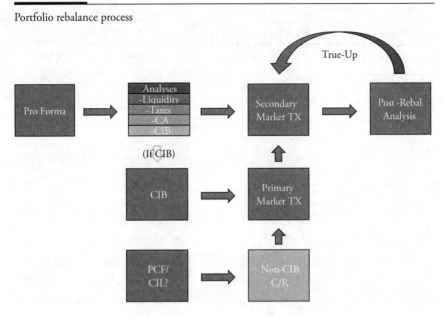

INDEX CALCULATION AND PRO FORMA FILES

For passive ETFs, the portfolio rebalancing process begins with the index, of course. Often the fund sponsor is also the index sponsor, which means the sponsor is "self-indexing." Self-indexing does not change the process, but merely means that the index (and the rebalance) is being generated by the fund sponsor. If the fund sponsor is self-indexing, then the information gathered in the process is material nonpublic information and must not be acted upon by the PM until the information becomes public. Typically, the index sponsor will post the index rebalance on its website.

If the fund sponsor is not the index sponsor, then the fund is licensing the index for use, and it will receive pro forma files from the index sponsor. We presented pro forma files in Chapter 4. These are the lifeblood of the PM's rebalancing activities, as pro formas express what the portfolio is expected to look like as a result of the index rebalance calculations. As soon as the first pro forma files arrive (often five days or more prior to the index rebalance date), the ETF PM can get a first glimpse at what a rebalance trade might look like, at which point the analysis phase can begin.

REBALANCE ANALYSES

Once the rebalance is codified through the pro forma files, the PM should be looking at the following:

- Tax implications and wash sales
- Anticipated corporate actions
- Transaction costs and liquidity analysis
- Custom in-kind basket analysis

Tax Implications and Wash Sales

With an assist from fund accounting and the tax files described in Chapter 9, the PM should have a clear idea of where the fund stands with respect to realized and unrealized gains and losses on a position-by-position basis. Overlaying the required rebalance trades will give the PM a clear indication of what the expected change in these gains and losses will be. Note that this takes a particularly granular approach to fund accounting: having the average cost basis for a stock, for example, is not as accurate as having it on a lot-by-lot basis. Lot by lot is clearly the way to go for accuracy.

Any transactions that have occurred within the wash-sale window should also be at the PM's disposal, so he or she knows what the impact on the portfolio will be from deferrals, for example (see Chapter 9). A good PM will get ahead of the portfolio rebalance at least 30 days in advance, making sure to understand the impact of any considered trade in the window prior to the portfolio rebalance so as not to potentially cause any wash-sale problems. This is especially important if it is the last rebalance of the fiscal year, where "mistakes" might cause capital gains to be reported for the year.

Anticipated Corporate Actions

Anticipated corporate actions might also play a role here: imagine the rebalanced portfolio has a name that has already been announced as an acquisition target. The type of corporate action that is forthcoming might dictate how the PM trades that particular position as part of the rebalance, or at the very least, what the implication for trading that position is on the net gain or loss the fund incurs as part of the rebalance. Any changes to the PCF to manage corporate actions should also be considered.

Transaction Costs and Liquidity Analysis

Understanding the impact of transaction costs on the portfolio and illiquidity is another important task for the ETF PM, one that requires strong coordination with the execution desk. In particular, liquidity analysis can be critical. Its importance depends on the size of the positions and the types of securities held. In an equity portfolio, if a name is held that is thinly traded and the PM requires liquidating that position, for example, then trading the whole lot on the index rebalance day will have a profound market impact. The desk might perform an ADV (average daily volume) analysis, which tells the PM what percentage of an average day's trading is expected for the order. This is done for every security that is expected to be part of the rebalance (i.e., bought or sold). If that percentage is considerable (and it could be 50%, 100%, or 300%, say), then it behooves the trading desk to develop a strategy for getting into or out of each position. We discussed best execution in Chapter 8. This is where the traders earn their money, so to speak: working the order early, finding pockets of liquidity, etc.

If the trading desk comes back to the PM and says that particular securities require more time to complete an order, then this can shift the entire timeline for the rebalance. It doesn't necessarily mean that every transaction needs to begin earlier, but when you have securities in markets that close at different times, earlier transactions can lead to tracking error as the PM rebalances part of a portfolio but not the whole thing at once.

MONITORING C/R ACTIVITY

CIBs aside, there is always the possibility that a fund will receive creation or redemption orders during a rebalance period. In some cases, this is hardly a problem, but in others, it can be. For many ETFs, if the portfolio is domestic, then all the trading tends to occur on the index rebalance day at the close (or near the close), subject to liquidity constraints. As long as the PCF for the rebalance day matches the pro forma close, then whatever comes into or goes out of the portfolio will match the end-of-day portfolio.

There are instances, however, where it is not that simple. Imagine that a creation order comes in on the day (T − 1) before a custom redemption order (T). All the securities that enter the portfolio have a cost basis of their closing prices on day T − 1, and any redemption orders that come in on T − 1 will take the lowest cost basis securities out of the portfolio per each name to maximize the tax effects of the redemption. This means that the activity on T − 1 can potentially impact which securities are chosen to be placed in a CIB redemption basket. As a second example, if international securities are to be traded and the order trade date is T − 1, orders going in on T − 1 for trade date T must account for the updated positioning in the portfolio.

MONITORING CORPORATE ACTIONS

Few things are more frustrating for an ETF PM than corporate actions in the middle of a rebalance. Index files are updating, pro forma files are updating, and the portfolio composition may be updating all at once. The key principle for a PM to remember is making sure there is an understanding of what the portfolio needs to look like on the close of the rebalance day and what, if any, special considerations/transactions need to be made in order to have the portfolio match the index. Unless a halt takes place (which is, of course, out of the control of the PM), the good news is that pro forma files are designed to incorporate corporate actions, so this is the PM's best source for what the portfolio changes need to be.

MARKET TRANSACTIONS DIFFER FROM INDEX "TRANSACTIONS"

Recall that in Table 4.7 we showed the "transactions" required for the index rebalance of the SWA Index. Remember, these transactions are not real transactions, but they are index transactions that occur instantaneously on the close at the closing prices of securities. In reality, traders can place market-on-close orders, but they have to fix the number of shares, for example, ahead of time, and so as prices move around, the amount traded might not be exactly what was ideal for the portfolio.

TRUEING UP AND POST-REBALANCE ANALYSIS

Despite all the technical details and processes that go into a rebalance, there is an art form to the entire process, and in the end if there's one thing this book demonstrates, it is that the process cannot, by definition, be perfect. Once the index rebalance date transactions are completed, it is incumbent upon the PM to review the portfolio; all aspects of the pre-trade should be mirrored in the post-trade. How do transaction costs compare with expectations? What was the impact of the trading activity? How did the unrealized gains and losses and realized gains and losses change as a result of the trading activity? How does the cash in the portfolio look (if prices moved considerably on the close or throughout the day of a CIB redemption, cash can be considerably off from expectations)?

Most importantly, the PM must ensure that the portfolio looks the way it is expected to, tracking the index as expected. If the misallocation and/or cash position is considerable, then the PM will true up the portfolio, submitting trades on T + 1 to bring the portfolio further in line. If there is no lag between calculation and rebalance, as we mentioned briefly in Chapter 7, then the PM will try to hit the close, which often requires true-up trades, given the inexact nature of the exercise.

PART V

Expanding the Product Set

So far, we have been able to demonstrate many of the principles underlying ETF portfolio management through the use of index-based, equity-focused ETFs. So much of the practice is underlying-agnostic, but there are nuances pertaining to particular asset classes or structures that are worth exploring. In the ensuing chapters, we focus on expanding the product set to include international underlyings (Chapter 14), actively managed ETFs (Chapter 15), and fixed-income securities (Chapter 16).* We then tackle leveraged and inverse exposures (Chapter 17), which is less about the underlying and more about the products' exposures to the underlying. All these areas create new and interesting challenges for the ETF PM to solve.

---

* There are, of course, other asset classes or products that are not covered here, such as commodities, currencies, and derivatives-based strategies.

CHAPTER 14

Managing an International ETF

An international ETF is like many things overseas: much the same as at home, but different. English in Great Britain is different from English in the United States: same language, but some words are different, some spellings are different, and of course, the accent is different. Driving in Australia (and in Britain) is kind of the same as it is here in the States, but you're driving on the other side of the road and the steering wheel is on the other side of the car. It's not that driving on the left side of the road is *harder* than driving on the right, but if you're used to driving in the United States, you'll have to be careful when driving in Australia. In this chapter we highlight some of the challenges for the ETF PM when we move from the domestic to the international.

While the majority of index-based ETFs in the United States comprise only US-listed securities, there is a sizable segment of the ETF marketplace that is either international in nature, comprising securities from multiple geographies, or country specific, holding securities from one country other than the United States. According to Bloomberg, over 76% of US-listed ETFs were international or country specific as of June 2020, so this is an important issue.[1] The selling point for these ETFs is obvious: US-based investors can gain access to overseas markets while maintaining trading accounts only in the United States. The ETF opens up markets that the US investor would find difficult to gain access to otherwise. This leaves the ETF PM in the position of managing an international or country-specific portfolio on behalf of the US-based investor.

FILES

For starters, all the files that we reviewed in prior chapters now have an additional layer of complication for PMs tracking indices: all the prices appear in both the local currency where the security trades and the base currency, which represents the currency in which the index is denominated (in our examples, the US dollar). Each of the files will provide the currency code that tells the PM in which currency the local price is quoted, and the exchange rate used to convert to the base currency is provided in the files as well. For our purposes (and for typical ETFs), the ETF's base currency will match the index's base currency. In Table 14.1, we show a hypothetical index close file for 1/11/2021 for SWA, assuming that its eligible universe included international stocks and that some of the tickers we have already encountered were tickers that traded abroad. Note that the additional columns may appear in domestic files as well, but they are not of much use.

TABLE 14.1

International Index Close File

Index	SWA Index
Date	1/11/2021
Index Level	99.24844

ID	Ticker	Country	Local Price	Currency	FX	Base Price	Weight	Index Shares	Index Value
US1001	AABA	US	81.63	USD	1	$81.63	4.95%	0.0602	4.9149
US1003	AAQZ	JP	7,706.65	JPY	114.50	$67.31	4.71%	0.0695	4.6772
US1004	AAWL	CA	76.20	CAD	1.3115	$58.10	4.78%	0.0816	4.7425

LOT SIZE

While equities in the United States allow for trades in shares rounded to the nearest share, sometimes securities that trade in overseas markets have lot sizes that are greater than 1, often in multiples of 100 or greater. It is not possible to place an order for, say, 87 shares, when the lot size of the overseas security is 100.

The immediate implication of larger lot sizes has been covered in Chapter 7 and should be obvious: if the index calls for a fixed number of shares but the market structure does not allow for that amount to be held, then the ETF will suffer from a larger tracking error. This is one contributing factor to higher tracking errors for international funds. An ETF with $10 million AUM tracking an equally weighted index of 100 securities at a particular time should hold securities each worth $100,000. If one of the securities is trading at a base price of $80, the portfolio would seek to hold 1,250 shares of the stock. However, if the lot size for the stock is 100, the PM will be off in his or her allocation by 50 shares. This translates to a misweight of 4 basis points.

This may not sound like a large misweight. Even a 10% move in the underlying stock would not result in a performance differential of 1 basis point. Imagine, however, a portfolio with multiple lot-size constraints. These can add up across the various positions in a portfolio, and as a result, it becomes part of the PM's job when managing an international portfolio to ensure that the misweights offset each other, with overweights offsetting underweights if the securities are correlated so that the tracking error doesn't compound. On the other hand, the larger the fund, the less the lot size impacts the tracking error since large amounts of holdings are required per security. There are implications for primary market activity, however.

Lot Size and Creation/Redemption Activity

When lot sizes are greater than one, the PCF needs to be adjusted accordingly. Recall that the PCF will dictate how many shares of a given constituent security will change hands in a one-unit transaction between the AP and the fund in the primary market. The PCF would be suboptimal if it were to dictate a number of shares that could not trade in the local market where the security is listed.

As a result, the PCF considers lot sizes when it rounds shares.* Below we produce a comparison of the PCF for 1/11/2021 versus the PCF we presented in Table 6.3, where now the lot size for each security is 100 shares, and the securities have been adjusted to reflect an international portfolio (see Table 14.2). Notice how the expected cash is significantly higher than in Table 6.3—over $60,000 compared with $525—as a result.

---

* Note that the flooring mechanism can be used in one-lot securities as well: an unrounded share count of 10.82 shares would be rounded down to 10 shares in the PCF. We employ the flooring methodology throughout this book.

TABLE 14.2

PCF with Larger Lot Sizes (1/11/2021)

SWA ETF			
Trade date	1/11/2021	Actual CIL	$ —
Settlement	T + 2	Actual cash	$1,250,000.00
Creation unit	50,000	Base market value	$1,188,850.92
NAV	$25.00	Basket shares	29,900
NAV per CU	$ 1,250,000.00	Estimated CIL	$ —
Shares O/S	400,000	Estimated cash	$ 61,149.08
Total net assets	$10,000,000.00	Estimated dividend	$ —

ID	Ticker	Shares	Local Price	Currency	FX	Base Price	Base MV	Weight	CIL
US1001	AABA	700	85.93	USD	1	$85.93	$60,151.23	5.06%	N
US1003	AAQZ	800	7903	JPY	114.50	$69.02	$55,216.99	4.64%	N
US1004	AAWL	1,000	78.91	CAD	1.3115	$60.17	$60,169.60	5.06%	N
. . .									

Lot-size rounding can mean additional problems for the PM in the case when multiple units are being created or redeemed. In the example above, if 1 unit were to map to 754 shares of AABA (as in Table 6.4), then a 10-unit create to the fund would ideally result in 7,540 shares coming from the AP. However, the rounding and flooring mechanism leads to the PCF only specifying a 700 count for this security, so when a 10-unit create comes in, the fund receives only 7,000 shares. This may, at first, seem odd, in the sense that the AP *could* deliver 7,500 shares since the security trades in 100-share lots. Multi-unit creation and redemption orders, however, do not allow for the AP to alter the standard PCF. As a result, the PM might consider trueing up the portfolio upon receipt of the shares (and cash) from the AP by purchasing an additional 500 shares in the market.*

TIMING

One of the key tenets of index-based ETFs is that the ETF can largely replicate the index performance, subject to transaction costs and fees. International

---

* Custom creation and redemption baskets allow for the PM to specify the *total* number of shares in a multi-unit order. Recall, however, that these are prearranged orders where the number of units in the order is already specified.

indices often use the closing prices of securities whose markets close at different times across the globe. This lack of timing synchronicity means that it might not actually be possible to replicate the index performance to the same degree as one might for a domestic index.

To isolate the issue, consider a transaction cost–free world where the PM could get the guaranteed closing price for any security, foreign or domestic. A given ETF holds half of its securities in the United States and half of its securities in Europe, which closes ahead of the United States.

The pro forma file on a rebalance day dictates that the portfolio should be equally weighted at the end of the day. The PM places an order for European shares just prior to the closing window in Europe, say 9:45 a.m. ET, that reflects a desired holding. At 10:00 a.m. ET, the orders are executed. Just after execution, the US market plummets. The value of the index is going to fall since it is dependent on prices from both markets. The positions required in the US market are going to be scaled back; otherwise the equity position will be overinvested. As a result, on the close it will appear that the European positions are larger than the US positions on a relative basis. When the market opens in Europe on the morning of the following business day, perhaps the positions will be down, or perhaps the PM would have to sell positions in Europe. Only when both markets are open will the PM know if the positions are equally weighted, but even then the PM is too late since the equal weighting was meant to take place on the close. Noncontemporaneous market activity can make index tracking difficult.

Timing also contributes to differences between index returns and NAV and closing price returns, as the indices that could be tracked for passive products may close at different times than the market closes for the ETF.

TRANSACTION COSTS AND LIQUIDITY

Oftentimes, transaction costs for overseas securities are higher than those for domestic securities. Not only may markets be wider in less liquid markets, but by design, overseas securities require two transactions: the purchase or sale of the security in local currency and the foreign exchange transaction to facilitate the movement of cash between the base currency and the local currency. These additional costs will have a larger effect on index tracking or ETF performance than a similarly constituted domestic portfolio.

TAXES AND WITHHOLDING RATES

When a US-listed company declares a dividend, the investor that holds the security prior to the ex-date receives the full dividend payment on the payment date. Investors declare their dividend payments to the IRS when they do their taxes. Foreign governments, however, often do not wait for investors to declare their dividends, but rather they take withholdings from the dividend payment directly, much like many Americans have withholdings taxes taken from their paychecks.

Overseas withholding taxes on dividends may result in minor increases in the performance differential to the index, depending on how the index to be tracked handles dividends of foreign companies. As we discussed in Chapter 3, index methodologies address dividend reinvestment primarily to determine how cash received from dividends is redeployed to securities in the index. Another specification required for international or country-specific indices is whether or not the index applies the withholding tax to dividend payments, and if so, what withholdings rate is used. A well-specified index will match the withholdings rate to the government-specified rates on a country-by-country basis. Table 14.3 shows a selection of countries and sample withholding tax rates for dividends.

TABLE 14.3

Withholding Rates for a Selection of Countries

Country	Withholding Rate
Australia	30%
Canada	25%
China	10%
France	28%
Germany	26%
India	20%
Japan	15%
Mexico	10%
Philippines	30%
South Africa	20%

Source: Solactive AG.

HOLIDAY CALENDARS

For a domestic index, specifying a holiday calendar is pretty straightforward; index companies often defer to the holiday calendar followed by the major exchanges (frequently the New York Stock Exchange). This means, formally, that index business days are days upon which the exchange is open for trading. If the exchange is closed due to a holiday, then that day is not considered an index business day, and no index level is published. For indices whose calculation dates and/or rebalance dates are impacted by a holiday market closure, the index methodology typically specifies that the date in question shifts to the day before or after the holiday.

International indices present a much more problematic landscape with respect to holidays, for the obvious reason that there are multiple geographies and therefore multiple holidays to consider. The ramifications are less obvious but no less significant. Will an index holding securities in multiple markets publish levels if one or more of the constituent markets are closed? What happens if a market is closed on a calculation date? What if a market is closed on the rebalance date?

These questions can wreak havoc on the ETF portfolio management process. Consider an ETF tracking an equity index that uses the NYSE holiday calendar but holds international stocks. An AP wishes to create a unit of the ETF on a date where an international market is closed. The AP does not own the shares of a constituent stock from that market prior to the create order, so the AP cannot include those shares in the basket. The AP might request that the fund accept cash in lieu of the shares dictated in the PCF. If the CIL is accepted, then the PM receives cash instead of shares and must wait until the local market is open to purchase the shares. Since the shares were valued at the last closing price for the stock, and the PM has to wait until the market reopens to purchase, the lengthier the delay, the more risk the portfolio has, which translates to tracking error.

By far, the most challenging impact on misaligned holiday calendars is when a foreign market is closed during a rebalance.* If a given market is closed on a calculation date, the index sponsor will typically use the last closing price of the security that trades on that market when performing the calculations necessary to produce a pro forma.

---

* Many indices are designed to avoid this.

Imagine an equally weighted index rebalancing scheme across stocks from 10 different countries where one of the markets, say Japan, is closed on the calculation date. Now consider what would happen if there were a market crash on the calculation date. Because there are no closing values for Japanese stocks, it would appear in the calculations that Japanese stocks were unaffected by the crash. While the other markets might be down 10% or 20%, Japan appears flat. To achieve the equal weight, the index methodology will unintentionally hold too few shares of Japanese stocks (the value must equal the value of the other stocks, but the price is artificially too high). If all the markets are open the following day, the positions in the Japanese markets will (likely) decline precipitously. Japanese stocks will be systematically underrepresented in what was supposed to be an equal-weighted index.

So far, all the impact of the calculation date holiday in Japan is only on the pro forma, not the actual index and therefore not the actual portfolio since the ETF has not yet rebalanced. In this case, while the PM might ultimately have to field questions about why the portfolio does not appear equally weighted (once the portfolio is eventually rebalanced), that is largely the extent of it. This is not the case when the holiday occurs on the rebalance date.

Consider the same example as above, only this time the Japanese market is closed on the rebalance date. The pro forma dictates trades in the Japanese stocks held in the portfolio, but the market is closed. The PM knows this ahead of time, and so he or she must either transact before the rebalance date or wait until the market reopens. If the PM has to purchase Japanese stocks for the rebalance, then the funds must be available to do so, or the PM will overdraw the cash account and be charged interest for the borrow. If the PM chooses to sell some of the stocks in markets that are open prior to the rebalance date to fund the purchase of the Japanese stocks, then he or she will have misweights in these stocks.

ORDER WINDOW FOR CREATIONS AND REDEMPTIONS

For international funds, the cutoff times for C/R may be ahead of T by a day. This gives the AP (and the fund) more lead time for when the order will come through so as to be able to prepare for the shares that go from the fund to the AP, or vice versa. An AP might look at today's PCF in anticipation of an order for tomorrow to get a sense of what will likely be included in a basket, and assuming it is not a rebalance date, the PCF will probably be fairly representative.

CIL AND ASSISTED TRADING

Portfolio managers of international ETFs must have the capacity to trade in a variety of overseas markets to replicate the indices they seek to track. That requires trading accounts in several geographies. Setting up these accounts takes time, and in some cases, it may not be possible due to restrictions on where the ETF sponsor may transact business. As a result, without an intermediary to assist in trading, the ETF will undoubtedly have tracking error to the international index.

Fortunately, custodians can offer "assisted trading" services, where they will transact in markets where the sponsor cannot. When orders come in through an AP for creations or redemptions, securities in the restricted countries will be marked "CIL" for cash in lieu. For a create, the AP will send cash to the fund, but when the custodian receives the cash on behalf of the fund, it will effect a trade by purchasing the securities in the restricted markets on behalf of the fund (see Figure 14.1), at which point the fund is made whole relative to the PCF. Conversely, if a redemption order is received, the fund will have the custodian sell the restricted securities on its behalf, at which point cash is delivered to the AP who placed the order.

FIGURE 14.1

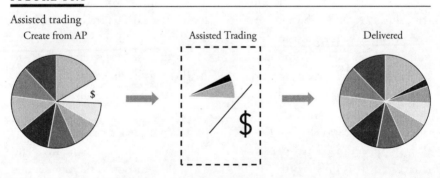

Assisted trading

Create from AP   Assisted Trading   Delivered

The most important things to keep in mind for the PM in cases like this are:

1. Understanding market access (which is usually a discussion with the compliance and legal teams for the ETF sponsor)
2. Specifying which securities will *automatically* be marked CIL
3. Setting up assisted trading with the custodian

FX TRANSACTIONS

International portfolios require foreign currency transactions to facilitate the purchase and sale of securities in overseas markets. When an overseas security is purchased, dollars are converted to the base currency of the security, and then that currency is used for the subsequent purchase. Similarly, sales are effected in the foreign currency, and then that currency is repatriated into dollars. Oftentimes the ETF PM is employed by a firm with a separate FX desk that will facilitate the currency transactions, or the PM can be assisted by the custodian as an alternative. Without one of these scenarios, the PM will be responsible for currency conversion.

A key risk with respect to FX transactions is currency appreciation or depreciation. As a simple example, consider a portfolio that owns 1,000 shares of hypothetical stock ABC, which is listed on the London Stock Exchange and is denominated in GBP. The stock is trading at £100 and issues a dividend of £1. The stock goes ex-dividend on February 12, and payment is one week later on February 19.

The ETF PM has a couple of things to consider. First, the weight in ABC will decrease, so if the PM is aiming to exactly replicate the index, then the dividend must be redistributed across the rest of the portfolio. Second, the dividend does not come into the portfolio until a week after the redistribution is required. Suppose on February 12 the GBP is trading at $1.30. The portfolio's reduction in stock is £1,000, and the value in dollars at this point is $1,300. The PM purchases $1,300 worth of stocks, which is likely to consist of stocks in multiple currencies. The PM may or may not have $1,300 in cash to employ; if he or she does not, that creates a need to borrow to fund the purchases.

The delay in receiving the distribution also creates a risk event for the PM. Suppose on February 18 the GBP falls to $1.20. When the dividend is received, it is only worth $1,200, not $1,300. And once the dividend is received, it will remain in the account in the foreign currency until the payment is repatriated into dollars. Every delay in repatriation creates a risk event for the PM. In the above example, the exchange rate may remain constant through the distribution, but if the GBP is not repatriated and the pound falls, then the portfolio will suffer a loss. This underscores a fundamental principle of index methodology—unless specified otherwise, transactions happen instantaneously, which creates tracking errors for any portfolio looking to track that index.

Currency forward transactions can guard against this kind of risk, and there are several currency-hedged ETFs that offset risks associated with holding foreign-denominated securities.

INTERNATIONAL CORPORATE ACTIONS

In Chapter 11 we discussed a number of corporate actions and how they can impact both an index and an ETF portfolio. Here we note that there are certain corporate actions that US account holders may not participate in, meaning that while the index can process an event as if it is impacting a security in the portfolio, the actual tracking portfolio may not be able to process the event.

An example of this is in rights offerings. Occasionally an ETF portfolio may hold the stock of a company that issues a rights offering that is not valid for security holders in the United States. Rights are options to the holders, and as such they have value to the investor. Unfortunately, in this case, the investor will not be able to capture that value, while the index containing that constituent likely will. There is a value loss related to the corporate action, and that appears as a NAV drop relative to the index move on the ex-date of the event.

Index tracking in an international portfolio clearly adds to the level of difficulty of the exercise. One way to get around this is to manage a fund actively, seeking to meet or exceed the performance of an international benchmark index without having to replicate its performance and constitution. In the next chapter, we delve into how the shift to an active platform yields different issues to consider.

Note

1. Bloomberg Finance L.P., Investment Company Institute.

CHAPTER 15

Actively Managed ETFs

W e have spent a lot of time on index-based ETFs, from the construction of the indices to be tracked to the management of index rebalances and the Three Ts and Three Cs. While the majority of ETFs (and ETF assets) cover underlying strategies that are index-based, a growing segment of the industry pertains to actively managed strategies, i.e., those that do not technically track any index.* These so-called actively managed ETFs (AETFs) allow for much more flexibility on the part of the portfolio manager with respect to what he or she might hold: an actively managed strategy could be just about anything, from a purely qualitative approach to security selection to highly mechanized model-driven processes.

Consider some of the largest AETFs in the market today, as shown in Table 15.1, and what some of their mandates are. The goal of MINT is to "provide maximum current income, consistent with preservation of capital," while ARKK invests "in equity securities of companies relevant to the theme of disruptive innovation."[1] The discretion afforded to the PM in each of these cases is effectively the investment case for the product itself; if the investor sought performance tied to an index, a passive product would be the more appropriate vehicle. The value proposition of an active product is that it can beat a particular benchmark or may provide alpha at a risk that is worth it to the investor on an after-fee basis.

---

* We say "technically," because it is quite possible for an actively managed ETF to track an index, but according to the relief under which the product was listed, the product could be considered active. This distinction has become less relevant after the adoption of the ETF Rule (6c-11).

TABLE 15.1

Largest Actively Managed ETFs (12/31/2020)

Ticker	Name	AUM ($B)
ARKK	ARK Innovation ETF	17.8
JPST	JPMorgan Ultra-Short Income ETF	15.6
MINT	PIMCO Enhanced Short Maturity ETF	14.3
ARKG	ARK Genomic Revolution ETF	7.7
LMBS	First Trust Low Duration Opportunities ETF	6.6
FPE	First Trust Preferred Securities ETF	5.9
ARKW	ARK Next Generation Internet ETF	5.3
ICSH	BlackRock Ultra Short-Term Bon ETF	5.2

Source: Bloomberg Finance L.P.

EXEMPTIVE RELIEF AND TRANSPARENCY

Prior to the ETF Rule, AETFs had to file for exemptive relief in the same manner in which their index-based brethren had to. Over time, the SEC became more restrictive around creation/redemption baskets, which made it more difficult to use CIBs except in some circumstances, limiting a key tax management tool that we discussed at length in Chapter 12. With the new ETF Rule, this no longer applies: AETFs that comply with 6c-11 will be allowed to use custom in-kind baskets for creation and redemption activity in a way that does not distinguish between index-based and actively managed funds.

Earlier exemptive relief for active products and the new ETF Rule require that AETFs publicly display their holdings on a daily basis, just like index-based ETFs. This "transparency" requirement is the reason many believe that actively managed funds are still lagging considerably in AUM relative to passive funds. The argument is essentially that since mutual funds only require holdings to be reported publicly (through Form N-Q filings) 45 days after the quarter-end, active portfolio managers could conceal their investment strategies better within the mutual fund construct, rather than give up the "secret sauce" of their investment strategies by managing the assets within an ETF. The transparency requirement has led to some innovative ETF structures, which we will discuss at the end of this chapter.

ACTIVE VERSUS PASSIVE ETF PORTFOLIO MANAGEMENT

Our goal here is to distinguish the active portfolio management process from its index-based counterpart we have covered already, or, in some cases, highlight the similarity between active and index-based portfolio management. There is far more overlap between the two than there are differences, and taking an index-based approach to the portfolio process can aid the active PM in running his or her portfolio. In what follows, we cover:

- The Three Ts and Three Cs
- Actively managed PCF construction
- ETF launch and initial baskets
- Reporting
- Transparency alternatives

THE THREE TS AND THREE CS

We framed our analysis of passive products around the concept of the Three Ts and the Three Cs. There are important differences with respect to those ideas as they relate to managing active products. The Three Ts are still quite relevant, if you take the right perspective: clearly, there is no index to be tracked and hence no tracking error; but with a slightly different perspective, you may be surprised at how close active funds can be to their passive cousins.

Tracking Error

Active strategies are not formally tied to an index, but they often seek to outpace a benchmark. In many ways, the benchmark of an active strategy often serves as a proxy for the underlying index in a passive ETF, and while active portfolio management is often perceived to be nonanalytical (don't PM's just wake up every morning and decide what they want to hold?), there's actually much more science involved than is typically given credit for. No place is this truer than in thinking about the risk and performance of an active strategy.

How do investors know if an active PM is doing a good job if there is no index to be tracked? Investors don't simply rely on a story to be told by the PM; they generally rely on the benchmark, a pre-established yardstick that will be used to tell investors whether or not the PM has delivered value and at what cost in terms of fees, risk, etc. Beyond straight performance, how much risk is the PM adding by taking the approach that he or she relies upon?

The standard framework for answering these questions is often the information ratio, or IR.* The IR tells us how much additional return per unit of risk a strategy provides relative to a benchmark. Providing alpha above and beyond risk is what active managers try to achieve; even smart beta strategies try to achieve this by designing an index with an attractive information ratio.

To calculate the information ratio, a little math is required, and we outline some methodology in the appendix to this chapter. If you compare the appendix in Chapter 7 with the appendix in this chapter, you will find that they are extraordinarily alike. Without delving into the calculations, we can get to the key message: Attributing outperformance in an active fund is not much different from doing so in an index-based fund. The difference is that in the index-based case, the comparative benchmark *is the index*. Once the index is designed, the ETF PM's job is to track it, not outperform it. In contrast, the AETF PM's job is to beat the benchmark without taking on too much risk. You can think of IR maximization as the tracking error minimization of active portfolio management.†

Another important difference is that in the active case, there are assets in the portfolio that are absent from the securities in the benchmark. In the index case, securities selected by the PM were always in the index when the PM managed to full replication. The exception was typically cash, as most indices do not have a cash component. Just as we stated above with respect to risk calculations, there's actually not as much difference as one might perceive at the outset: instead of cash being the only asset the index PM uses outside the index security set, cash and other securities form a larger set that the active PM may choose from in security selection. If we consider that not all index PMs seek full replication—some employ a representative sampling strategy—then once again the parallels between index portfolio management and active portfolio management become clearer.

An Alternative Perspective

There is another way to think about tracking error and its relation to AETF portfolio management, as long as the PM is willing to consider his or her portfolio through the lens of portfolio optimization.

---

* We broadly discuss arithmetic information ratios, but some advocate the use of geometric information ratios. For more on this, see, for example, http://www.automated-trading-system .com/geometric-information-ratio/#start.
† In fact, looking carefully at the IR formula in the appendix, you can see that the denominator of the IR is, in fact, the tracking error, so for a given level of outperformance, a lower tracking error results in a higher IR.

When an AETF PM chooses to hold a portfolio, we can imagine that this portfolio expresses an optimal choice, i.e., the ideal portfolio for a PM who, subject to some basic constraints around the fund objective, can choose almost anything to put into the portfolio. We might think of *this* portfolio as an index of sorts. Recall from Chapter 3 that index calculation agents (ICA) send out index files on a daily basis. Well, imagine that the AETF PM played the role of the ICA, formally capturing the portfolio as if it were an index. Now imagine that the PM is considering a trade for the purposes of capturing an unrealized loss in one of the names in his or her book. Table 15.2 shows the "index" of holdings for the active PM as of 4/15/2021, which mimics the portfolio of the passive PM and the unrealized gains/losses associated with each position.

TABLE 15.2

Active Tax Harvesting (4/15/2021)

Security	Sum of Weight	Unrealized G/L	Redistribute	Cash	Overweight AKXI
Cash	0.00%	$ —	0.00%	4.94%	0.00%
AKRY	4.94%	$(180,721.71)	0.00%	0.00%	0.00%
AGFZ	4.73%	$(107,802.67)	4.97%	4.73%	4.73%
AAQZ	4.48%	$ (96,120.36)	4.71%	4.48%	4.48%
AIAD	4.97%	$ (84,085.78)	5.23%	4.97%	4.97%
AMGP	4.98%	$ (62,076.16)	5.23%	4.98%	4.98%
ACOP	4.49%	$ (57,507.45)	4.73%	4.49%	4.49%
AKXI	4.95%	$ (44,603.38)	5.21%	4.95%	9.89%
AABA	4.17%	$ (24,431.47)	4.38%	4.17%	4.17%
ACGN	5.05%	$ (22,064.37)	5.32%	5.05%	5.05%
AHBP	4.51%	$ (15,254.23)	4.74%	4.51%	4.51%
AHJQ	5.69%	$ (8,139.23)	5.98%	5.69%	5.69%
ADXK	5.40%	$ (4,708.85)	5.68%	5.40%	5.40%
ADZI	4.88%	$ (1,687.80)	5.13%	4.88%	4.88%
AAXX	4.77%	$ 5,522.47	5.02%	4.77%	4.77%
AKZO	5.03%	$ 7,644.12	5.29%	5.03%	5.03%
AKEK	5.12%	$ 7,712.39	5.38%	5.12%	5.12%
AHGG	5.58%	$ 31,649.29	5.87%	5.58%	5.58%
AFOJ	5.27%	$ 71,282.26	5.54%	5.27%	5.27%
ALTO	5.50%	$ 143,079.84	5.79%	5.50%	5.50%
ACBU	5.50%	$ 155,077.75	5.79%	5.50%	5.50%

The unrealized loss for ticker AKRY is substantial, and as we saw in Table 9.8, the bang for the buck is also significant. And while AKRY is in the portfolio—meaning in theory that this stock is part of the optimal portfolio for the active PM—the PM has no obligation to hold it. Any deviation from a 4.94% weight in this name, however, is a deviation from the assumed optimum. In index-based portfolios we have a name for what that imposes on the portfolio: tracking error—the first of the Three Ts.

Through this index lens, it is now pretty straightforward to figure out the impact on the tax harvesting trade in a way that mimics the index-based analysis. Just as we showed in Chapter 9, the AETF PM can redistribute the weight from AKRY to the remaining portfolio (as depicted in the "Redistribute" column in Table 15.2), keep the weight in cash ("Cash"), or deploy it to a substitute security or set of securities that may or may not already be held; this last case is depicted by redistributing the weight entirely in AKXI ("Overweight AKXI"), something the passive PM is less likely to do without extraordinary comovement between the two securities. The key here is recognizing that each of these choices is a deviation from the optimal portfolio for the purposes of harvesting tax losses, and the PM can use analytics (e.g., some of the techniques described in the appendix to Chapter 7 and those described in Chapter 19 regarding representative sampling) to get a sense of the tracking error relative to his or her optimal choice. As always, because of wash-sale considerations, we expect the harvesting trade to be held for just over 30 days.

The irony in this example is that the best way to manage the active portfolio is to treat it as an index-based portfolio, though we allow for that fact that many active managers will not manage their portfolios in this manner.

Tracking Error Versus Benchmark Risk

When an active strategy specifies a benchmark, the PM must be aware that the benchmark is, of course, not static. The benchmark will rebalance like other indices. At the point of a rebalance, the active PM makes an *active* decision whether or not to follow the index rebalance and perform similar transactions in his or her portfolio that would mimic what the benchmark is doing.

Recall, for example, that stocks AAWL and AKMW were removed from the SWA Index in the 2021 Q1 rebalance and were replaced by AAXX and AKEK. In the passive case, the PM is going to sell AAWL and AKMW and replace the holdings in the portfolio with some holdings in AAXX and AKEK (subject to their new weights, of course). For an active PM, it might be the case that something about the story behind AAWL resonates with the PM; perhaps he or she has spent time examining why the market cap of the company fell below the index benchmark threshold and feels confident that there is plenty of alpha in the stock. The active PM must make the call about whether or not keeping the security in the portfolio makes sense; the decision will no doubt impact active risk to the benchmark index.

In short, active risk to a benchmark can occur not only when the PM makes an active decision but also when the benchmark changes as a result of a rebalance. This is a spin on the age-old adage that deciding not to act is an act in and of itself.

Transaction Costs

The basic premise of the second of the Three Ts, minimizing transaction costs, pertains to all ETFs whether they are passive or active. Seeking best execution is a given. What the active construct affords the ETF PM is flexibility. In the previous section, we touched on how there is no tracking error per se. This means that the PM might not feel as pressed to match weights in a benchmark index as a passive PM would with respect to matching an index to be tracked. Still, if active risk is a consideration, then as benchmarks change, so too will the PM need to consider the cost of transacting to maintain his or her risk tolerances.

Taxes and CIBs

The rules regarding taxes around purchases and sales of securities within an ETF are independent of whether the ETF is active or passive. As a result, so much of what we have covered in the chapter on taxes still holds here. Actively managed and index-based ETF PMs have the same goal when it comes to taxes (the third T): distribute zero capital gains to the end investor at the end of the fiscal year.

Actively managed products typically make more use of tax-loss harvesting in lieu of CIBs. Index-based ETF PMs often manage their portfolios using perfect replication, and as a result are somewhat hamstrung by a desire to track the underlying index; AETF PMs have much more leeway to substitute securities when a security might offer tax relief by realizing capital losses. Active managers will often use analytical tools that provide alternatives to a security holding that have similar characteristics—just like index-based ETF PMs might do, as we discussed above—thus allowing for a tax trade without suffering decay in the overall strategic goal of the fund. Wash-sale timing will no doubt inform many of those tax-loss harvesting trades. The set of opportunities open to the active PM may be broader than that of the index-based PM.*

Of course, the ETF Rule changes the tax management game for active ETFs by allowing CIBs. In Chapter 12 we presented a very systematic approach to the construction of the CIB for the index-based ETF PM. The CIB came into play during index rebalancing and utilized an approach whereby a combination of custom in-kind activity and market trading resulted in the desired post-rebalance portfolio while capturing losses in the portfolio.

In the AETF case, one obvious difference is that there is no formal index to be tracked and therefore no index rebalance. The PM is free to rebalance at any time however he or she sees fit. Nevertheless, the active PM can treat a repositioning of the portfolio as a rebalance and use the CIB mechanism to effect part (or all) of the necessary transactions required. Often the active PM will review the portfolio on a standard frequency, e.g., monthly or quarterly; this is particularly so if the strategy of the fund is model-driven despite being characterized as active. This review effectively mimics the index rebalance process.

The difference here can be interpreted as one of endogeneity: in the index-based CIB case, the index dictates what the resulting portfolio needs to look like at the end of the rebalance day. In the actively managed case, it is the PM that determines the portfolio composition: it might be the case that this composition is a function of the tax losses that can be generated by selling out of certain positions.

Cash

Cash management is a critical part of ETF portfolio management in passive and active funds, but the philosophy behind cash differs. For index-based funds, cash is about minimization, having just enough around to potentially fund transactions but not enough to meaningfully lead to tracking error to the underlying index, i.e., cash drag.

For active managers, cash is less about minimizing and more about lining up cash flows coming in and going out. There is no index, and therefore no associated cash minimization mandate. An active manager can use cash to

---

* For more on the tools that an AETF PM might use, refer to Chapter 19 on representative sampling.

dampen volatility, to preserve for an impending investment, or to reduce a position before a new allocation is established.

Corporate Actions

In what is becoming a bit of a theme, what active ETFs allow the PM to do in the case of corporate actions is to maintain flexibility. Simply put, if an index processes a corporate action, the passive ETF PM is going to track that corporate action, one way or another. The active PM, on the other hand, may not wish to do anything when faced with a corporate action. In fact, perhaps the portfolio was positioned for the purpose of taking advantage of a corporate action. In an acquisition, for example, where an index may not have the acquiror in it and thus the PM would sell the target, the active PM may choose to hold the acquiror shares once a stock-based deal is completed. Tender offers might work to the portfolio manager's advantage; rights offerings may be acted upon in full without having to redistribute any assets across other positions in the portfolio. In short, active strategies provide much more flexibility than passive ones.

(TRANSPARENT) ACTIVELY MANAGED PCF CONSTRUCTION

PCF construction lies at the heart of the primary market transactions that fuel the ETF market. Index-based PCFs could be based on holdings or on the index weights themselves. For index-based funds, these two things lined up pretty closely, since the PM is trying to track the underlying index. With AETFs, however, there are no relevant index weights, nor are there any index files. The only obvious basis for the PCF is the portfolio holdings. Since publishing a holdings-based PCF is akin to publishing holdings, we proceed with this discussion for transparent actively managed ETFs; later in this chapter we focus on semi-transparent and non-transparent actively managed ETFs.

Using a holdings-based PCF approach will likely be sufficient for the purposes of many AETFs. Some changes at the margins might be necessary, such as scaling up the positions in order to present a basket with zero cash. Consider an ETF that has 100 creation units outstanding and a small amount of cash in the portfolio (e.g., 20 basis points); the ETF portfolio manager will not necessarily want to bring in more cash in a creation and can comfortably handle an all-securities basket in the case of a redemption, so it makes sense in this case to simply remove cash from the basket and to gross up the units of the securities in the portfolio to construct the PCF. Similarly, some actively managed portfolios might contain derivatives (e.g., swaps or futures) that the PM may not want to be reflected in the PCF. As with the treatment of cash, the PM can alter the PCF to reflect a nonderivatives-based portfolio.*

AETF PMs can also utilize CIL in a PCF the same way an index-based ETF PM can. Corporate actions might be the most prevalent reason for CIL-ing a security, but the PM might also be in the middle of changing the weighting of a position, for example, and would like to manage the position without interference from C/R activity (though this could signal to the market what transactions are occurring in the fund in a way that might be disadvantageous to the fund's shareholders). CIL can also be used to prevent securities with unrealized losses from leaving the portfolio through a redemption without capturing the loss, especially for funds that by design take in cash-only creations while offering in-kind redemptions.

ETF LAUNCH AND THE INITIAL BASKET

When an ETF launches, it is the AP that delivers securities and/or cash to the ETF as ETF shares are delivered to the AP. In the case of the index-based ETF, the goal is to track the index through the launch, so that performance immediately ties out to the best of the PM's ability from day one.

With an actively managed ETF, this goal is no longer applicable. This leaves the actively managed portfolio manager with two choices: either ask for a basket consisting purely of cash in order to take in the funds to invest in the desired basket, or communicate the desired basket of securities to the AP. In the first case, it is a straight cash-for-shares swap (potentially using futures or swaps to gain exposure while legging into the strategy). In the second case, the same considerations that we reviewed in the index-based case in Chapter 6 apply here, namely how to address the initial NAV for the ETF; the PM may choose to fix or float the NAV or take a zero-cash approach.

All of this is a matter of preference and to be agreed upon up front between the AP handling the initial create and the ETF sponsor, though it should seem reasonable that it is far more likely for an actively managed ETF to launch with an all-cash basket than an index-based ETF. From day one the

---

* It is important to note that under 6c-11 certain changes to the PCF that would not have been considered "custom" baskets under the earlier regime might now be considered as such. PMs should consult with their legal and compliance departments.

PM is typically uninterested (or at least less interested) in tracking an external benchmark, so starting with cash and allowing the portfolio to leg into positions at the outset makes far more sense for an actively managed ETF.

REPORTING

Whereas the index-based ETF PM is extremely concerned about cash drag and misallocation, the active PM is less inclined to think about these matters in order to minimize the headline tracking error statistic. Internally, though, the PM is concerned with tracking relative to a benchmark and may have other objectives in mind to track on a regular basis.

In our discussion of the Three Ts and Three Cs, we highlighted the importance of reporting to the index PM the cash reports, the dividend reports, and the over/under reports. All these are tools to give the index PM the greatest opportunity to achieve his or her objectives. The active PM *also* benefits from reporting, but the flavor of the reporting might differ. This is particularly true for misallocation, for example. Often an AETF will target a certain strategy: in the case of JPST, for example, the name of the fund— JPMorgan Ultra-Short Income Fund—makes clear that duration is a key metric for the ETF. Rather than report on overweights/underweights relative to an index, the relevant reporting for this portfolio might be a summary statistic of the duration of the book. If the stated target of an equity fund is a beta of 1.2 to the S&P 500, then the portfolio beta is the relevant statistic. The key here is recognizing that the active PM should be every bit as interested in reporting as his or her index-based counterparts and should design the reporting structure to fit the fund's needs.

TRANSPARENCY ALTERNATIVES: SEMI-TRANSPARENT AND NON-TRANSPARENT ACTIVELY MANAGED ETFS

We began this book with a story about disruption, one in which a change in an existing rule allowed for the birth of the ETF industry. Today, we are in the middle of what some hope is a next-generation disruption to the ETF industry itself: non-transparent and semi-transparent exchange-traded funds.

One of the foundational principles of ETFs has been their transparency: every day, ETF holdings are published, and a basket of securities representative of the portfolio is constructed (the PCF) and disseminated broadly.

There is no guesswork in what an ETF holds, whereas with a mutual fund, by contrast, an investor only sees what the portfolio holds once a quarter—and on a lagged basis at that.

Active portfolio managers are often concerned about widespread knowledge of their portfolios, under the theory that if their positions are known, then others could "free-ride" their portfolios by reverse-engineering their strategies. Others could "front-run" their portfolios by trading securities ahead of when they believe the active PM will trade, thereby impacting the prices at which the PM could transact, harming the end investor.

In theory, if an active PM held stock ABC in large quantities, and market participants knew this and believed that the PM would sell ABC imminently, they could sell short the security, wait for ABC to sell (at a presumably lower price), and then buy the shares back (perhaps even from the selling fund itself), thereby locking in a profit and forcing the PM to sell at a lower price. This is particularly worrisome for larger portfolios, where a wholesale change in or out of a position may take more than one trading session: if others see the start of a transition as reflected in an increase or decrease in a holding, then they may try to get ahead of future transactions over the subsequent days. Smaller portfolios that can transition a position in or out in one trading day are less subject to this phenomenon.*

Mutual fund managers are only required to reveal their holdings 45 days after a quarter-end, so this tends to be less of an issue; the daily holdings requirement of ETFs leaves some active PMs skittish about the structure.

There are a number of approaches that various companies have devised to work around the transparency requirement, and those we discuss below have all been submitted to (and approved by) the SEC.† Some have been called "semi-transparent," others "non-transparent" or "highly transparent." Regardless of the nomenclature (which is mostly a marketing exercise), the relief applications have a similar feel to them: they all effectively ask the SEC to allow the fund (or the structure that a fund would use to list) to avoid the transparency requirement, and then they provide an alternative mechanism

---

* Index-tracking portfolios are also subject to this type of behavior, especially since index changes are published ahead of time.

† One product we do not include in this section—by design—is Eaton Vance's NextShares. NextShares are exchange-traded mutual funds that trade at the next NAV plus or minus a spread. They are registered investment companies just like ETFs, but because they are not traded at prices determined by market supply and demand, they are not considered ETFs and hence are not part of our discussion on nontransparent ETFs.

that achieves certain goals that they believe proxy the transparency requirement.

With each structure we ask a simple question: "What would change in what we have discussed already if the fund were to list under this structure?"

Precidian

In 2019, Precidian Funds LLC filed an exemptive relief petition with the SEC—which was subsequently approved—for a new structure relating to actively managed ETFs, designed to maintain secrecy surrounding the portfolio holdings of an actively managed portfolio. The approved structure, which is available for licensing to other active ETF sponsors, is known as ActiveShares.*

The ActiveShares construct is relatively simple. Most importantly, the funds are not required to post their daily holdings, in contrast to typical ETFs. This alleviates part of the concern around transparency but does not completely eliminate it. Recall from Chapter 2 that the ETF ecosystem relies heavily on the interaction among the PM, the NSCC, and the AP when it comes to defining the basket of securities required to be included in a creation or redemption order, i.e., the PCF. When the file is posted, it is in the public domain, thereby allowing a view into the portfolio holdings.

This is where the innovation in the ActiveShares construct comes in. The fund, through the custodian, directly transmits a file to an "AP representative," who sits between the custodian and the AP and acts as a confidential intermediary between the sponsor and the AP. Each AP would have an AP representative, and the file, akin to the PCF, is held in confidence with the AP representative and is only used at such time as when the associated AP wishes to create or redeem shares. The AP representative transacts in the shares in a confidential account on behalf of the AP and clears the account at the end of each business day.

To balance the lack of transparency that comes with the absence of daily holdings, ActiveShares also publishes a verified indicative intraday value (VIIV), which is effectively an IV that ticks every second. While VIIVs are meant to be accurate every second and to keep secondary prices in line, this is not necessarily the case, as intraday transactions do not accrue to the VIIV (or the IV in ETFs broadly).

---

* For more information, see http://www.activeshares.com.

It is fair to say that the jury is out on whether or not this structure will take off, and questions remain about how the ActiveShares construct will work in practice, what the effect will be on spreads relative to VIIV, etc. For our purposes, the question is simply if any actions on behalf of the PM should differ based on whether the holdings are public or held in secrecy. In the ActiveShares case, there is no additional or different trading activity required on the part of the PM during the creation or redemption process. ActiveShares do not, as of this writing, however, have custom in-kind basket relief, and they are not covered by the ETF Rule (6c-11). Therefore, this creates an additional burden on the ETF PM to tax-manage the funds without this important tool.

Blue Tractor

Blue Tractor's solution to the transparency puzzle is its Shielded Alpha^{SM} ETF wrapper. In this structure, the publication of daily holdings is no longer required, and the Shielded Alpha hides a complete picture of the portfolio by adding randomization to the PCF construction. Rather than take a pro rata slice of the portfolio holdings, the Blue Tractor methodology creates a "dynamic" portfolio that has over 90% overlap with the actual PCF based on undisclosed holdings, but randomizes each holding so that none of the actual percentages match their dynamic portfolio counterparts. In addition, the PM has the ability to go in and tweak the dynamic portfolio, including the ability to freeze a security weight while the PM is actively changing that position. Because of the 90% overlap, Blue Tractor calls its approach "highly transparent."*

Blue Tractor has filed with the SEC to allow for CIB relief, but as of this writing, it is believed that application is still outstanding.

Fidelity

Fidelity offers a tracking basket, which is "comprised of select recently disclosed portfolio holdings (Strategy Components), liquid ETFs that convey information about the fund's investments that are not otherwise fully represented by the Strategy Components, and cash and cash equivalents."[2] Fidelity publishes the "Tracking Basket Weight Overlap" every day to gauge how much risk is inherent in the basket relative to the actual holdings, and the

---

* For more information on Blue Tractor, see bluetractorgroup.com.

tracking basket becomes the creation/redemption basket.* Just as for the Blue Tractor structure, the PM does not receive or give up exactly what he or she would get in the transparent case.

Natixis/NYSE

Natixis and the NYSE have partnered on an active non-transparent structure that was approved by the SEC in 2019.† At its core is their proxy portfolio, which contains more components than the actual portfolio, and is constructed using a 5- to 15-day lag on purchases and sales occurring in the actual portfolio. And just as it was for Blue Tractor and Fidelity, the baskets differ from the transparent cases.

T. Rowe Price

According to T. Rowe Price's filing, its proxy portfolio is "structured so as to minimize the potential for market impact. The Proxy Portfolio will be the Fund's most recent quarterly portfolio holdings or, in some cases, a broad-based securities index—and in either case, each Fund will consistently invest such that at least 80% of its total assets at the time of purchase . . . will overlay with the portfolio weightings in its identified Proxy Portfolio."[3] Once again, this structure does not align with a transparent basket.

Implications for Portfolio Management

Several of these structures have important consequences for the PM: Because the various forms of proxy portfolios serve as the basis for the standard creation and redemption baskets, the weights, in general, will not match the holdings in the portfolio. As a result, the ETF PM will not generally receive (in the case of a creation) or give (in the case of a redemption) exactly what he or she would want, which makes it more likely that the PM will end up having to true up around creation and redemption activity. While there is the potential for creation and redemption fees to offset transaction expenses incurred by the PM as a result of the post-C/R activity, this may impact spreads and is still an additional area to be aware of when managing a non-transparent product.

---

* See sec.gov/rules/ic/2019/ic-33683.pdf.
† For more information, see sec.gov/Archives/edgar/data/1018331/000119312518323642/ d649748d40appa.htm.

APPENDIX

In the appendix to Chapter 7, we provided a mathematical framework for defining tracking error and overperformance or underperformance to an index. In this appendix, we take a similar approach, comparing portfolio performance with a benchmark.

Define the performance on the benchmark for a given day as

$$r_t^{BM} = \sum_i^M w_{it}^{BM} r_{it},$$

the performance for the portfolio on a given day as

$$r_t^P = \sum_i^M w_{it}^P r_{it} + \varepsilon_t,$$

and define the outperformance for a given day, α_t, as the difference:

$$\alpha_t = \sum_i^M (w_{it}^P - w_{it}^{BM}) r_{it} + \varepsilon_t$$

where

r_{it} = the return to security i at time

r_t^f = the return to cash at time t

M = the number of assets in the eligible universe of investments (including cash), not restricted to those solely in the benchmark

$i = 1$ which represents the cash asset

w_{it}^P = the weight of security i in the portfolio at time t

w_{it}^{BM} = the weight of security i in the benchmark at time t

The portfolio weights sum to one:

$$\sum_i^M w_{it}^P = 1$$

The benchmark weights also sum to one:

$$\sum_i^M w_{it}^{BM} = 1$$

We group the daily fee, securities lending income, and transaction costs into ε_t where

$$\varepsilon_t = -fee_t + SL_t - TC_t$$

There will be multiple elements of w_{it}^P that are zero (those that refer to weights in positions held in the benchmark but not in the portfolio) and multiple elements of w_{it}^{BM} that are also zero (those that refer to weights in positions held in the portfolio but not in the benchmark). For starters, in many benchmarks

$$w_{1t}^{BM} = 0$$

The noncash weight in the portfolio is captured by

$$w_t^{*P} = 1 - w_{1t}^P$$

Normalizing the portfolio weights on the securities to add up to 100%, we have

$$\alpha_t = w_t^{*P} \sum_{i=2}^{M} \frac{w_{it}^P}{w_t^{*P}} r_{it} + w_{1t}^P r_t^f - \sum_{i=2}^{M} w_{it}^{BM} r_{it} + \varepsilon_t$$

or

$$\alpha_t = w_t^{*P} \sum_{i=2}^{M} \tilde{w}_{it}^P r_{it} + w_{1t}^P r_t^f - \sum_{i=2}^{M} w_{it}^{BM} r_{it} + \varepsilon_t$$

Since

$$\sum_{i=2}^{M} w_{it}^{BM} r_{it} = w_{1t}^P \sum_{i=2}^{M} w_{it}^{BM} r_{it} + w_t^{*P} \sum_{i=2}^{M} w_{it}^{BM} r_{it}$$

we have

$$\alpha_t = w_t^{*P} \sum_{i=2}^{M} (\tilde{w}_{it}^P - w_{it}^{BM}) r_{it} + w_{1t}^P \left(r_t^f - \sum_{i=2}^{M} w_{it}^{BM} r_{it} \right) + \varepsilon_t$$

The first term is a misallocation contribution of the portfolio securities relative to its benchmark, while the second term is cash drag relative to the benchmark return.

As we stated in the appendix to Chapter 7, the expected outperformance would be $E[\alpha_t]$, and the tracking error relative to the benchmark would be the standard deviation of α_t.

The information ratio IR is simply the ratio of the expected outperformance to the tracking error:

$$IR = \frac{E[\alpha_t]}{\sigma[\alpha_t]}$$

Notes

1. Bloomberg Finance L.P.
2. Institutional.fidelity.com/app/proxy/content?literatureURL=/9894623.PDF.
3. https://www.sec.gov/Archives/edgar/data/80255/000119312519127691/d738735d40appa.htm.

CHAPTER 16

Fixed-Income ETFs

The underlying principles of ETF portfolio management are portable with respect to asset class. Whether a PM is managing a corporate bond portfolio, an equity portfolio, or a commodity portfolio, balancing the multiple goals of minimizing transaction costs, taxes, and (in the case of index-tracking products) tracking error is paramount. Because the overwhelming majority of ETFs and ETF assets are equity-based—75% as of July 2020[1]—we have used the equity asset class to demonstrate many of the principles of ETF portfolio management in this book. The second largest ETF asset class is fixed income, and with that in mind, in this chapter we seek to highlight some of the nuances that arise in managing a fixed-income portfolio.

FIXED-INCOME BASICS

A quick refresher or introduction for those less familiar with fixed income may assist the reader with the rest of this chapter.* By no means is this exhaustive, but it should help with some concepts. In general, fixed-income securities are those that pay a specified amount periodically (a coupon) before returning the principal, or face value, of the security. A 10-year corporate bond might specify an annual coupon rate of 4% paid semiannually (2% every 6 months). At the end of the 10-year period, the face value of the security is paid to the investor. The investor pays a price for this security that can

---

* There are whole libraries full of fixed-income books covering the basics and advanced topics. See, for example, Frank J. Fabozzi, *The Handbook of Fixed Income Securities*.

be above the face value (above par) or below the face value (below par) of the security.

Callability and Sinkability

Some securities are callable, which means that the issuer of the note can pay out the principal before the due date, and there can be terms that specify under what conditions or when the security can be called. Callability is an option for the security issuer, not for the investor.

A sinkable bond is an issue that may be retired early on a schedule. This allows the issuer to reduce the overall principal to be paid at the maturity of the bond. The sinkability provision results in the holder of the issue receiving cash in exchange for a percentage of the holding.

Yield

The yield on a security is the expected return of the security, based on the price paid for it, and the expected cash flows, based on coupons and principal. When the security is held to maturity, the expected yield is called, unsurprisingly, the yield to maturity (YTM). However, in the case of callable securities, a different yield is often quoted—the yield to call (YTC). YTC is typically calculated as if the security were to be called on the first date that calling the security is allowed under its terms (or the next callable date if there is a schedule and the first callable date has passed). For callable securities, yield to maturity and yield to call are often compared, and the *lower* of the two is called the yield to worst (YTW). This should give the investor an idea of a worst-case scenario.

Sensitivity to Rates

Fixed-income securities are heavily dependent on interest rates. When rates go up, the prices of the securities go down, and vice versa. The sensitivity of a security to a change in interest rates is called the "duration." A closely related measure, the dollar value of a basis point, or DV01, reflects the change in value of a fixed-income security when rates increase by 1 basis point. Duration can be thought of as the time-weighted average of payments from the security; a zero-coupon bond maturing in 10 years has a duration of 10 since the average payment is received 10 years hence. A coupon-paying bond also maturing in 10 years has a duration less than 10 since some of the payments occur prior to maturity. Duration can be measured in slightly different ways, but for our purposes here, a broad generalization is sufficient. Durations also change with rates, and the sensitivity of duration to a change in rates is known as "convexity."

Accrued Interest

Accrued interest is the portion of an upcoming interest payment that has accumulated, based on the time since the last interest payment, but that has not yet been paid. A 4% coupon-paying bond that pays coupons semiannually will have a 2% coupon every six months. Three months into that quarter, the bond will have accrued 1% (half the coupon), which will be accrued interest but not paid. Accrued interest is quite important. When a bond is sold, the purchaser may become the holder of record to receive the full interest payment, even though the sale took place between coupon payments. As a result, the purchaser must compensate the seller for the interest that accrued during the time the seller held the position. The price that includes the accrued interest is often called the "dirty" price, while the price that does not is called the "clean" price.

Negative Accrued Interest

Just as stocks have ex-dividend dates, bonds have ex-coupon dates, upon which the owner of record due to receive the coupon is the owner of the bond at the close prior to the ex-date. When a sale of a bond falls between the ex-date and the coupon date, the owner of record of the coupon (the "prior" owner) will not be the owner on the coupon date (the "current" owner). As a result, the accrued interest that accumulates between the sale and the coupon date will be paid to the prior owner and not the current owner, which means that when the sale of the bond takes place, the accrued interest between the sale date and the coupon date is subtracted from the clean price of the bond. This is analogous to calculating a dirty price by adding accrued interest, only here there is negative accrued interest. Negative accrued interest occurs in some overseas bond markets, including markets in Australia, Denmark, New Zealand, Norway, Sweden, and the United Kingdom.[2]

Lot Sizes

Just as equities trade with minimum lot sizes, so too do fixed-income instruments. Lots may be in sizes as small as 1,000 or 2,000 or as large as 50,000 or even 100,000 (often in overseas markets).

Securitization and Prepayment

Finally, some fixed-income securities are "securitized" baskets of payments from other fixed-income securities. Mortgage-backed securities, for example, take payments from a basket of mortgages and pass them through to investors. Other kinds of fixed-income securities offer those payouts to investors in tranches, dictating who will receive the payments according to a predefined order: the first payments go to the most secure, or highest-rated, issues, while the last payments go to the lowest.

Some mortgages, as homeowners may know, are prepaid prior to the term of the mortgage, often to refinance at a lower rate. When this happens, principal is given to the investor that presumably gets invested at lower rates. Thus, "prepayment risk" is an element of securitized products that is tracked by fixed-income PMs.

FIXED-INCOME INDICES AND INDEX FILES

For index-based FI (fixed-income) ETFs, all roads start and end with the index methodology and the associated index files, just as they do for equity-based ETFs. And just as we see with equity indices, fixed-income indices can be weighted in any number of different ways, from market capitalization, which takes into account the size of a particular issue as opposed to the equity valuation of a corporation, to equal weight or even fundamental weighting. Rebalancing may take place monthly, quarterly, or less frequently, and just as we see with equities, there will be a calculation date and a rebalance date; the rebalance date may be the same as the calculation date or a number of days later.

Fixed-income PMs rely on index files, pro forma files, and corporate action files, just as equity PMs do. Index files related to bond indices can include a wide array of information and typically include index-level information in a way that equity index files do not.

Table 16.1 presents the summary information for the Solactive USD Investment Grade Corporate Index (SOLUSICG) on 5/26/2020. In addition to the index level, we see the market value of the securities in the index, as well as a breakout of this value between the instrument itself and cash associated with the instruments. Unlike equity counterparts, fixed-income indices might hold cash without reinvesting it. Typically, in equity indices dividends are instantaneously reinvested, either in the total index pro rata or back to the particular stock that issued the dividend. In a fixed-income index, however, it is possible for the sponsor to dictate that coupons (and paydowns if applicable) that are paid be held in cash until the next rebalance, in which case it is not uncommon to have a cash holding in a fixed-income index (something rarely, if ever, seen in an equity index). According to the SOLUSICG index methodology, "Coupon and other cash payments will be reinvested on each Rebalancing Day," which is the last business day of each month.[3]

TABLE 16.1

Summary Information for the SOLUSICG Index

Date	5/26/2020		
Index close	2,152.49		
Date rebal	4/30/2020	Average yield to maturity	2.57135
Index close rebal	2,131.33	Avg. duration to maturity	8.376984
Month-to-date return	1.00%	Avg. duration to maturity	8.253564
Daily return	−0.0155%	Average DV01	0.096
Index MV	$6,558,210,000,000	Average term	11.90169
Index cash	$ 18,971,070,086	Average convexity	1.289157

Duration is Macaulay duration.
Source: Solactive AG.

In addition to cash, we also see summary statistics for the index, including:[4]

- Average yield to maturity
- Duration (Macaulay and/or other measures)
- Average DV01 (dollar value of a basis point)
- Average term
- Average convexity

From a quick glance, a seasoned fixed-income PM can tell a lot from this summary information without having to delve into the line-by-line details of each particular issue. That can be important because some fixed-income indices can reference hundreds or thousands of bonds (SOLUSICG had 6,166 on this date).

For the individual securities in the index file, an extensive amount of information per position is often included. A PM, however, should expect to see:

- Security identifiers (CUSIPs, SEDOLs, etc.)
- Country (if international) and currency
- Amount outstanding (of the entire issue)
- Maturity and coupon
- Price, accrued interest, and market value
- Cash
- Weights (which may be calculated including cash and excluding cash)
- YTM, YTC, YTW, DV01, duration, and convexity
- Seniority and rating (for rated instruments)

As is the case with equity indices, understanding the details of the index methodology and what is being reported in the index files is absolutely critical when tracking a fixed-income index.

Pro forma files for fixed-income indices act just like equity pro formas. Corporate action files are also similar to their equity counterparts; however, the set of corporate actions relevant to the index is different. Stock splits and rights offerings are of no interest to a corporate bondholder, but callability, for example, is of significant interest. A nonexhaustive selection of corporate actions specific to fixed-income securities includes:[5]

- **Early redemption:** This would include callable bonds being called, tender offers (much like equity tenders), and buyback programs initiated by the issuer.
- **Exchange offers:** Issuers propose a redemption of the bond in exchange for cash, other bonds, stocks, etc.
- **Distressed debt exchange:** The principal on a note is reduced in exchange for higher security or other provisions related to the bond when an issuer is in distress.
- **Default actions:** A coupon or principal payment is missed, or an issue already in default makes a payment.

Provisions for how these events impact the index should be covered in the index methodology and would be handled in the portfolio much like what we discussed in Chapter 11 with respect to corporate actions.

TRACKING THE INDEX AND REPRESENTATIVE SAMPLING

Fixed-income indices can be difficult to track using full replication; the liquidity and sizing of some positions that are in an index might make it challenging for the PM to hold the right amount of a given issue or even any amount of an issue at all. As a result, fixed-income managers often employ representative sampling to overcome some of these challenges. Representative sampling may not be "better" than full replication in terms of tracking, but it is an explicit capitulation to the challenges of fixed-income portfolio management that will signal to investors up front that the fund will not track the underlying index perfectly.

Fixed-income funds that use representative sampling are generally not just matching issuers when a particular issue is illiquid or unavailable. Rather, the techniques used in representative sampling can be more complex and model-driven than in the equity space. FI PMs may try to match a number of statistics on the portfolio or subsets of the portfolio, including:

- **Duration matching:** By matching duration of a sampled portfolio with an index portfolio, the PM is ensuring that changes to the underlying rate environment impact the portfolios similarly.
- **Convexity matching:** When rates change, not only does the value of a portfolio change, but the sensitivity to future interest rate moves changes as well. If the convexity and duration of two portfolios match, then as interest rate moves impact the value of the portfolio, the two portfolios will maintain duration profiles so the PM's portfolio will not require a duration rebalance.
- **Matching of prepayment risk.**
- **Fundamentals or industry and sector matching.**

We discuss more on representative sampling in Chapter 19.

FIXED-INCOME PCFS

The PCF is the backbone of the creation and redemption process, dictating what is included in the basket of securities (and cash) that exchanges hands between the portfolio and the authorized participant. This is the starting point for understanding the primary market transactions for fixed-income ETFs, just as it is for equities.

In Chapter 5, we highlighted the PCF construction using holdings in the portfolio or the index file as a basis for production. Because of the prevalence of representative sampling in index-tracking fixed-income ETFs and the difficulty sourcing certain issues, putting all the securities from an index into the PCF is a recipe for disaster: a PM won't have all the securities for a redemption and wouldn't want to receive all the securities in a creation because he or she would have to manage that full basket of securities. A pro rata slice of the holdings in a portfolio can be the basis for PCF construction, though depending on the exemptive relief, the PCF may reflect a representative sample of the portfolio.

PCFs for FI have summary information and security-level information just as we would expect. Imagine that alongside the SWA ETF that we have been using as an example throughout this book, the fund sponsor also lists a "BWA"* ETF, which is a collection of bonds from issuers whose equity tickers start with the letter A. In Table 16.2, we present the summary-level informa-

TABLE 16.2

BWA PCF Based on Holdings Files—Portfolio-Level Detail

BWA ETF			
Trade date	2/1/2021	Actual CIL	$ 589,421.75
Settlement	T + 2	Actual cash	$1,074,869.65
Creation unit	50,000	Base market value	$1,375,000.00
NAV	$ 50.00	Estimated total cash	$1,125,000.00
NAV per CU	$ 2,500,000.00	Estimated CIL	$ 590,011.17
Shares O/S	10,000,000	Estimated cash	$ 534,988.83
Total net assets	$500,000,000.00	Estimated dividend	$ 7,346.00

---

* BWA, just like SWA, is solely hypothetical. Any relation to any fixed-income index and/or ETF is completely unintentional.

tion for the PCF. As we can see, the PCF is still anchored by the value of a creation unit. By definition, the value of the basket must equal the value of the creation unit. In the case of bonds, though, this is not as straightforward as it appears. In particular, the market prices for bonds are typically quoted as "clean prices." As mentioned above, clean bond prices are prices that do not include accrued interest.

Given that the prices in the PCF are clean prices, it should now be clear why this might be problematic from the equivalence requirement of the PCF. If we simply add up the market value of the securities in the portfolio based on clean prices, we would be missing the value of the accrued interest.

This is why, in the summary section of the PCF for a fixed-income ETF, the total accrued interest is calculated, and this amount will become part of the *cash* portion of the basket, since interest accrued is not in-kind. Alternatively, adjusting the file to incorporate dirty prices would ensure equivalence as well.* This is similar to the treatment of dividends in the equity context. Expected dividends on the ex-date become part of the estimated cash calculation, just as expected interest becomes a part of the estimated cash calculation in the FI PCF. In Table 16.3, we reconcile the figures in the summary section of the PCF.

TABLE 16.3

Cash Reconciliation for BWA PCF (2/1/2021)

NAV per CU	$2,500,000.00
− Basket market value	$1,375,000.00
= Estimated total cash	$1,125,000.00
− Estimated CIL	$ 590,011.17
= Estimated cash (non-CIL)	$ 534,988.83
− Estimated dividend	$ 7,346.00
= Other cash (plug)	$ 527,642.83

For security-level information, the information set largely mimics what we discussed in the index section above. One important caveat concerns prices. Equity closing prices are well known and stream on exchanges, whereas fixed-income prices are often more subject to debate. ETF sponsors

---

* Coupons paid after a trade but before settlement would require a cash adjustment as well.

often employ third-party valuation services to value fixed-income securities, and while each security in a basket must be valued, individual prices may not be revealed in the PCF. Instead, a file might include the overall valuation of the basket of securities with par amounts, along with residual or expected cash. The file we present here does indicate pricing, but it allows for the possibility that a file may not.

While there are still security identifiers and the names and weights of the securities, several data points are unique to fixed income, as they pertain to the individual securities. The PCF will likely include:

- **Original face value:** The par value of the bonds in the basket
- **Interest:** Accrued interest on the bonds since the last interest payment
- **Interest factor:** The accrued interest as a percentage of the face value

Lot-size constraints are prevalent, just as they are in the equity space, but note that lot-size constraints in fixed income can lead to considerably more residual cash in the valuation process if the lot size is high enough, as we've discussed.

Table 16.4 depicts a few lines of security-level detail in BWA.

CIL IN FI PCFS

As is the case with equities, marking bonds cash in lieu can make a considerable impact on capital gains and losses. If a security is placed into the PCF and a redemption comes in, the lots with the lowest cost basis get included, and it might be possible to "recycle" unrealized gains through the redemption mechanism without having to realize them. In the case of a particular bond, it might be that all the lots are in losses, and by including the security in the basket, the PM is losing an opportunity to convert unrealized losses into realized losses.*

This is where marking certain securities CIL can be advantageous for the FI ETF PM. Any security that would leave the portfolio with an unrealized loss can be marked CIL so that the PM has the opportunity to sell the security in the secondary market rather than passing the security to the AP

---

* To be fair, the inability to convert unrealized losses to realized losses in a redemption when all the lots in a security are in losses is not unique to fixed income; the same applies to equities.

TABLE 16.4

BWA PCF Based on Index Files—Security-Level Detail (2/1/2021)

ID	Description	Shares	Original Face	Interest	Base Price	Base MV	Weight	CIL	Lot Size
US1001B	AABA Corp	20,000	20,000,000	$37.34	$ 99.42	$1,988,400.00	1.20%	N	2,000
US1003B	AAQZ Corp	18,000	18,000,000	$42.02	$104.31	$1,877,580.00	0.83%	N	2,000
US1004B	AAWL Corp	22,000	22,000,000	$13.41	$102.23	$2,249,060.00	0.70%	N	2,000
US1009B	ACBU Corp	20,000	20,000,000	$21.87	$101.88	$2,037,600.00	0.65%	N	2,000

in the primary market transaction, thereby converting the unrealized loss to a realized loss. In a symmetric basket construct, where creations and redemptions are based on the same file, the AP would pass cash to the PM in lieu of the security, and then the PM would have to purchase the security in the secondary market should he or she wish to. C/R variable fees would often be collected in this case to compensate the PM for transaction costs. The PM should be aware of wash sales in the case of creations where the PM would be transacting rather than taking securities from the AP.

NEGOTIATED BASKETS

Having spent considerable time discussing fixed-income PCFs, we now address why, in fact, the PCF is very often *ignored* in the creation and redemption process for fixed-income ETFs. To be clear, the PCF is *valid* for use in a standard creation or redemption, but most of the time, orders are completed using negotiated baskets.

A negotiated basket is a customized portfolio just like a CIB. In the fixed-income space, availability and liquidity of securities are paramount. It may be difficult for an AP to source bonds that are listed in the PCF or sell bonds that are delivered to the AP as a result of a standard redemption. Lack of liquidity could lead to larger spreads on products as the market makers' arbitrage bounds are pushed due to expected slippage in the secondary markets for trading constituent fixed-income securities. Rather than accept the standard baskets, however, APs often negotiate the basket with the fund sponsor, or more specifically (and importantly), with the fund's portfolio manager.

What does this negotiation look like? Suppose an AP wishes to create but does not have that basket of bonds from Table 16.4 on hand. Instead, the AP has an inventory of bonds that includes the bonds in Table 16.5:

TABLE 16.5

AP Inventory (2/1/2021)

ID	Description	Shares	Original Face	Interest	Base Price	Base MV	Lot Size
US1001B	AABA Corp	20,000	20,000,000	$37.34	$99.42	$1,988,400.00	2,000
US1002B	AABD Corp	20,000	20,000,000	$28.76	$101.01	$2,020,200.00	2,000
US1006B	AABW Corp	20,000	20,000,000	$19.99	$99.28	$1,985,600.00	2,000
. . .							

The AP will typically present the menu of choices to the PM, and the PM will choose which bonds to accept and in what size as part of the negotiation for what the creation basket will look like. This is no simple task for the PM.

When reviewing the selection set, the PM—likely using a sampling approach—will have to consider the relevant characteristics of the set of securities he or she would receive:

- Duration
- Convexity
- Sector or industry
- Quality

There may be other factors. In the case of this model ETF, the PM might consider whether the inventory offered reflects issues whose stock tickers begin with the letter A. There is often a back-and-forth with the AP before a finalized selection set is established, and once the basket is agreed upon, that basket becomes the basis for the creation. A similar process is completed for a redemption.

NETTING ORDERS

From the perspective of the ETF PM, standard orders are easily "netted" because they reflect the PCF: if a fund receives a one-unit standard create and a two-unit standard redeem, from the PM's perspective the fund can effectively process a one-unit redemption. Offsetting standard orders is effectively a nonevent for the PM. Of course, these orders may come from different APs, so the actual orders themselves are not netted, and the fact that so many C/R orders are negotiated means that netting is less relevant for fixed-income PMs. It also means that the process described above—reviewing the negotiated list of securities with an AP—can happen with multiple APs at the same time. This creates a real need for a considerable effort to manage the C/R process for a fixed-income ETF in a way that does not generally present itself for an equity-based ETF. Portfolio analytics become "mission critical," especially for funds that have considerable AUM and steady C/R activity.

WASH SALES AND TAX LOTS

Wash sales do not eliminate losses, but they do defer losses, and without careful attention to the timing of transactions, wash sales can turn a negative tax year (a good thing) into a positive tax year (a bad thing).

What makes the discussion about wash sales in equities *relatively* straightforward (it's a complicated topic, of course) is that a stock is a stock is a stock: there's little question about the underlying security that relates to the wash sale in most equity cases.* In the fixed-income universe, this question is far more complicated. Consider two bonds issued by the same company, one that expires in five years and one that expires in seven years. Are those two securities "substantially identical" in the eyes of the IRS? What if the company has two bonds that expire on the same day but one has a coupon of 4% and one has a coupon of 3%? Are those substantially identical?

This is where the fund accountants will earn their money. The key thing for the FI ETF PM is that he or she knows the answers the fund accountants are comfortable with before transacting in a security that may or may not fall subject to the wash-sale rule. The last thing a PM wants is to transact in a security and then find out afterward that the transaction deferred losses beyond the end of a fiscal year.

REBALANCES

We have spent considerable time discussing the rebalancing of an index-tracking ETF in the context of an equity portfolio, and the mechanics involved are really no different in the fixed-income space. Just as we depicted the rebalancing process in the equity setting in Figure 13.1, that process applies here as well, and we refer the reader to Chapters 12 ("Custom In-Kind Baskets") and 13 ("Portfolio Rebalance") for review.† Important considerations to note in the fixed-income arena are negotiating a CIB with an AP (CIBs are allowable for fixed-income ETFs compliant with the ETF Rule) and accounting

---

* This gets more nuanced when the equity underlyings are themselves ETFs, such as two ETFs that track the same index.

† Like their equity-based counterparts, prior to the adoption of the ETF Rule, fixed-income ETFs were subject to the same regulatory framework of exemptive relief as equity-based products. With the implementation of the ETF Rule, both active and index-based fixed-income ETFs can utilize CIB as a significant part of the tax management strategy.

for the liquidity, time, and transaction costs it may take to complete certain desired bond issues.

Notes

1. Bloomberg Finance L.P., ICI.
2. https://thismatter.com/money/bonds/bond-pricing.htm.
3. Solactive AG.
4. Ibid.
5. Ibid.

CHAPTER 17

Leveraged and Inverse Exposures

ETFs are typically nonleveraged investment vehicles: an investor with $10,000 worth of ETF shares usually carries exposure to $10,000 worth of stocks, bonds, or whatever the ETF holds. If the basket of securities that the ETF holds gains 5%, then (absent fees), the ETF NAV increases by 5%. There exists, however, a set of ETFs where this traditional relationship breaks down. For these ETFs, when the underlying exposure goes up or down by a certain percentage, the ETF seeks to provide a return that is a multiple of that percentage, and that multiple can be positive or negative. These are called "leveraged" and "inverse" products, respectively.

ETFs that provide leveraged exposures have been around since 2006. They cover a range of asset classes, from equities to fixed income to commodities. A small sample of these products is found in Table 17.1.

For example, consider TQQQ, the ProShares UltraPro QQQ ETF. TQQQ is a 3X leveraged ETF, seeking "investment results which correspond to three times (300%) the daily performance of the NASDAQ-100 Index."[1] If the Nasdaq-100 goes up by 5% on a given day, the TQQQ PM's job is to try to provide a return to the investor of 15% (less fees). If the Nasdaq-100 goes down 3% on a given day, then the target performance for the ETF is −9%.

For an inverse, or −1X, leveraged exposure, the ETF PM's job is to provide a return to the investor that is the negative of the daily return of the underlying. SH, for example, ProShares' Short S&P 500 ETF, seeks "daily investment results that correspond to the inverse (opposite) of the daily per-

TABLE 17.1

Leveraged and Inverse ETFs (12/31/2020)

Ticker	Name	Total Assets ($M)	Leverage Amount
TQQQ	ProShares UltraPro QQQ	$9,717	3
QLD	ProShares Ultra QQQ	$3,937	2
SSO	ProShares Ultra S&P 500	$3,202	2
FAS	Direxion Daily Financials Bull 3X	$2,189	3
TECL	Direxion Daily Technology Bull 3X	$2,033	3
SOXL	Direxion Daily Semiconductors Bull 3X	$2,006	3
UPRO	ProShares UltraPro S&P 500	$1,829	3
SH	ProShares Short S&P 500	$1,807	−1
SPXL	Direxion Daily S&P 500 Bull 3X	$1,723	3
TNA	Direxion Daily Small Cap Bull 3X	$1,549	3
SQQQ	ProShares UltraPro Short QQQ	$1,371	−3
UVXY	ProShares Ultra VIX ST Futures	$1,305	1.5
NUGT	Direxion Daily Gold Miners Bull 2X	$1,149	2
UCO	ProShares Ultra Bloomberg Crude Oil	$ 900	2
JNUG	Direxion Daily Junior Gold Miners Bull 2X	$ 777	2
AGQ	ProShares Ultra Silver	$ 754	2

Source: Bloomberg Finance L.P.

formance of the S&P 500 Index."[2] When the index is down 1%, the target return for the day is +1%, and when the index is up 2%, the target return for the day is −2%.

How does the PM achieve these target returns (or get close to these target returns), and what are the implications for managing a leveraged portfolio?

HOW TO CREATE LEVERAGED EXPOSURES

When a portfolio manager (or any other investor, for that matter) borrows money to add exposure to an already fully invested position, he or she is "leveraged": the total exposure is greater than the net investment on the part of the investor. Leverage is far more common than you might think; in fact, if you have a mortgage, you have a leveraged investment in your home.

To set the stage, suppose an individual purchases a home worth $1 million and applies—and is approved—for a $500,000 mortgage. The individual takes $500,000 of his or her own cash along with the $500,000 provided by the mortgage bank and pays the current homeowner to complete the $1 million sale. If the value of the home rises from $1 million to $1.2 million—a 20% increase—the value of the new homeowner's equity goes from $500,000 to $700,000, a 40% increase (see Figure 17.1). This is because the investor is *leveraged*. The ratio of the value of the position ($1 million) to the outlay on the part of the investor ($500,000) is 2:1, so when the value of the home increases by $X\%$, the value to the investor increases by $2X\%$.

FIGURE 17.1

Leveraged returns—home mortgage

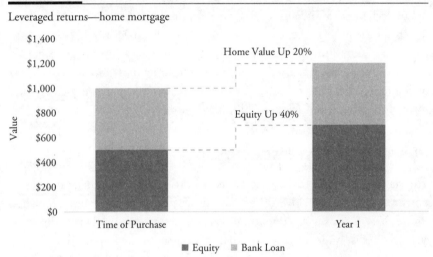

When it comes to leverage in ETFs, the principle behind the mortgage example largely applies: the total investment on the part of the investor is a multiple of the outlay on the part of the investor. This can happen in a number of ways, the most prevalent of which are probably through swaps and futures.

Swaps

A swap is an agreement between two parties to exchange cash flows. Oftentimes that could mean a fixed payment to one counterparty in exchange for a floating payment from another, and that floating payment can be (and often is) related to an index. For example, a swap agreement could provide one counterparty the ability to receive a daily-resetting* leveraged exposure to an underlying index while paying a fixed fee. The party providing that payoff would be responsible for hedging that exposure: creating the payoffs with which to fund the necessary agreement.

Futures

A future is a derivatives contract that is tied to an observable value on a specified date. Futures trade on futures exchanges, like the CBOE Futures Exchange. A buyer of a futures contract agrees to pay a specific price for an underlying on the expiry date of the contract; the seller agrees to sell the underlying for that price. If a buyer purchases a futures contract at a price of $100 and the price on the date of expiry for the underlying is $110, then the buyer is able to purchase the underlying at a discount of $10 and can presumably turn around and sell it to bank the profit. Of course, if prices decline, the buyer would be forced to pay a premium to the market price for a loss. Futures are not tied to leveraged payouts, but a PM of a leveraged fund would know how much exposure he or she requires at the end of each day and then would manage the exposure through purchases and sales of additional contracts.

HOW TO CREATE INVERSE EXPOSURES

The classic case of an inverse exposure is shorting a stock. When an investor borrows a security, the investor has an inverse exposure to the security: when the security increases in value, the investor loses money, and when the security declines in value, the investor makes money. If called upon to do so, the investor would be required to "buy back in" to recapture the security to give back to the lender in order for the owner to potentially sell the security.

There are other ways to create short exposure. Having gone through instruments through which one can achieve leveraged exposures, it is not hard to envision how to achieve the opposite effect, i.e., inverse exposure. In the case of the swap contract, the swap counterparty offers the investor a return in the form of a negative of the return of the underlying index.[†] In the case of a futures contract, a PM can sell futures contracts to create short exposure. As in our brief example above, when prices rise, there is a loss to sellers

---

* More on daily-resetting exposures below.

† It should not be lost on us that the counterparty is then responsible for creating the inverse exposure to pass along to the investor.

of futures contracts. Futures contracts require margin, so there is a cash management role that PMs must play when managing a futures-based portfolio.

DAILY-RESETTING LEVERAGE (OR INVERSE) EXPOSURE

One of the key aspects of leveraged and inverse ETFs is that the leverage ratio (LR) is generally static on a day-to-day basis. That means that each day, the leverage exposure to the underlying index is the same. For this to happen, the ETF PM must *reset* the leverage on a daily basis.

Consider a 2X exposure to an underlying index, accomplished through a swap or futures exposure. A $100 investment implies a $200 exposure to the underlying return on day T. Imagine that the underlying index returns 10% on a given day. The $200 investment grows to $220, and (absent borrowing costs for simplicity) the capital invested increases to $120 at the end of day T + 1 prior to any transactions. At this point, the leverage ratio is now *less* than 2:1, as shown in Figure 17.2.

FIGURE 17.2

Daily-resetting leverage during an up move

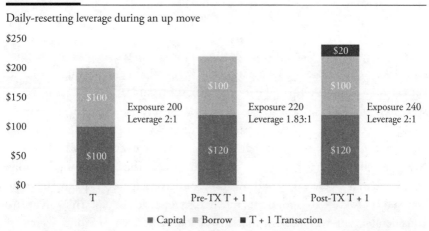

The leverage ratio of 1.83 must increase going into the next day if the PM is going to maintain the mandate of a daily exposure of twice the underlying index return. To accomplish this, the PM must *increase* his or her leverage: for $120 in capital, the strategy will need $240 in investments, requiring an increase of $20 in the position. This is the "daily-resetting" transaction for the portfolio.

Conversely, if the underlying return is −10%, then the total capital invested is $80, while the total investment is $180 (see Figure 17.3). As a result, the leverage ratio is *higher* than 2:1, and to reset it, the ETF PM must *reduce* the exposure by $20 to achieve an exposure of $160, i.e., twice the capital on the part of the investor.

FIGURE 17.3

Daily-resetting leverage during a down move

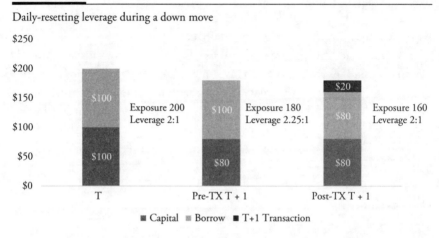

In Figures 17.4 and 17.5, we show how the inverse exposures require end-of-day daily-resetting transactions as well. What is interesting is that in the case of a positive return, the inverse exposure requires an increase in exposure, and in the case of a negative return, the inverse exposure requires a decrease in exposure. This is exactly the same as was the case for leveraged 2X exposures. It is often assumed that if there is a positive return, the inverse PM needs to sell. As the figures show, that is incorrect. The broader implications of this are that *all* leveraged and inverse products trade directionally the same way subject to how an underlying moves over a particular day. This can create considerable one-way flow in markets tied heavily to inverse and leveraged products.

FIGURE 17.4

Daily-resetting inverse leverage during an up move

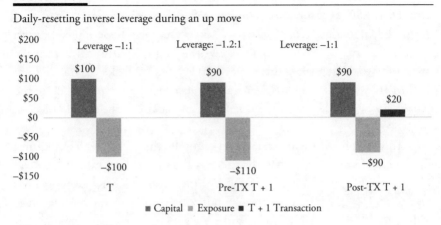

FIGURE 17.5

Daily-resetting inverse leverage during a down move

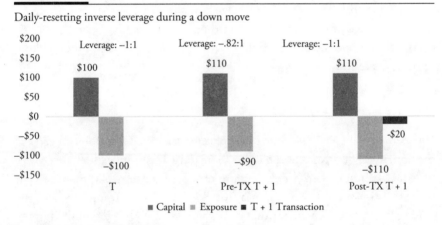

HITTING THE CLOSE

In the prior examples, we calculated how much of an increase or decrease was required in positioning to maintain the constant leverage ratio going into the following day. The problem, however, is that the required purchase or sale was only known conditional on knowing the closing level of the underlying index. There is a catch-22: the PM needs to know the index closing level to calculate the purchase or sale, but the required purchase or sale must be conducted before the market closes.

This paradox creates a headache for an ETF PM. It can be shown that for a 2X or –1X exposure, the required purchase is twice the daily return of the underlying index.* For a 3X or –2X exposure, the transaction is *six times* the daily return. This means that the PM is trying to continually match the transaction to the return, as there is less and less time to make the transaction: the PM tries to "hit the close," or transact just the right amount before the market closes in order to get the leverage ratio as close to the stated objective as possible.

This is not just theoretical. As an example, the S&P 500 VIX Futures Short-Term Excess Return MCAP Index is the underlying index for several VIX-related ETFs (VIX is the CBOE Volatility Index). To replicate it, PMs need to trade VIX futures. For those funds to appropriately establish leverage at the end of the day to VIX futures, the PMs try to hit the close by transacting as close to the end of the business day as possible. Intraday volume charts for front-month VIX futures routinely show that the lion's share of transactions occurs just prior to the close of trading, when the index marks the positions. This is undoubtedly attributable to leveraged and inverse funds seeking to track the index.

INDEX AND PRO FORMA FILES

Unless the ETF PM is interested in replicated leveraged positions on each of the underlying securities in the index to be tracked, the index files are of very little use to him or her. The key figure necessary for portfolio management is the real-time value of the index as it ticks toward the closing level and the closing level itself. Remember that once the closing level is established, there is no longer an opportunity to trade during market hours. There may be an opportunity to trade in an after-hours market (like the VIX afternoon session, for example), but there one is simply trueing up the position, much like a PM would do the morning after an index rebalance.

Similarly, there is often little need for the pro forma files associated with the index for the same reason: as long as the PM is tracking the index at the index level, and not at a more granular level by tracking positions, the rebalanced nature of the index is irrelevant for portfolio management purposes.

---

* See, for example, q-group.org/wp-content/uploads/2014/01/Madhavan-LeverageETF.pdf.

PCFs

As we learned in Chapter 5, for a passive ETF, the PCF is meant to reflect holdings and/or the index to be tracked. For an active ETF, it is meant to reflect the holdings of the fund. For unleveraged products this makes a lot of sense, and while there is movement from the time the PCF is constructed to the time at which it is in force (i.e., the close of the business day), the estimated cash is often very close to actual cash that changes hands upon a create or redeem.

For leveraged and inverse funds, however, the holdings at the end of day T, which are likely the basis for the PCF on day T + 1, are generally quite different from the required constitution of the fund at the close of T + 1, due to the daily-resetting feature of these products. As a simple example already used in this chapter, if the underlying index to be tracked in a passive product goes up by 10% for a 2X leveraged product, the required exposure must increase by 20% of the beginning-of-day assets; that 20% would be a huge differential between estimated and actual cash to change hands. APs understand the dynamics of these funds, and the fund sponsors can set the PCFs to be all-cash baskets. The estimated cash, of course, would then simply reflect the NAV without any market movements, but once the NAV is set for the day, the cash that changes hands would reflect the updated NAV based on the market moves for the day.*

For the ETF PM running such a fund, the real issue here is what the cutoff time is for orders. The PM must be ready to upsize or downsize the portfolio exposure based on the orders coming in for the day. The cutoff is generally set for products of this nature with enough time before the market closes so that the PM can adjust accordingly. This means that the daily trade is not only a function of the daily reset, but also a function of the overall desired exposure subject to C/R activity.

THE THREE Ts AND THE THREE Cs

As we have seen with index files, some of what we have learned about ETFs tends to go off course with leveraged and inverse funds. Corporate actions, for example, may not be relevant in an index that tracks commodity futures

---

* Some funds allow for EFRP (exchange for related position), which effectively means that futures can change hands as opposed to cash. See https://www.cmegroup.com/education/courses/market-regulation/efrp/what-is-an-efrp.html.

or volatility-based instruments. Below we highlight a few key points with respect to leveraged and inverse products.

Tracking Error

Unlike traditional ETFs, which generally fall nicely into the framework we developed in Chapter 7 regarding tracking error, leveraged and inverse funds derive virtually all their tracking error (absent fees) from misallocation and cash drag, which, when you're tracking one underlying, can be effectively two sides of the same coin.

Consider the case where the underlying index is a rolling futures index. For every $100 in AUM in a 2X product, $200 worth of exposure is required. If the PM ends the day with only $198 of exposure, then he or she is effectively $2 short. That is the cash drag component. If the composition of futures in the basket is different from the composition of futures in the index to be tracked, then that is the misallocation component. If the PM uses a swap with a bank counterparty to track the index, then the composition is no longer a factor, as exposure is tied directly to the index, but the exposure amount can vary from what is required in the same way as if the PM didn't purchase or sell enough futures to match the required exposure. Leveraged and inverse tracking errors can be substantial as a result of the difficulty in hitting the close.

Another issue with tracking error for leveraged and inverse funds is that the indices that are tracked often close at times that differ from the closing price time. As a result, there appears to be a difference between index returns, NAV returns, and closing price returns.

Transaction Costs

In general, expect a lot of transactions for daily-resetting leveraged products. Every day there are transactions that are, by definition, multiples of the return in the underlying. Standard turnover should not be expected in such instruments, and transaction costs will be a higher percentage of the fund than in almost any other fund in comparison.

Taxes

Taxes are, of course, an issue for all ETFs, whether or not there is leverage (or inverse leverage). The underlying exposure and the structure of the ETF will be an important component in determining tax considerations. Some funds are structured as partnerships, and as such, investors receive K-1 forms, as required by the IRS, when doing their taxes; other funds are open-ended investment companies that don't receive K-1s. In addition, the heavy transactions-based process of maintaining leverage makes it difficult to construct tax trades for these products.

The Three Cs

In general, because of swap-based or futures-based exposures in some of these products and exposures linked to commodities or volatility, corporate actions are less relevant. Of course, there are leveraged and inverse products linked to indices comprising equities or fixed-income products, and therefore what we discussed in Chapter 11 largely applies in those situations if underlying positions are being tracked. To the extent there are futures or swaps on the indices, this is again less relevant.

We've already mentioned how cash is a critical component of leveraged and inverse products, especially with respect to cash drag and margin for futures products, and one would not expect CIBs to be a component of ETF portfolio management for leveraged and inverse products that track commodity or futures indices. For indices that rebalance in a more substantive way, as opposed to futures indices that often simply roll to the following futures contract when one contract expires, CIBs can address some of the same issues that we covered in Chapter 12.

RISK OF 100% LOSS

With any portfolio where leverage or inverse leverage is present, a 100% (or greater) loss becomes possible. In the case of a leveraged product where the leverage ratio is LR, the threshold move in the underlying index (assuming perfect replication) that would result in a 100% loss is $-1/LR$. For a 2X leveraged product, a downward threshold move in the underlying of -50% would result in a 100% loss because of the 2X leverage. For a $-X$ product, an *upward* move in the underlying of 100% would result in a loss of 100% in the inverse product.

At the end of the day, it is the job of the index-based ETF PM, of course, to track the underlying index with the target leverage, but the PM will likely trade out of positions to avoid the zero threshold, though this isn't always possible in a fast-moving market. Once the portfolio is deemed worthless intraday, it will generally no longer hold any value, and its closing

NAV will be zero. Further losses will accrue to the fund sponsor and not the ETF holder, whose liability is limited to the amount invested. Tracking what a portfolio holds intraday, however, is a bit of an art form, since calculation agents usually cannot print intraday indicative values based on real-time transactions. It is therefore possible to have the IV hit the zero threshold when the PM has actually traded out of positions and has kept the value of the portfolio positive.

However, if the underlying reverses course after the PM has liquidated positioning, while the portfolio may avoid the zero threshold, it may not capture the day-to-day movement one might expect from the fund. This would obviously result in a case where there would be significant overperformance or underperformance in the fund.

Notes

1. Source: Bloomberg Finance L.P.
2. Ibid.

PART VI

When the Going Gets Tough

I n this final part of the book, we touch on three areas all related to the challenges of managing an ETF. First, we discuss extreme market turbulence in Chapter 18, using the global COVID-19 pandemic to illustrate some of the difficulties that present themselves to the ETF PM.

In Chapter 19, we discuss a different approach to ETF portfolio management for index-based products: representative sampling. We have largely adhered to a full replication model so far in the book, but we have alluded to times when full replication is simply untenable. The nature of the index to be tracked in a passive product may force the hand of the PM to employ a different portfolio management style.

Finally, in Chapter 20, we discuss what happens when the fund sponsor decides the fund ought to be closed and what steps the PM takes to wind down the positions in the portfolio.

CHAPTER 18

Market Turbulence

As the world prepared to celebrate New Year's Eve and usher in the year 2020, the World Health Organization reported on December 31, 2019, that a concerning new virus was emanating from Wuhan, China, rendering dozens of people ill with pneumonialike symptoms. Within weeks, China had reported its first death from the illness, and by mid-January, the United States had its first death, a man who had visited Wuhan.[1] What we now know as the novel coronavirus (or COVID-19) would come to infect millions of people and kill over a million people worldwide over the ensuing months. But by late February, despite the growing threat, markets globally seemed to still shrug off warnings of a global pandemic and economic disaster: On February 19, 2020, the S&P 500 Index hit an all-time high. And the Euro STOXX 50 Index, tracking the 50 largest European firms, reached an all-time high on the same day.[2]

Then the markets woke up to the threat, as confirmed cases and growing concern from epidemiologists and economists alike came to the forefront; fear seemed to set in. Seven consecutive negative sessions on the S&P 500 closed out the month of February and took the index down almost 13%, and by March 23, the S&P 500 was down an incredible 34%.[3] European markets were down over 38%. While *annualized* volatility on the S&P 500 up to the peak was approximately 12%,* between February 20 and March 24, the index experienced moves of 3% or greater on 15 of 22 days, with an almost unthinkable stretch of 8 straight days of more than 4.9% moves (see Figure 18.1).

---

* Based on the 30 prior trading days.

FIGURE 18.1

Market volatility during the onset of the COVID-19 pandemic

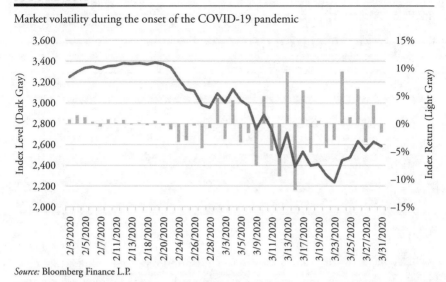

Source: Bloomberg Finance L.P.

Enough happened with respect to public health, the markets, the economy, the government response, etc., to fill many, many volumes. For our purposes, however, the critical question is this: How are ETFs managed in times of market stress such as this pandemic, and what are the implications of such events on ETF performance?

The short answer is that everything is magnified. Transaction costs, both direct and in the form of bid-ask spreads, can increase; the impact of asynchronicity of market closures for international portfolios can drastically impact portfolio rebalances; price discovery can be challenging, potentially coming more swiftly to the ETF than the underlying securities it holds; and arbitrage opportunities may appear to be prevalent as secondary market prices veer away from intraday indicative values. The COVID-19 pandemic is a case study in market turbulence, and we will reference data for that period to highlight some of the concerns the ETF PM faces during fast-moving markets.

MARKET HALTS

We have discussed the impact of trading halts on individual securities both as part of an index and as part of corporate actions impacting the ETF portfolio management process. Turbulent markets can lead to complete market halts, where all securities on a given exchange are halted and no trading is allowed for a predetermined period of time.

Take, for example, the "circuit breakers" imposed on the New York Stock Exchange. As a means to try to give the market a collective deep breath as markets precipitously fall, the New York Stock Exchange imposes tiered trading rules based on the following moves on the S&P 500 Index:[4]

- **Level 1:** 7% down from the prior day's S&P 500 close
- **Level 2:** 13% down from the prior day's S&P 500 close
- **Level 3:** 20% down from the prior day's S&P 500 close

If Level 1 or Level 2 is breached, a 15-minute trading pause goes into effect. After a Level 3 breach, trading is suspended for the remainder of the session. Level 1 and Level 2 breaches can only be triggered from the open (9:30 a.m. ET) through 3:25 p.m. ET, at which point only the Level 3 circuit breaker remains in effect.

Orders may be canceled during a marketwide halt, but new orders will be rejected during the closure. For index-based ETFs, where most trading occurs on the close, the Level 1 and Level 2 breaches may be less concerning, and only extreme events would lead to a Level 3 breach. For active and index-based managers alike, however, midday market closures can have consequences, especially if some part of a reallocation is achieved before the halt but the remainder has not been completed and is forced to resume after the halt, as new price discovery takes effect.

On March 16, in the middle of the COVID-19 pandemic, the S&P Index opened down at 2,508.59 from a prior closing level of 2,711.02, a decline of 7.47%. Markets were immediately halted at a Level 1 trading pause and reopened 15 minutes later. According to Bloomberg, only 95 stocks in the S&P 500 actually opened for trading that morning, meaning that many of them were not available for trading at the open.[5]

TRANSACTION COSTS

As the markets become more turbulent, the need for repositioning may increase, leading market makers to widen their spreads to protect against overpositioning in a security and thereby forcing market participants to accept higher transaction costs.

This might be perceived as a phenomenon applying only to small, less liquid securities, but even the most liquid securities in the world come under pressure in turbulent times. Consider the equity of Apple, Inc., one of the world's largest, most liquid and heavily traded securities (see Figure 18.2). Average bid-ask spreads on Apple stock in 2019 were just over $0.02, or just over 1 basis point. Then COVID-19 happened. As market volatility skyrocketed, Apple stock widened to multiples of that average range; on March 16, the bid-ask spread on Apple topped $0.50, over 20 basis points of the closing price.[6]

FIGURE 18.2

Apple's spread during COVID-19

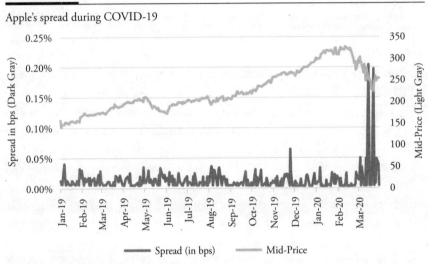

Source: Bloomberg Finance L.P.

While Apple's spread adjustment was dramatic, it is not the type of spread that is going to crush a portfolio in need of a rebalance. For some securities, it might be difficult to find a price at all; "price discovery" can be a challenge.

PRICE DISCOVERY

The very notion of a price of a security is much more specific than investors, or portfolio managers, generally think about. The price of a security is not *just* the price of the security, but rather it might be the particular price that was paid for a security at a specific period in time, or it might be an indication of a price that a buyer is willing to pay or a seller is willing to receive at a specific point in time. As soon as that moment passes, however, for all intents and purposes that price is stale. What was a market price an instant ago no longer applies.

Price discovery is uncovering the prevailing value for a security at a particular moment; it is especially relevant for ETFs, as intraday indicative values of funds are a function of real-time prices of the securities held by the ETF.* What happens, though, if a "real-time" price for a security is unavailable? What if a price is available, but the transaction that this particular price reflected was stale, say from a few minutes prior, or even hours or days prior, to the "real-time" moment for which the indicative value is being calculated?

In practice, what happens is that IVs are calculated using the stale prices. This is undoubtedly a suboptimal outcome, but the alternative is not publishing an IV if there is a lack of pricing for any component in the basket. While the new ETF Rule does not require intraday indicative value publication as was previously required, many funds will continue to publish IVs to assist investors with trading the funds and keeping spreads tight. In turbulent markets, any hint of illiquidity in a security in the form of pauses in price discovery can be magnified, because the movement in the general market from the time of a stale print to the present can be significant.

Consider the hypothetical example in Figure 18.3. An equally weighted ETF has 25 stocks in it (labeled A through Y), each at a weight of 4%. All the stocks are highly correlated with similar levels of volatility and betas to the market. Stocks A through X trade every second between 12:00:00 p.m. ET and 12:00:15 p.m. ET. Stock Y, however, trades at 12:00:00 p.m. ET and then does not trade again until after 12:00:15 p.m. ET. Suppose stocks A through X in the basket of stocks all decline in value by 2% between noon and 15 seconds past the hour. What does the IV for the ETF reflect in those 15 seconds? One might expect a 2% decline, but if the stale price for Y is used, then the answer is 1.92%, or 8 basis points away from what is most likely the "value" of the basket of securities.

---

* A subtle, but important, point to note is that the intraday indicative values do not generally update the portfolio for intraday transactions, but rather reflect what the portfolio began the day holding.

FIGURE 18.3

Impact of stale price on IV

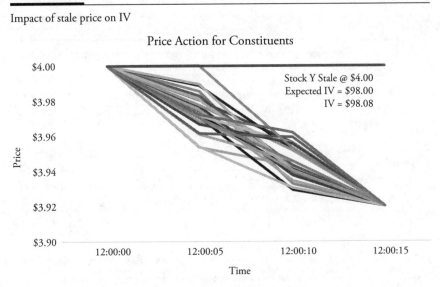

Price Action for Constituents

Stock Y Stale @ $4.00
Expected IV = $98.00
IV = $98.08

How does this play out in real life? In this hypothetical example we only covered 15 seconds; what happens if it is 15 minutes or hours, or more than a day? The COVID-19 pandemic put this phenomenon in the limelight, as fixed-income ETFs had a particularly difficult time with price discovery in the fast-moving markets of mid-March 2020. AGG, the iShares Core US Aggregate Bond ETF, traded more than $5 away from its IV on March 12 and again on March 18, whereas typical spreads between the secondary price and IV were in pennies as opposed to dollars. On traded prices in the $105–$115 range during this time, this spread approached 5% of the secondary price. And it was not alone. Many products traded far away from their IVs and NAVs as a result of the difficulty of price discovery.

Another instance of extreme price movement of ETFs relative to the IVs, took place on August 24, 2015. An overnight plunge in U.S. equity futures contributed to an erratic open, with several stocks failing to open for trading at 9:30 a.m. With the price discovery mechanism failing, selling pressure in several ETFs pulled their secondary prices considerably below their intrinsic value, with some ETFs trading at less than 60% of their previous closing values. The prices corrected over the course of the first hour of trading—small solace for those who sold their ETF shares at the bottom.

CREATION/REDEMPTION AND ARBITRAGE BREAKDOWN

One of the key reasons why ETFs work—and why they were approved—is that they are designed to allow the arbitrage mechanism to keep exchange-traded prices tight to NAVs. If APs could create at the NAV and sell at a premium risk-free or buy at a discount and redeem at the NAV, they would in theory do it all day. Here we now see that this process seems to have broken down. Wasn't there an arbitrage opportunity? That depends on your definition. Technically, we tend to think of arbitrage as a *riskless* attainable profit. If we know we can buy an asset at one price and sell it at a higher price at the same instant, there is an arbitrage profit to be had. Here, however, what we've learned is that price discovery was all but impossible in certain cases, and the asynchronous price discovery created a wrinkle in the system, not because of secondary prices, but because the value of the securities was not adequately reflected in the IV.

REBALANCING IN THE MIDDLE OF AN EVENT

In Chapter 3, we discussed the role of the index committee at the index sponsor. The index committee has complete responsibility for the indices it oversees. Over the normal course of business, a committee will review its policies, the construction of indices, corporate actions, etc. In times of market stress, however, index committees might decide, by fiat, that a particular index should change the way it is calculated and/or rebalanced. Any PM managing an ETF that tracks that index must be up to speed on these index committee changes. The index committee will publish any changes to notify subscribers so that appropriate actions can be taken.

In the midst of the COVID-19 onset, S&P Dow Jones Indices decided to postpone an index rebalance for the S&P 500 Equal Weight Index. This action was completely legitimate and well within the rights of the index committee. S&P duly informed subscribers by posting an announcement that it would hold off on the Q1 2020 rebalance due to occur on March 23, 2020. It postponed that rebalance until April 24. One index-based ETF tracking this index, however, apparently believed that the March rebalance would simply be skipped and that the next rebalance would take place in June. As a result, the fund missed the April rebalance and ended up underperforming significantly. The ETF sponsor suffered a loss of over $100 million as a result of the error.[7]

HETEROSKEDASTICITY

"Heteroskedasticity" is the technical term for nonconstant volatility. We tend to think about a security's volatility, but just like its price, that metric is contingent on a lot of parameters, such as what time period is being examined and exactly how is volatility being measured. The reality is that volatility is constantly changing. Consider the volatility of the S&P 500 Index. In Figure 18.1, we showed returns in February and March 2020. The index became increasingly volatile after the onset of COVID-19 in the United States: annualized volatility in February 2020 was 25%, while annualized volatility in March 2020 was over 93%.

Not only do turbulent markets impact the volatilities of indices, but they also impact individual securities and the correlations and covariances between them. It is a standard Wall Street saying that correlations "tend to one" in periods of stress, meaning that assets that were less correlated become more correlated in such times. This, of course, makes intuitive sense—when the market is precipitously falling, many stocks are along for the ride.

What is the impact of heteroskedasticity on ETF portfolio management? We've already discussed spread-widening and price discovery, but two additional areas are worth mention: how it increases in tracking error/active benchmark risk and how it affects representative sampling.

With respect to tracking error and active benchmark risk, these measures are inherently reflective of volatility. When volatility increases, one can expect to see larger impacts of a misallocation or a variation in weight relative to the index or a benchmark. It is only natural to expect larger tracking errors under these conditions. Representative sampling is also heavily dependent on volatility. Optimizing a portfolio relies on correlations and covariances; and in the fixed-income space, in periods of stress, rates can move quite significantly as well, causing some of the metrics that go into matching a representative sample to an index to be stressed as well.*

WHEN TRACKING ERROR BECOMES INTRACTABLE

On April 20, 2020, the unthinkable happened: The price of oil went *negative*. To be clearer, the price of the front-month crude oil futures contract, which

---

* For a technical discussion regarding the impact of heteroskedasticity on portfolio optimization, see Scott M. Weiner, "Should Stochastic Volatility Matter to the Cost-Constrained Investor?," *Mathematical Finance*, Vol 14.1, January 2004.

trades on the New York Mercantile Exchange (NYMEX), went negative, as shown in Figure 18.4. Why did this happen, and what were some of the implications in the ETF market?

FIGURE 18.4

Front-month oil contract

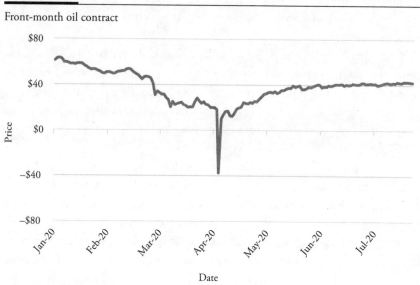

Date

Source: Bloomberg Finance L.P.

First, the why. The front-month oil contract does not cash-settle, meaning that settlement of the contract results in the actual delivery of oil. The recipient of the oil must have the ability to store the oil upon receipt; if he or she does not have that capacity, then as the future nears expiry, he or she will be become desperate to sell the contract, so much so that the investor might actually pay someone to take the contract and accept delivery instead. When the price of the front-month contract closed at *negative* $37.63, the market price effectively said that contract holders were willing to *pay* $37.63 per barrel to whoever would take the oil for delivery. The oversupply of oil in the midst of the pandemic leading up to this crisis resulted in a lack of storage space for future delivery, resulting in the price action.

What impact does a negative price have on ETFs? USO (United States Oil Fund) had the stated investment objective (per the product prospectus) to trade the "daily changes in percentage terms of the spot price of light, sweet crude oil delivered to Cushing, Oklahoma, as measured by the daily changes in the price of the futures contract on light, sweet crude oil as traded on the New York Mercantile Exchange (the 'NYMEX') that is the near-month contract to expire, except when the near-month contract is within two weeks of expiration, in which case it will be measured by the futures contract that is the next month contract to expire, less USOF's expenses (the 'Benchmark Oil Futures Contract')."[8] In short, the ETF tracked the front-month futures price, unless the future was nearing expiry, at which point the ETF tracked the next expiry as a target.

So what happened to USO on 4/20/2020? USO did not hold the front-month contract, because of the rollover discussed above, but it did hold the following expiry, and it held so much of it that, according to multiple reports, it was coming up against CFTC concentration limits specifying that no one party could hold more than 25% of an outstanding futures contract.* Two key things, then, were about to occur.

First, the concentration limit imposed by the market would lead to tracking error. Second, the concern that the *following* expiry price would fall negative (just as the front-month expiry had done) would mean that the ETF PM would have to either trade out of those contracts before they turned negative or risk having the NAV of the fund turn negative. Were the latter to happen, the investors would have a worthless instrument, but the fund sponsor would hold the futures and would suffer losses. To mitigate against this scenario, the fund sponsor announced that it would no longer specifically track the front-month futures contract.[9] This was effectively a realization that under the "new normal," a world with the possibility of negative prices, tracking the front-month future was no longer a reasonable goal for the fund without risking the principal of the fund's investors and/or coming up against concentration problems once again. As such, the fund effectively—overnight—became what amounts to an active ETF, targeting oil prices but no longer explicitly tying performance to a benchmark index or price as it had done before.

———————

The COVID-19 pandemic is just one example of extreme turbulence in markets, and as we have seen in this chapter, such volatile markets can have serious consequences for ETFs. Some funds may choose to rethink their investment

———————

* See, for example, https://www.etf.com/sections/features-and-news/oil-etf-chaos-natgas-etf-2019-plunge.

objectives and/or portfolio management strategies. Some may end up closing altogether.

Notes

1. www.abcnews.com/health/timeline-coronavirus-started/story?id=69435165.
2. Bloomberg Finance L.P.
3. Ibid.
4. http://www.nyse.com/markets/trading-info.
5. Bloomberg Finance L.P.
6. Ibid.
7. http://www.bloomberg.com/news/newsletters/2020-05-08/money-stuff-oil-prices-were-a-beautiful-mystery.
8. https://www.sec.gov/Archives/edgar/data/1327068/000119312512265421/d335842d424b3.htm.
9. http://www.sec.gov/ix?doc=/Archives/edgar/data/1327068/000117120020000259/i20262_uso-8k.htm.

CHAPTER 19

Representative Sampling

n Chapter 7, we introduced tracking error as an unavoidable consequence of trying to replicate an index. There are simply too many things that are beyond the control of the ETF PM to achieve perfect replication. As a result, some ETF PMs do not even try to perfectly replicate the underlying index, instead opting for a method known as "representative sampling." Representative sampling (RS) is like snagging a lunch reservation at a three-star Michelin restaurant during Restaurant Week when you can't get one for the Saturday night of your anniversary: you know you won't get the same menu or experience per se, but you'll get most of it (at a fraction of the cost!).

The ETF sponsor will make clear in the prospectus that the PM will not be seeking to achieve perfect replication, admitting that those Michelin star reservations are too hard to come by. RS is designed to give the investor something that closely reflects an exposure to the underlying index, but not necessarily with the precision implied by replication.*, †

All else equal, RS will undoubtedly contribute to a higher tracking error to the underlying index than full replication. The questions for the ETF PM

---

* By contrast, an active ETF may state directly in the prospectus that it will not seek to track any index, though it might specify conditions that it seeks to attain in the portfolio, such as duration or sector weighting.

† Representative sampling can be (and often is) based on portfolio optimization or modern portfolio theory. While this book is keenly focused on practical portfolio management and less on portfolio theory and modeling, we note that in making the case for representative sampling, some theory is required. There are plenty of sources that delve far more deeply into portfolio theory; here we only touch the surface, and by no means is our treatment meant to be complete.

are what are the reasons for using RS, and what might make RS worth the additional tracking error?

REASONS FOR RS

We highlight four important reasons underlying the need for RS as a portfolio management option:

- Large numbers of constituents in the strategy
- Illiquidity/cost
- Restricted holdings
- Factor optimization, including flexibility in tax management

For strategies that require large numbers of securities, it can be overwhelming to manage the portfolio, and PCF construction/AP transactions in the primary market become increasingly complex. Some fixed-income indices, for example, may hold thousands of different bonds. With lot-size considerations, it is very possible that the portfolio ought to hold fractions of lots over multiple holdings. The portfolio manager can instead opt to hold just a selection of the securities in the index, rather than several thousand.

Even if the number of securities is manageable, it is also possible that the liquidity of the constituents may lead to more efficient portfolios through RS. In international portfolios with smaller-capitalized holdings, for example, thinly traded securities can be difficult to source both for the PM and for the AP and may trade particularly wide. This may lead to more significant costs in transactions tied to those securities than the PM might otherwise incur for securities that may represent the holdings well in a portfolio context. The saving in transaction costs is the benefit to offset the risk. For funds of funds, lower-priced fund alternatives may be a factor in representative sampling.

There can be structural impediments to full replication, including some we have already discussed. For example, a fund may not be able to trade in a particular market that is included in an index to be tracked. In another case, the fund might be quite large relative to some of the holdings' assets outstanding, causing concentration limits to impede full replication.

Finally, RS adds a tremendous amount of flexibility relative to full replication. The PM is not bound by the set of securities in the index and not bound by stringent weight considerations. Instead, RS can allow the PM to optimize exposure to certain factors or manage the portfolio in a tax-efficient manner without the typical tracking error constraint being as tight as it might be otherwise. A fund that seeks to track within 5–10% will have much more flexibility to create factor tilts or implement tax harvesting trades, for example, than a fund that seeks perfect replication and a minimal tracking error.

IS RS WORTH IT?

Every fund is different, so it is impossible to answer that question with one broad stroke. Are some funds worth managing in this manner? Absolutely. Characteristics-based strategies, such as fixed-income strategies focused on duration, convexity, credit ratings, etc., are particularly strong candidates for this type of portfolio management style, as the individual positions are less critical to the strategy than the features they represent. Indices with liquid underlyings, no structural impediments, and a relatively small number of holdings would be poorer candidates for RS.

Ultimately it is up to the fund sponsor and PM to determine the best method and the cost-benefit to its use. In what follows, we walk through an example of representative sampling just to give a flavor of the types of things a PM can do in this construct. Oftentimes, RS goes hand in hand with portfolio optimization, though it is not required per se. Still, portfolio optimization can be a strong tool to allow the PM to abide by certain guidelines around RS while optimizing performance by minimizing tracking error, maximizing an IR (yes, just like active strategies), etc. It can also be the very reason for RS: track the index, but try to beat it.

PORTFOLIO OPTIMIZATION AS AN RS STRATEGY

To lay the foundation for representative sampling, we will employ modern portfolio theory (MPT). MPT shows how to construct portfolios based on the relationship between risk and reward, seeking optimal returns for a given level of risk. The basic inputs to the model are the expected returns of each of the assets in the model (and a risk-free asset) and the covariances between assets. We have generally tried to keep the mathematics to a bare minimum, so the reader may want to refer to the appendix at the end of this chapter for more on the model.

To set the stage for some RS exercises, in Table 19.1 we present the expected returns and the covariance matrix for a set of securities, A through E. Consider a hypothetical equally weighted index that consists of only four holdings, A through D. Figure 19.1 plots the expected return versus volatility for the index as well as for each of the constituents.

TABLE 19.1

Risk and Return Characteristics for an Equally Weighted Index

Annualized Return	A	B	C	D	E
	7.28%	4.00%	5.33%	7.86%	9.24%
Covariance Matrix	A	B	C	D	E
A	14%	5%	7%	9%	10%
B	5%	6%	4%	4%	4%
C	7%	4%	11%	9%	11%
D	9%	4%	9%	35%	41%
E	10%	4%	11%	41%	58%
Correlation Matrix	A	B	C	D	E
A	100%	57%	58%	43%	37%
B	57%	100%	54%	28%	19%
C	58%	54%	100%	48%	43%
D	43%	28%	48%	100%	91%
E	37%	19%	43%	91%	100%

FIGURE 19.1

Risk and return characteristics for an equally weighted index

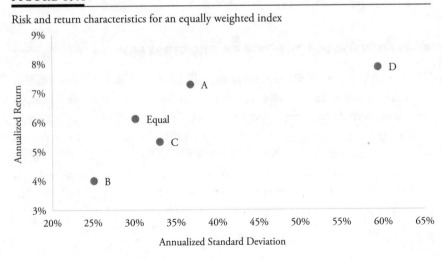

We are going to pursue four RS strategies in tracking the hypothetical index:

- Performance enhancement (i.e., improved Sharpe)
- Optimization with required overlap
- Restricted holdings
- Optimization subject to tracking error constraint

Performance Enhancement

The portfolio weights ascribed to the equal-weighted index do not necessarily result in the optimal portfolio allocation for the risk and return profile of the constituent securities. In Figure 19.2, we overlay the efficient frontier onto Figure 19.1.

FIGURE 19.2

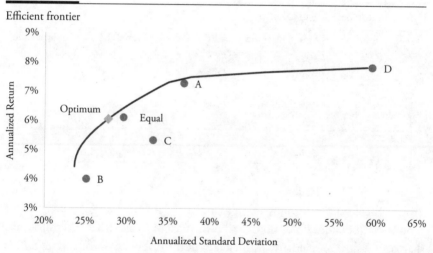

Efficient frontier

For those less familiar with MPT, two things should immediately stand out. First, any portfolio that lies to the "northwest" of another portfolio is preferable to that portfolio: it has a greater expected return and a lower level of risk. The second thing to note is that the index portfolio is *not* on the efficient frontier: for a given level of risk equal to that of the index, the PM can expect a higher expected return if he or she alters the weights.

The optimal portfolio, if we choose this metric of return per unit of risk as our objective, is highlighted by the point on the efficient frontier labeled "Optimum."*

Optimization with Required Overlap

Generally, RS schemes dictate that there must be *some* level of overlap in the construction of the index to be tracked. In our hypothetical index in this chapter, we have four assets. Suppose a fifth asset, E, also traded in the market. How much of E could the portfolio have? The fund prospectus might state that the RS portfolio seeks an overlap of 80%. This means that 80% of the portfolio must be representative of the index. Consider Table 19.2, which shows a hypothetical allocation that differs from equal weighting for the assets in the model.

TABLE 19.2

Hypothetical Allocation and Overlap

Stock	Portfolio Weight	Index Weight	Over/Underweight	Absolute Value
A	25%	25%	0%	0%
B	25%	25%	0%	0%
C	15%	25%	−10%	10%
D	25%	25%	0%	0%
E	10%	0%	10%	10%
			Sum	20%
			Sum/2	10%

If there is an underweight in one security, there has to be an offsetting overweight if both portfolios are fully invested.† In Table 19.2, we overweight E by 10% (the index holds no E) and underweight C by 10%. This still means that A, B, and D are exactly as they are meant to be: 25%. But though C is meant to have 25%, it only has 15%. E is meant to hold 0%, but it holds 10%. This portfolio would satisfy the overlap constraint. That should make sense too, since 90% of the portfolio is exactly allocated to A, B, C, and D. The question, though, is which portfolio that satisfies the overlap constraint is *optimal*? In

---

* This assumes the risk-free rate is zero.

† We can show that the overlap constraint here can be written as follows, with the notation found in the appendix to the chapter:

$$\sum_i \frac{w_i^P - w_i^I}{2} < 1 - \gamma$$

Figure 19.3, we show the risk-return space again, only this time we highlight the range of portfolios that not only satisfies the overlap constraint but is also preferable to the index portfolio from a risk-return perspective. We maintain the original optimum from Figure 19.2 in this figure, and zoom in in Figure 19.4 to see further differentiation between that optimum and the constrained optimum ("Optimum Overlap"). Note that the restricted portfolio does not match the original optimum. This means that the constraint is binding.

FIGURE 19.3

Optimal allocation satisfying overlap constraint

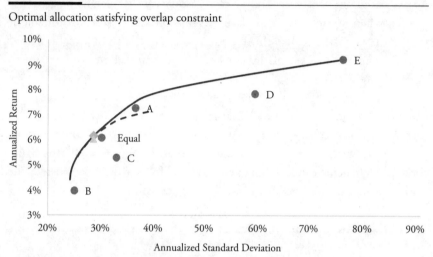

FIGURE 19.4

Optimal allocation satisfying overlap constraint (zoom)

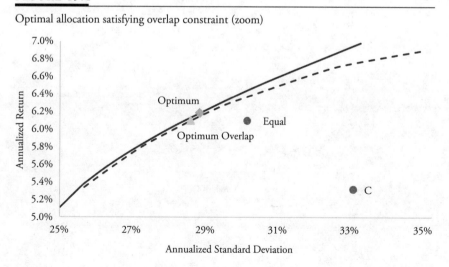

While we generically label the non-index asset E in our example, there are several possibilities besides a particular security or set of securities that a PM may hold outside of the index assets. A PM may opt to hold another ETF that provides a profile that matches his or her desired profile; hold a set of swaps, futures, and/or other derivative contracts that provide a related exposure; or simply hold cash if necessary.

Restricted Holdings

As we stated at the outset, one of the reasons why RS might be advantageous is when restrictions are in place that make trading a security difficult or impossible. Constraints like this for a portfolio are relatively straightforward to handle in the context of the construct of the model we have set up to demonstrate RS.

In Figure 19.5, we show our now-familiar efficient frontier; only this time we also show several points that relate to portfolios in which asset A is unavailable. As such, the portfolio would have to hold the remaining securities, or other securities not in the index (such as E in our model). The figure shows the efficient frontier available to the portfolio, which sits "inside" the initial efficient frontier because of the holding constraint.

FIGURE 19.5

Representative sampling with restricted holdings

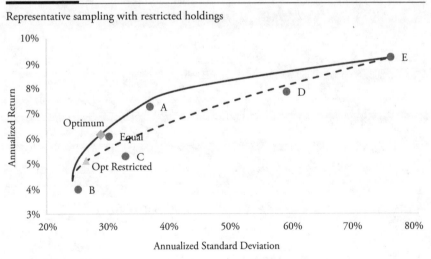

Optimization Subject to Tracking Error Constraint

The expected tracking error of an RS portfolio can be calculated from the respective weight vectors and the covariance matrix.* Recall that the weight vectors and (annualized) covariance matrix would have all assets collectively in either the index or the portfolio. With this construct in hand, it is now easy to specify a tracking error constraint, such as

$$TE < 5\%$$

In Figure 19.6, we again show the efficient frontier, the equally weighted portfolio, and the portfolio optimized for the highest return per unit of risk subject to the tracking error constraint above. We see that because the equally weighted portfolio is guaranteed to satisfy this constraint, any optimized portfolio would have a higher risk-reward profile than the index. The optimized portfolio does not, however, rest on the original efficient frontier, as we can see more closely in Figure 19.7.[†]

FIGURE 19.6

Representative sampling with tracking error constraint

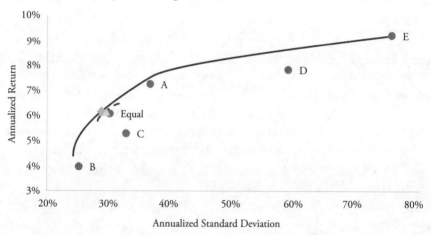

---

* Using the notation from the appendix, we have
$$TE = \sqrt{((w^P - w^I)'\Sigma(w^P - w^I))}$$

† Note that mean-variance optimal is not necessarily the objective for the ETF PM tracking an index with RS. There may be other objectives the ETF PM is trying to obtain.

FIGURE 19.7

Representative sampling with tracking error constraint (zoom)

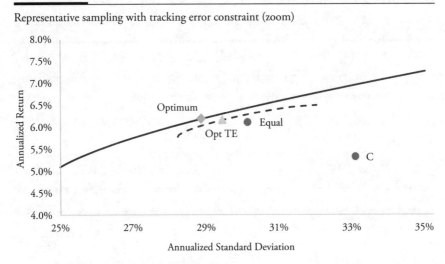

COMPLICATIONS

RS can be a powerful tool to manage a portfolio, but there is a laundry list of concerns that any portfolio manager should consider when performing RS with a portfolio. It begins with all the concerns that one would have with the model to be employed. For example, in our hypothetical exercise above, we used mean-variance optimization and modern portfolio theory. A whole set of assumptions underlies MPT that, if not correct, could deal a fatal blow to the output of such a model. At the top of that list might be whether or not the parameters change over time or whether or not the variables in question exhibit behavior consistent with normal distributions. One might question whether or not there is enough data for the number of parameters to be estimated. Or the model might not be appropriate for nonlinear instruments such as options. The list goes on.

Furthermore, implementing the result might raise related questions: How often should parameters be updated? If I optimize today and then optimize tomorrow (or next week or next month), should I consider when I next plan to optimize when optimizing today? It quickly becomes apparent that all the optimality decisions are, in effect, tied together. Clearly, the challenges in RS can be significant, but so too can the payoffs.

APPENDIX

The framework for the analyses in this chapter is modern portfolio theory. While providing a detailed description of the complete methodology is beyond the scope of this book, here we provide some of the basics in order to better follow some of the constraints discussed as a part of representative sampling.

We begin by defining terms:

- w_{it}^P is the weight of security i in the portfolio at time t
- w_{it}^I is the weight of security i in the index I at time t
- μ_{it} is the expected return to security i at time t
- σ_{ij} is the annualized covariance for security i and security j
- Σ is the covariance matrix, with elements σ_{ij}

Returns are linear, so the expected return of a portfolio is the weighted average of the expected returns of the components. So, for example,

$$\mu_t^P = \sum_i w_{it}^P \mu_{it}$$

is the expected return of the portfolio. Similarly,

$$\mu_t^I = \sum_i w_{it}^I \mu_{it}$$

is the expected return of the index.

Volatility is *not* linear, so the annualized volatility for a portfolio is not a weighted average of the annualized volatilities of the constituents. Portfolio volatility for a two-asset portfolio, as an example, is calculated as follows:

$$\sigma = \sqrt{w_a^2 \sigma_a^2 + w_b^2 \sigma_b^2 + 2 w_a w_b \sigma_{ab}}$$

Using matrix notation, we can generalize to the following:

$$\sigma^P = \sqrt{w^{P'} \Sigma w^P}$$

where the ' symbol reflects the vector transpose and σ^P is portfolio volatility.

We can define a misallocation vector as $\tilde{w} = w^P - w^I$, and therefore the tracking error of the portfolio as

$$TE = \sqrt{\tilde{w}'\Sigma\tilde{w}}$$

Modern portfolio theory works by selecting a weight vector that minimizes risk subject to a fixed level of return, thereby creating a frontier of optimal combinations of risk and reward. As we detail in the chapter, constraints can be added to the optimization, such as capping tracking error or limiting the amount of misallocation.

CHAPTER 20

Closing an ETF

We close with a discussion of what happens when the life of an ETF comes to an end. In fact, many ETFs are closed; we saw at the outset that despite many product listings, some ETFs fail to garner assets. There are fixed costs in launching an ETF related to fund administration, trust fees, etc., that mean that without enough assets and a fee applied to those assets to offset the costs, launching an ETF can be a losing battle; the fund will close eventually.

THE CLOSING PROCESS

Should the fund sponsor decide to close the fund, several steps will happen well in advance of a proposed closing date. First, the ETF's board of trustees will approve the closure, and an announcement will go out to the public (a press release or a posting on the fund's website, for example) indicating that the fund will be delisting from the exchange where it trades. Generally, the announcement will make clear when the fund will no longer accept creation orders and when the final trading date on the exchange will take place. The fund will also make clear when any securities in the portfolio will be liquidated and when the distribution of assets will take place, much like a standard distribution of funds to shareholders, by specifying a record date and a distribution date.

THE PM'S RESPONSIBILITY

The ETF portfolio manager's responsibility in a closure is to liquidate the holdings in the portfolio according to the schedule laid out by the fund sponsor. Redemptions may well occur prior to the delisting upon notification, and those redemptions may be in-kind much like redemptions at any other time, but the remaining assets get liquidated by the PM.

An index-based ETF may also specify a date upon which the ETF will no longer be tied to the underlying index: this date can line up with the delisting date. It is possible, however, that to liquidate less liquid securities by the date in question, PMs must send orders early or liquidate parts of the portfolio ahead of time. It is obvious that in these scenarios the ability to track the underlying index is compromised.

CONCERNS AND COMPLICATIONS

The closing process is not complicated, but there are a few things to be aware of. First, index tracking for index-based ETFs can become a problem in the final days of an ETF. This is largely a function of the liquidation timing process. If the fund is small enough to sell remaining shares on the liquidation date at the close, this is less of a concern. But imagine what happens when a larger fund decides to shutter; there could be substantial positions in the fund that might require several days to unwind. Furthermore, once the closure is announced, other market participants know there will be selling pressure on those holdings, contributing to potential underperformance in the fund's final days. Redemptions during the wind-down period may be the PM's best friend, allowing in-kind transfers of securities out of the portfolio without having to transact in the secondary market.

Second, for those transactions that do occur in the secondary market, like transactions at other times in the ETF's life, they may incur capital gains.

Finally, it is possible for a portfolio to contain a security that has been halted prior to the liquidation. If this is the case, then it may not be possible to convert the position to cash to distribute to the ETF shareholder. Several possibilities might exist: for example, the fund could try to find a counterparty willing to accept the halted shares, or the fund could withhold from the distribution the value of the halted shares to potentially be returned at a later date.

CONCLUSION

For the ETF portfolio manager who has managed the fund from its infancy, the closure of the fund might feel like a failure. Managing an ETF, however, is distinct in large part from growing assets in an ETF. Yes, if the strategy is successful, invested assets will grow; but there is a whole marketing and distribution effort that goes side by side with performance to build assets in a product, and that effort has a lot of competition. An ETF PM should look back not on the asset raise, but on the key metrics that we have discussed in this book when reflecting on his or her performance. Did an index-based ETF track the index well? Did the PM declare capital gains when he or she might have been able to manage those gains by employing some of the strategies we have discussed? Did the active ETF PM manage the portfolio effectively by trying to optimize performance relative to a benchmark? Did the PM work with his or her traders to execute effectively? And in the end, did the PM fulfill his or her obligation to manage the portfolio in the best interests of the shareholder? The answers to these questions are the true barometer of performance.

ETFs are here to stay. They have become a critical part of the financial landscape in the early part of the twenty-first century, and until the next disruption in the investment management industry, ETFs will likely be the dominant investing tool for years to come.

Glossary

ADV	Average daily volume
AETF	Actively-managed ETF
AP	Authorized participant
AUM	Assets under management
C/R	Creation/redemption
CFTC	Commodity Futures Trading Commission
CIB	Custom in-kind basket
CIL	Cash in lieu
CU	Creation unit
DTCC	Depository Trust & Clearing Corporation
DV01	Dollar value of a basis point
ETF	Exchange-traded fund
FI	Fixed income
FINRA	Financial Industry Regulatory Authority
FX	Foreign exchange
ICA	Index calculation agent
ICF	Index closing file
IOF	Index opening file
IOPV	Indicative optimized portfolio values
IR	Information ratio
IV	Indicative value

LIBOR	London Interbank Offer Rate
LMM	Lead market maker
MF	Mutual fund
MOC	Market on close
MOO	Market on open
MPT	Modern portfolio theory
NAV	Net asset value
NSCC	National Securities Clearing Corporation
NYSE	New York Stock Exchange
PCF	Portfolio composition file
PLF	Portfolio listing file
PF	Pro forma
PM	Portfolio manager
RS	Representative sampling
SEC	Securities and Exchange Commission
SPDR	Standard and Poor's Depositary Receipts S&P 500 ETF Trust
SWA	Starts with A
TC	Transaction costs
TE	Tracking error
VIIV	Verified intraday indicative value
VIX	CBOE Volatility Index
YTC	Yield to call
YTM	Yield to maturity
YTW	Yield to worst

Index

Page numbers followed by *f* and *t* refer to figures and tables, respectively.

About the Author

Dr. Scott M. Weiner is the Head of Quantitative Strategy and senior Portfolio Manager for the Exchange-Traded Products team at Janus Henderson Investors. He is a member of the firm's Index Committee and serves on the Board of Directors for the Janus Henderson Foundation.

Prior to his tenure at Janus Henderson, Dr. Weiner was the U.S. Head of Equity Derivatives and Quantitative Strategy at Deutsche Bank and was a lecturer at Oxford University. His research has been published in *Mathematical Finance*; *The Journal of Money, Credit and Banking*; and *The Journal of Business and Economic Statistics*. Dr. Weiner earned a bachelor's degree in economics from the Wharton School of the University of Pennsylvania, received his master's and doctoral degrees in economics from Oxford University, and completed the Advanced Management Program at Harvard University.

He is the founder of Veterans on Wall Street (VOWS™).

———————

Follow Dr. Weiner at linkedin.com/in/ScottMWeiner or visit swetf.com.